Marxism and the State

Also by Paul Wetherly

Marx's Theory of History: The Contemporary Debate (*editor*, 1992)

Marxism and the State

An Analytical Approach

Paul Wetherly
Principal Lecturer in Politics
Leeds Metropolitan University

First published 2005 by
PALGRAVE MACMILLAN
Houndmills, Basingstoke, Hampshire RG21 6XS and
175 Fifth Avenue, New York, N. Y. 10010
Companies and representatives throughout the world

PALGRAVE MACMILLAN is the global academic imprint of the Palgrave Macmillan division of St. Martin's Press, LLC and of Palgrave Macmillan Ltd. Macmillan® is a registered trademark in the United States, United Kingdom and other countries. Palgrave is a registered trademark in the European Union and other countries.

ISBN-13: 978–0–333–72478–1   hardback
ISBN-10: 0–333–72478–X   hardback

This book is printed on paper suitable for recycling and made from fully managed and sustained forest sources.

A catalogue record for this book is available from the British Library.

Library of Congress Cataloging-in-Publication Data
Wetherly, Paul.
    Marxism and the state : an analytical approach / Paul Wetherly.
        p. cm.
    Includes bibliographical references and index.
    ISBN 0–333–72478–X
        1. State, The. 2. Historical materialism. 3. Capitalism. 4. Communism.
I. Title.

JC131.W47 2005
335.4′119–dc22   2005042517

10   9   8   7   6   5   4   3   2   1
14   13   12   11   10   09   08   07   06   05

Printed and bound in Great Britain by
Antony Rowe Ltd, Chippenham and Eastbourne

For *Barbara, Rebecca and Laura*

Contents

Preface

This book offers a restatement of an 'old-fashioned' Marxist theory of the state. According to that theory the character of the state, in so far as it is part of the 'legal and political superstructure' of a society, is determined or explained by the nature of the prevailing economic structure.

More specifically, it is claimed that the state is functionally explained by the needs or functional requirements of the economy – for example, that the state in capitalist society is functionally explained by the extra-economic conditions that must be secured if capitalist relations of production are to be maintained and reproduced, or stabilised. What this means is that certain state actions (laws, policies) are explained by their having a functional (stabilising) effect on the economy. Or it can be said that such actions are explained by the disposition of the economy to be stabilised by them. It is this functionality that the concept of 'the capitalist state' is intended to capture.

The characterisation of Marxism as a functional theory is not new, but has for long figured in discussions of Marx's writings on the state. But by far the most rigorous and convincing statement of this view is found in the contemporary stream of 'analytical' Marxism and, more specifically, the book that was one of the primary sources of that stream: G.A. Cohen's *Karl Marx's Theory of History: A Defence*. Cohen's functional interpretation of the theory of history provides the theoretical framework for this book, whose purpose can be summarised as to elaborate the relatively neglected 'second stage' of the theory – the functional connection between the economic structure and the legal and political superstructure.[1]

This book is concerned with the capitalist state and does not deal with the base-superstructure connection or the theory of history in more general terms. Thus it does not deal with pre-capitalist societies, the origins of capitalist relations of production and the capitalist state, or the possibility of a post-capitalist society and the implications for the state. It should be noted that the plausibility of the functional explanation of the capitalist state does not depend on the plausibility of the theory of history in total. It could be true in capitalist society that the nature of the economic structure functionally explains the character of the legal and political superstructure even if this is not true for any other kind of society.

It should also be noted that the theory of history deals with the capitalist state only in so far as it is part of the legal and political super-structure. The terms 'state' and 'superstructure' are not to be treated as synonymous. This means that there is more to the Marxist theory of the state than the theory of history, as a wider range of political phenomena may be explained in terms of class interests and struggle than are relevant to the theory of history. The theory of history contains a partial theory of the state within Marxism, and Marxism should probably be seen as a partial theory of the state within the wider field of state theory.

A functional theory or explanation of the state appears vulnerable to a range of criticisms, such as these:

- Functional explanation is inadmissible in the social sciences. In particular, one event cannot be explained in terms of its effect or consequences, unless the functional explanation is restated as an intentional explanation where actions are explained by their intended outcomes.
- Functional explanation depends on a concept of 'system needs', whereas in fact social systems have no needs and no interests in their own survival. Such 'needs' must really be the wants of actors.
- Functional explanations can only be accepted in the company of plausible mechanisms (or elaborations) showing how the effect of some event explains its occurrence.
- Functional explanation involves economic reductionism or determinism since features of the economic structure (its needs, or disposition to be stabilised by certain state actions) are seen as sufficient or privileged explanations of non-economic (legal and political) phenomena. This denies the multiple causes that may combine to explain such phenomena. More specifically, the structural cast of the functional explanation – explaining legal and political phenomena in terms of the nature of the economic structure – seems to deny the role of agency.

These criticisms are countered in this book by arguments to show that:

- A capitalist economic structure can be analysed in terms of 'system needs' or 'functional requirements'. In fact this idea is widely accepted in the form of recognition that there are certain crucial extra-economic conditions for a capitalist economy to function and be reproduced.

- Instrumentalist and structuralist arguments can be adduced to provide plausible mechanisms of functional explanation of the state.
- The inter-relationship between these mechanisms can be understood in a way that makes sense of the structure-agency dilemma.
- Functional explanation as a form of economic determination is compatible with a notion of the relative autonomy of the state. This involves an understanding of economic determination as a strong tendency.

Chapter one sets out the overall approach of the book in more detail and, in particular, clarifies the relationship between Marx's theory of history and the theory of the state.

Chapter two is a commentary on the apparently diverse approaches to the state in Marx's writing. These approaches can be analysed in terms of answers to these questions: what is the state? what is the purpose or role of the state? and, how is this role explained? Marx is often interpreted as advancing two views of the state – primary and secondary – according to whether it is seen as an instrument in the hands of the capitalist class or as autonomous with respect to class interests. However a more fruitful approach replaces the either-or dichotomy with a view of the state as both an instrument and as operating within structural constraints, and as both largely explained by the economic structure and possessing a capacity for autonomy.

Chapters three and four examine the nature of instrumentalist and structuralist (or class- and capital-theoretical) accounts of the state and their interaction. It is mistaken to counterpose these causal mechanisms since instrumentalist explanation in terms of class interest has a crucial structural dimension. Instrumentalist accounts rely on a theory of the shaping of objective class interests by positions or roles in the economic structure, whereas structuralist accounts rely on a theory of the shaping of actions of state managers by structural constraints arising from their dependence on the healthy functioning of the economic system.

Chapter five analyses the base-superstructure distinction. Cohen's presentation of the theory of history defines the economic structure only in terms of positions or roles in relations of power over economic resources, and not as 'a way of producing'. Structure, in this way, is distinguished from process. But this conception is too narrow for the purpose of functional explanation of the legal and political superstructure. This is because what needs explaining is the stabilisation of relations of production as forms of development of the productive forces. But it is only as a way of producing – the circuit of capital and accumulation – that capitalist production relations perform this progressive role. Therefore the state must secure the extra-economic conditions of capital's self-expanding circuit. This leads to a more expansive concept of the needs of capital, understood as a subset of the interests of the capitalist class.

Chapter six provides an analysis of the needs of capital, defined as functional requirements or conditions that must be met for capitalism to continue. Doyal and Gough's theory of human need provides a conceptual framework for understanding system needs in terms of an 'ultimate system need', 'basic needs', 'intermediate needs', and 'specific satisfiers'. The ultimate goal or system need is defined as the maintenance of capitalism, that is, the maintenance or stabilisation of the relations of production which comprise the economic structure. This is understood not narrowly in terms of the ownership positions of capitalists and proletarians but in the wider sense of the renewal of the circuit of capital. The needs or functional requirements of capital constitute the point of reference for functional explanation of the state: in this view some actions of the state are as they are because of the way such actions satisfy these functional requirements.

Chapter seven considers the apparent tension between economic determination as a principle of explanation and the notion of the relative autonomy of the state. The misleading dichotomy of determinism versus autonomy is rejected in favour of an understanding of economic determination as a strong tendency, or the primacy of economic determination. The notion of relative autonomy is analysed using Lukes's conceptualisations of autonomy and freedom, as the non-constraining of the purposes of an agent (i.e. the extent to which such purposes are the agent's own) and the non-constraining of the agent's ability to realise these purposes.

In chapter eight four types of constraint are analysed as mechanisms of economic determination – these are the possible combinations of internal or external and personal or impersonal constraints. In other words, economic determination is conceived as working via the ways in which state autonomy is constrained by the nature of the economic structure. The four constraints are characterised as: ideological dispositions of the state elite, the rationality of the state system, pressure from above, and structural constraints.

Chapter nine examines the implications of the globalisation debate for the central themes of this book. In essence this introduces a spatial dimension that is largely absent from Cohen's interpretation of the theory of history. The question here is: is there a plausible account of economic globalisation that is consistent with the central claims of the theory of history and, more specifically, the theory of the state?

I am very grateful to my editor at Palgrave, Alison Howson, for the opportunity to write this book, and for the patience and understanding she showed when I missed a succession of extended deadlines for completion of the final manuscript. I am also grateful to Leeds Metropolitan University for the support I have received for this work, particularly the award of a one-semester sabbatical that helped me finally to meet a deadline for Alison.

Two anonymous referees provided very helpful comments on the book at different stages of its completion and made me think again about my approach. The book is better as a result of their efforts.

As the writing of this book progressed a large number of people contributed to the development of my understanding and thinking in smaller and larger ways by providing helpful comments and criticisms, and I won't try to name them all here. Some of these comments have come in various conferences at which some of the arguments in the book have been presented. The Political Studies Association Marxism Specialist Group, convened by Mark Cowling, has been a particularly helpful forum and I am grateful to members of that group.

The original proposal for the book was based on my PhD thesis, and some of the chapters from that thesis are reproduced here in revised form. I owe an enormous debt of gratitude to Mark Cowling, who was the supervisor for my PhD at the University of Teesside and who has continued to support and influence my work as a close friend and colleague. Alan Carling has been a constant source of advice and support over many years and I have benefited from many discussions with him about some of the themes of this book.

If Alison Howson has found it necessary to apply some gentle pressure to get me to complete the manuscript, she has had an ally in my 12-year-old daughter Laura who has often asked 'you know that book you're writing, when are you going to get it finished?'. Laura is a great writer and, if she decides it is what she wants to do, I am sure she will write many books.

This one is dedicated to Barbara, Laura and Rebecca.

1
Introduction: The Theory of History and the State

This book is concerned with Marxist state theory, but from a particular angle: that is, the theory of the state insofar as it is contained within Marx's theory of history. As far as the theory of history goes, the book draws heavily, but not uncritically, on Cohen's masterful exposition and defence in *Karl Marx's Theory of History: A Defence* (Cohen, 1978).[1] Cohen's treatment of the base-superstructure connection is rather limited, in contrast to the detailed argument in respect of the forces and relations of production, and this book attempts to go some way to remedy that deficiency. The commitment to an 'analytical approach' is also inspired by Cohen's work on the theory of history, though, more precisely, the inspiration comes from the broad rather than the narrow meaning of analysis. In other words, it is the 'precision of statement ... and rigour of argument' in Cohen's work that is to be aspired to, not the commitment to methodological individualism that is to be emulated (Cohen, 2000, p. xviii).[2]

This book is concerned with the Marxist theory of the state insofar as it is contained within the theory of history, but an initial answer to the question how far that is must be that it is not all the way. The theory of history certainly makes important claims about the state, but it does not provide a complete explanation. A related qualification is that the theory of history does not exhaust all that Marxism has to say about the state. To make these points clearer we need to begin with a preliminary concept of the state, and an understanding of its relationship to the historical materialist concept of 'legal and political superstructure'.

There is no distinctive concept of the state in Marxism or, more specifically, the theory of history. Rather, Marxism employs a conventional conception of what the state is (Carnoy, 1984; Mann, 1986a;

1

Hall & Ikenberry, 1989; Pierson, 1996; Hoffman, 1995; Hay, 1996a). It might be doubted whether there is any kind of agreed concept for it has been argued that the state is a 'baffling phenomenon' (Berki, 1989, p. 12), 'contradictory and mystifying' (Hoffman, 1995, p. 3), a 'messy concept' (Mann, 1988, p. 4), perhaps even the most problematic concept in politics (Vincent, cited in Hoffman, 1995, p. 2). It is clear that in order to develop an analysis or theory of the state a coherent definition is a prerequisite. It is difficult to see, for example, how the relationship between the state and civil society can be elucidated if the phenomenon of the state itself remains baffling. Thus there must be a way for conceptual clarification and tidiness to replace mystification and messiness. And in fact there is. For, in practice, it turns out that there is substantial agreement on what the central features of the modern state are. Thus Pierson observes that 'there has been a surprisingly broad area of agreement about what constitutes the essential elements of the modern state' (1996, p. 6), and Hall and Ikenberry similarly note that 'there is a great deal of agreement amongst social scientists as to how the state should be defined' (1989, p. 1). This broad area of agreement constitutes an organisational view of the state that sees it as a distinct set of *institutions* (Dunleavy & O'Leary, 1987, p. 1; Burnham, 1994, p. 1) or focuses on the organisational *means* adopted by the state (Pierson, 1996, p. 7). This contrasts with a functional approach that defines the state in terms of the functions it performs or, in other words, its *purposes* or *objectives* (Mann, 1986a, p. 112). Functional approaches tend to obliterate the distinction between the state and 'civil society', and to enlarge the concept of the state, because the state comes to comprise all institutions which perform the prescribed functions. For example, Gramsci's (1971) conception of the 'extended state' 'comprises not merely the machinery of government but all aspects of civil society (press, trade unions, church, mass culture) which stabilise existing power relations' (Burnham, 1994, p. 2; see also Sassoon, 1980). The fundamental objection to the functionalist approach is that it results in a highly elastic concept of the state depending on the specification of its functions. If the function of the state is to create or maintain social order or cohesion it may be pertinent to ask whether there are any institutions which might not conceivably be incorporated into it.[3] A related problem of defining the state in terms of specific ends is that the organisational means of the state (however defined) may be utilised in the service of a plethora of ends. Therefore, 'the state cannot be defined in terms of its ends' (Weber, 1991, p. 77).

There is wide agreement on an organisational definition of the state according to which it is a particular type of organisation or, more accurately, set of institutions.[4] Hall and Ikenberry (1989, pp. 1–2) offer a composite definition which comprises the following elements:

1. 'the state is a set of institutions ... The state's most important institution is that of the means of violence and coercion'
2. 'these institutions are at the centre of a geographically bounded territory'
3. 'the state monopolises rule making within its territory'.

This is very close to Weber's classic definition of the state as 'a human community that (successfully) claims the *monopoly of the legitimate use of physical force* within a given territory' (1991, p. 78). Both emphasise the coercive and territorial aspects of the state. The third element suggested by Hall and Ikenberry makes clear that the fundamental role of the state is one of law or rule making and this allows us to think of the means of violence or coercion in terms of compliance or law enforcement. As Bottomore expresses it, 'the state is one of the important agencies of social control, whose functions are carried out by means of law, backed ultimately by physical force' (1971, p. 151; see also Hall, 1984, p. 4). Though the state is not defined simply as a coercive apparatus its most important institution is that of the means of violence and coercion because it provides the ultimate backing for the state as a system of rule. In other words

the state is a phenomenon principally and emphatically located within the sphere of political power ... What we should consider as unique to political power, as conceptually intrinsic to it, is control over the means of violence (Poggi, 1990, pp. 4–5).

Political power, understood in these terms, is distinguished from two other forms of social power: economic power, whose source is control over material resources; and, ideological or normative power, whose source is control over the means of communication and consent (Miliband, 1984, p. 329; Poggi, 1990). This distinction between forms of social power is closely related to the idea of 'institutional differentiation' (Burnham, 1994, p. 2): the set of institutions that comprises the state is 'so differentiated from the rest of society as to create identifiable public and private spheres' (Dunleavy & O'Leary, 1987, p. 2). It is true that the boundary between public and private cannot be sharply drawn but, nevertheless, according to Jessop 'it is acceptable to define ... [the] institutional boundaries [of the state] in terms of the legal distinction between "public" and "private"' (1984, p. 222). The point is that the making and enforcing of rules is assigned to a specialised set of political offices which are distinct from the roles and relations which constitute the economic sphere. Differentiation is, as Poggi observes, implicit in the definition of the state as a distinct organisation, or set of institutions, and is 'at a maximum when the organisation in question performs *all* and *only* political activities' (Poggi, 1990, p. 20).

The modern state, while in essence, as we have seen, a system of rule backed by physical force, is much more than that. Thus Weber observed that 'force is certainly not the normal or the only means of the state ... but force is a means specific to the state' (1991, p. 78). This points us to the aspects of the state which are concerned with the securing of consent to its rule. Equally, although the state is fundamentally about rule it also has many other functions. Thus the bald definitions offered by both Weber and Hall and Ikenberry might be thought deficient in failing to give due weight to the extra-coercive aspects of the state. In particular, to define the state solely in terms of rule making and coercion seems to exclude from view the direct provision of goods and services in the forms of state welfare and public enterprise, the fiscal and monetary powers of the state, and its associated capacity for economic management.

To define the state in terms of these activities would, of course, be problematic. Welfare, for example, is not of the essence of what the state is: in the absence of welfare provision by the state it would not be any the less a state. By contrast rule making and coercion do constitute the irreducible essence of what it is to be a state. Further, the capacity of the state to be a welfare state with the associated capacity to raise taxation to finance expenditure is founded on the state's being a system of rule. However, although welfare is not essential to the contemporary state it is in many advanced capitalist societies certainly weighty: it is not fundamental to what the state is in principle but it is fundamental to what the state is as a reality. It is this reality of the complex, extended state that theory must address.

On this basis we can distinguish between a narrow and a broad concept of the state, the first confined to essential characteristics and the second including aspects that are more contingent. The first highlights the essential character of the state as a coercive apparatus, while the second draws attention to the expansion of the modern state system including, for example, the development of the 'welfare state'. The latter approach sees the state as largely synonymous with the 'public sector' (Jessop, 1990, p. 117). It is this 'publicness' that is the connecting thread between the two conceptions. The point is that the state withdraws or abstracts control of the means of physical force from the private realm of civil society and locates it in a specialised public institution or apparatus.[5] And it is clear that the capacity of the state to provide welfare services to its citizens (or to its capitalists), or engage in a host of other activities, depends on its capacity to raise revenue through taxation, and the ultimate guarantor of this capacity is its ability to secure compliance through the threat or use of physical force.[6]

One reason why the theory of history cannot provide a complete explanation of the state in its broad sense is that, arguably, no theory can do this. As a set of institutions and a repertoire of practices, 'the state' is not a single thing and the term is too vague to constitute a definite explanandum. We need to ask what is it about this complex state system that a particular theory sets out to explain. This does not rule out explanations pitched at a high level of abstraction or generality, and such explanations are indeed central to the theory of history. But such general explanations will, by definition, be less informative about the concrete details of the form and functions of the state. The point is to specify the scope and limits of different approaches in state theory.

The scope and limits of the theory of history are more confined than Marxist state theory taken as a whole. This is because the relevant historical materialist concept is the 'legal and political superstructure' rather than the state. The theory of the state is contained within the theory of history to the extent that the state is contained within the superstructure, and it is so only partially. The superstructure might be something more than the state, and there might be more to the state than what is included in the superstructure. The superstructure consists of non-economic phenomena, but only such phenomena as are economically relevant. This means only those phenomena that are functionally explained by the needs (or functional requirements) of the economic base. Thus non-economic phenomena are defined as superstructural only in virtue of being causally related in a certain way (i.e. functionally) to the economic structure. This means that the contents and boundaries of the superstructure can only be determined by elucidating this functional relation – they 'depend on the data' (Cohen, 1988, p. 160). In what Cohen refers to as a 'restricted' (as opposed to inclusive) version of the theory of history it is not claimed that the nature of the economic structure explains 'the rest of society', and Mills was wrong to conceive the superstructure as a 'residual category' (Mills, 1962, p. 104). It also follows that the superstructure might not be comprised of the same set of phenomena in all forms of society, because each type of economic structure will have its own functional requirements. Yet there are good reasons to think that the superstructure in all societies involves at least some aspects of the state (or their equivalents). The designation of the superstructure as 'legal and political' shows that Marx thought this, though it does not, of course, show that he was right. The fundamental reason lies in the instability of economic power and thus production relations in the types of societies that the theory of history is chiefly concerned with – class societies.[7] The claim is, in short, that economic power requires political power for its stability. This is because class societies are inherently conflictual, and members of the subordinate class are liable to contest and seek to restrict or overthrow the relations of power that embody this subordination. The functional requirement for political power is to keep such class conflict in check. Focusing on the law, Cohen shows that economic powers may require legal rights to render them more stable by making them legitimate (1978, pp. 231–4). However the law is made and enforced by the state, and the state's capacity to rule is ultimately backed up by control of the means of physical coercion (political power in its narrow sense). Hence economic power requires political power in all class societies and, in capitalism at least, political power is located in the state.

This does not mean that only the essence of the state, as a coercive apparatus, is included in the superstructure, for other aspects of the state as a set of institutions and repertoire of actions may be functionally explained by the nature of the economic base. In capitalism this may, for example, include areas of welfare provision connected to the reproduction of labour power. Evidently a functional theory of the capitalist state must begin with an analysis of the functional requirements of capitalist production relations, or needs of capital. It may be that the theory of history explains a good deal about the capitalist state, but it does not exhaust Marxist explanation. In other words, there may be aspects of the state that do not come within reach of the theory of history but may still be explained within a Marxist framework of economic determination. Thus Cohen, following Wright, presents the distinction between restricted and inclusive historical materialism as one between the theory of history and Marxist sociology (1988, p. 176). Within the framework of Marxist sociology the nature of the capitalist economic structure may provide explanations of a range of political (and other non-economic) phenomena that are not relevant to the theory of history. For example, aspects of social or economic policy that are not functional for capital can be explained in terms of class struggle – pressure from below from trade unions and other workers' organisations, or pressure from above from capitalist firms or associations. In other words, class interests at play in political struggles are not confined to the needs of the economic structure that are the specific concern of the theory of history.[8]

Finally there may be political (and other non-economic phenomena) that elude Marxist explanation altogether since, not only is the superstructure not to be seen as 'the rest of society', but the larger ambitions of Marxist sociology do not amount to a theory of society as a whole. For example, developments in spiritual life – such as the emergence of Protestantism – may occur autonomously, for non-economic reasons (Cohen, 1988, pp. 158–65). Spiritual phenomena might be unaccounted for not only by the needs of the economic structure but also by class interests. That is, they might not be accounted for either in terms of the theory of history or Marxist sociology. The same might be said in relation to some political phenomena, such as certain aspects of economic or social policy. In that case a state-centred explanation might be in terms of an autonomous political logic and/or distinctive political interests – the push of interests from inside the state system. For example, it might be argued that state managers have an interest, in virtue of their positions within the state system, in expanding budgets and increasing the span of political control in society (Poggi, 1990).[9] Economic repercussions might arise from spiritual developments, and perhaps more obviously so from an 'invasive state'. Such repercussions, to be compatible with the theory of history, must not block the capacity of production relations to serve as forms of development of the productive forces. If the repercussions are that the economic structure is stabilised (i.e. the repercussions are functional) then the spiritual or political phenomena in question can only arise for non-economic reasons and be compatible with the theory of history if the specific functional effects can be explained by the phenomena adapting to the needs of the economy (Cohen, 1988, pp. 160–65). Thus, just as Cohen makes this argument in relation to a system of religious ideas – Protestantism – it might be made in relation to a system of political ideas. Political ideologies such as conservatism and liberalism might take hold and persist for non-economic reasons and have economic repercussions, yet their capitalist-promoting aspects might be explained by the adaptation of these ideologies to a developing capitalist economy.

This book is concerned with the Marxist theory of the state insofar as it is contained within the theory of history but, more specifically, it focuses on the state in capitalist society. Further, the argument takes as given certain aspects of the form of the state in capitalist society, notably its institutional separation from society and internal complexity (as a set of institutions comprising the state system). These aspects of the form of the state – separation and complexity – problematise its functionality. In other words economic power cannot be translated automatically into political power – plausible causal mechanisms have to be elucidated to show how this translation may be effected.[10] The central questions are: What are the functional requirements of a capitalist economy? What are the implications for the functions of the state? What causal mechanisms can be elucidated to support the functional explanation?

Although this is a book about Marxism and the state in capitalist society it is not a survey of Marxist state theory.[11] However it does confront some central theoretical issues or problems within the Marxist tradition: the relationship between class struggle and the logic of capital (or agency and structure); how to reconcile economic determination with the relative autonomy of the state; and, the possibility of a general theory of the state as against the more limited analysis of specific conjunctures.

The theory of history is a general theory of a highly ambitious kind – it advances the general claim that throughout history (in all class societies) certain non-economic phenomena (comprising the superstructure) are functionally explained by the needs of the economic structure. This book analyses this claim in relation to capitalist society: the nature of the capitalist economic structure functionally explains the character of the legal and political superstructure (including aspects of the state).[12] If the arguments in this book show that this claim about the state in capitalist society is plausible they will provide reinforcement of the theory of history. However the book does not defend the theory of history as such. So it could be true in capitalist society that the base functionally explains the superstructure without this being true in (all or any) other types of society. The base-superstructure thesis would have to be true as a general historical claim for the theory of history to be true, since economic structures can only serve as forms of development of the productive forces if they are stabilised by superstructures. But the claim that the set of production relations a society has is functionally explained by the level of development of the productive forces could be false even if the base-superstructure thesis is true. Thus, in relation to the concerns of this book, it could be true that important aspects of the state can be functionally explained by the needs of capital, regardless of the explanation of the historical emergence of capitalism. The claims made about the state could be true whether or not capitalist production relations were selected because they were best suited to develop the productive forces.

Equally, the claims about the capitalist state could be true regardless of the truth of what the theory of history says about the fate of capitalism. According to the theory capitalism will be stabilised only so long as it performs its progressive historical role or mission of developing the productive forces, beyond which it is destined to give way to socialism through proletarian revolution. The superstructure will, accordingly, be (more or less rapidly) transformed and, in this case, the state will wither away. The primary purpose of the theory of history is, of course, to guide this politics of emancipation (Carling, 1997) but assessing the plausibility of this final historical transition is beyond the scope of this book. However the point here is that the theory of the capitalist state and the theory of proletarian revolution can be detached – the plausibility of the former does not depend on the judgement that is made as to the plausibility of the latter.

2
Marx, the State and Functional Explanation

Introduction

It is generally accepted that there is no single theory of the state to be found in Marx's writings but a variety of themes and perspectives, some of which appear to be at odds with each other (Miliband, 1965; Jessop, 1977 and 1984; Barrow, 1993; Wetherly, 1998; Hay, 1999). A common distinction is between an 'instrumentalist' conception of the state (most famously expressed in *The Communist Manifesto*[1]) and an idea of the state as autonomous from the dominant class (found in *The Eighteenth Brumaire of Louis Bonaparte*[2]). For Miliband (1965) these constitute, respectively, Marx's 'primary' and 'secondary' views on the state. According to Elster 'the central question in the Marxist theory of the state is whether it is autonomous with respect to class interests, or entirely reducible to them' (Elster, 1985, p. 402).

However this way of presenting Marx's views is unhelpful because it suggests a false dualism or even antithesis.[3] Elster's 'central question' actually conflates two, and each is most fruitfully posed not in 'either-or' but 'both-and' terms. The first concerns whether the state can be understood simply in instrumental terms, however conceived, or whether there are non-instrumental causal influences that need also to be taken into account. An instrumental account need not be confined to the influence of class interests alone, still less to the interests of the capitalist class, but might also include non-class interests and social forces. Non-instrumental causal influences may include, in particular, structural constraints faced by the state. Although instrumental and non-instrumental forms of explanation might be conceived as alternatives, a more productive approach is to investigate how they may be combined. State actions can be the effect of *both* the exercise of power by a dominant class *and* structural constraints emanating from the nature of the capitalist economic system. The second question concerns the limits of independent action by the state, or state autonomy. Reductionist theories reject the concept of the state as a subject with its own interests and capacities but see it as reducible to, or a reflection of, society-centred influences and forces. State-centred theories, on the other hand, emphasise the independent interests and capacities of the state.[4] However, a society-centred approach need not assume reductionist form, just as a state-centred view need not conceive the state as a closed system. State actions can be the effect of both the push of interests from inside the state and external pressures of an instrumental and/or non-instrumental kind.

Identifying these two central questions makes clear that the state should not be seen as *either* autonomous *or* reducible to class interests. For example, the state can be autonomous from the capitalist class but still conceived as an instrument controlled by other social forces and, equally, the state can be conceived non-instrumentally without being autonomous in virtue of structural constraints. Further, by posing these questions in 'both-and' terms we can see that an instrumental account of the state can be combined with understanding of the force of structural constraints, and these society-centred influences on the state can be combined with a state-centred account of the capacity of the state to pursue its own interests. Thus the autonomy of the state is a question of degree, and this *relative autonomy* is an aspect of instrumental and non-instrumental (structural) causal influences and their theoretical combination.

The over-arching framework for this approach to the theory of the state can be found in Marx's theory of history, insofar as the state is included in the superstructure. The theory of history constitutes Marx's *general* theory of which the *particular* theory of the state is a constituent element. The key text is the Preface to *A Contribution to the Critique of Political Economy* in which Marx characterises the relationship between the economic and political realms in terms of the famous 'base and superstructure' metaphor.

> The totality of ... relations of production constitutes the economic structure of society, the real foundation, on which arises a legal and political superstructure ... At a certain stage of development, the material productive forces of society come into conflict with the existing relations of production ... From forms of development of the productive forces these relations turn into their fetters. Then begins

an era of social revolution. The changes in the economic foundation
lead sooner or later to the transformation of the whole immense
superstructure (Marx, 1987, p. 263).

In this highly abstract formulation there is no direct reference to
strategic actors or, more specifically, the relation between the state
and classes. Instead there is a 'structural' explanation or relationship: between the economic structure, which comprises the relations
of production, and the legal and political superstructure, which includes the state. It is this passage, above all, which expresses the
principle of economic determination, the idea that the character of
the superstructure is to be explained in terms of the nature of the
economic structure. This can be seen as a *particular* theory which
ought to exemplify the explanatory principles specified in the *general*
theory of history.[5] This means that a *single theory of the state* (insofar
as it is part of the superstructure) can be found in Marx, albeit one
pitched at a high level of abstraction or generality, rather than a
variety of perspectives.[6]

However the Preface does not specify what kind of explanation this
is or the causal mechanisms involved. According to Cohen (1978), the
central claims of the theory of history are functional explanations.
The character of the 'legal and political superstructure' is determined
by the nature of the relations of production which, in turn, is explained by the development of the productive forces, and each of these
two stages involves functional explanation. In other words economic
determination is the principle of explanation, and functional explanation is its specific form.[7] It follows from Cohen's argument that Marx is
committed by his general theory to a functional explanation of the
state.[8] However this still leaves open the precise causal mechanisms
whereby the nature of the economic structure functionally explains
the character of the state. There are, it will be argued, two fundamental
causal mechanisms, which may be termed the 'instrumentalist thesis'
and the 'structural constraint thesis'. These causal mechanisms, and
their interrelations, provide elaborations of the functional explanation
of the state which the historical materialist principle of economic
determination entails. This view involves a departure from much
commentary on Marx and the state, which generally fails to make a
clear link with the theory of history and presents Marx's writings as
fragmentary. Therefore it is necessary to begin with a critical look at
some of this writing as a prelude to outlining our own more unified,
historical materialist conception.

Principle of Explanation	Economic Determination
Form of Explanation	Functional Explanation
Causal Mechanisms	State as 'instrument'
	Structural constraints

The state of the *Communist Manifesto*

The Communist Manifesto contains probably the best-known and most often-quoted statement on the subject of the state to be found in Marx's writing which, it has been suggested, constitutes 'the classical Marxist view on the subject of the state' (Miliband, 1965). Here it is claimed that

> each step [in the economic development] of the bourgeoisie was accompanied by a corresponding political advance of that class. ... [T]he bourgeoisie has at last, since the establishment of Modern Industry and of the world market, conquered for itself, in the modern representative state, exclusive political sway. The executive of the modern state is but a committee for managing the common affairs of the whole bourgeoisie (Marx & Engels, 1976, p. 486).

The *Communist Manifesto* appears to make a rather simple and bold claim: political or state power has been conquered or taken over by the capitalist class (thus suggesting deliberate political action by the class) and is used exclusively (i.e. to the exclusion of other classes) to defend and advance the interests of the class. Hence the *Communist Manifesto* advances a class (or 'class-theoretical') analysis of politics and, more specifically, an 'instrumental' view in which the state is viewed as an instrument controlled by the bourgeoisie for its own purposes.[9] More specifically, 'political power, properly so called, is merely the organised power of one class for oppressing another' (1976, p. 505). In this conception the principal function of the state is to maintain class domination and the state is portrayed, rather more narrowly than in the opening statement, as an essentially oppressive or coercive instrument. The underlying characterisation of capitalism is as a society riven by class conflict (the intensity of which rises with capitalist development) such that the capitalist class requires a coercive apparatus, the state, to maintain its position as the economically dominant class. Here is at least one possible answer to the question why the economic structure needs to be 'stabilised' by the state. Following the same reasoning the revolutionary overthrow of capitalism requires the proletariat to organise itself as the ruling class through the seizure of state power into its own hands.[10] Hence the working class will have to use the state as an instrument to enforce its own rule against resistance from the capitalist class, until 'in the course of development, class distinctions will have disappeared, ... [and then] ... the public power will lose its political character' (ibid., p. 505), that is, its coercive aspect. We see here the idea that the state, as a coercive apparatus, arises in the context of class conflict as an instrument for one class to oppress another and that in a classless society this instrument, accordingly, 'withers away' (McLellan, 1980, pp. 211–2).

The instrumentalist thesis, as formulated in the *Communist Manifesto*, involves three major claims. First it characterises state power as primarily coercive – the state is, fundamentally, a coercive apparatus. In this sense there a close parallel between the Marxist and Weberian conceptions of what, in essence, the state *is*. The state is defined in terms of the means specific to it, namely the use of physical force. But Marx adds to this conception a crucial class dimension so that we have the second, more specific, claim that political or state power is 'the organised power of one class for oppressing another'. In capitalist society this means that it is the organised power of the capitalist class for oppressing the proletariat. Hence Carnoy says that 'it is the notion of the state as the *repressive apparatus of the bourgeoisie* that is the distinctly Marxist characteristic of the State' (1984, p. 50). This is a claim about what state power is *for* – it is to enforce the dominant position of the capitalist class against the threat from the proletariat. In other words the *Communist Manifesto* advances a particular, and rather narrow, conception of the class interests, or 'common affairs', of the bourgeoisie. It is worth noting however that the basic conception that the state manages the common affairs of the bourgeoisie is compatible with more expansive notions of what these comprise.[11] The third claim, which may be seen as the essence of the instrumentalist thesis, tells us *how* it comes to be that the state manages the common affairs of the bourgeoisie rather than, say, acting for the public and the 'common good': the state is an instrument in the hands of the bourgeoisie and used in the interests of that class. However the precise sense in which the state is an instrument 'in the hands of' the capitalist class or this class achieves 'exclusive political sway' clearly needs to be elucidated. In these phrases the instrumentalist thesis is merely suggestive.

The state of the *Communist Manifesto*

- What the state *is*: primarily a coercive apparatus of rule
- What the state is *for*: to secure the dominant position of the capitalist class against the threat from the proletariat (to manage the common affairs of the bourgeoisie)
- How the state's role is *explained*: the state is an instrument in the hands of the bourgeoisie

---

Primary and secondary themes?

According to Miliband this is the primary view of the state in Marx, and the *Communist Manifesto* provides its most explicit expression. However there are other views against which it needs to be set. Indeed Jessop asserts that 'there are at least six different approaches' in 'the classic texts on the state' (1977, p. 354; see also 1984, chap. 1). Similarly, though not in exactly the same terms, Hay identifies 'five principal conceptions' (1996, p. 5). These are not all strictly comparable since they deal variously with what the state *is*, what state power is *for*, and *how* the role of the state is explained.

Hay points out the already noted similarity between Weberian and Marxist definitions of the state, noting that key aspects of the Weberian definition were anticipated by Engels. One approach identified by Jessop treats the state as a set of institutions or 'institutional ensemble', and this has to do with 'how Marx and Engels actually defined the state itself' (1984, p. 20). This state system is institutionally differentiated from civil society allowing us to define the state roughly in terms of the conventional boundary between 'public' and 'private' realms. Insofar as this differentiation intrinsically involves the abstraction of political power from society and its separation 'over and above' the people it is linked to the conception of the state as an expression of 'alienated politics' identified by Hay. There is some similarity between this idea of alienated politics and the view of the state as a 'parasitic institution' which exploits and oppresses civil society. Although this view is expressed in both *The Eighteenth Brumaire* and *The Civil War in France*,[12] it essentially belongs to the critique of Hegel where Marx argues that 'the state becomes the private property of officials in their struggle for self-advancement' (Jessop, 1977, p. 354) and predates the development of a class theory of state. This view remains of interest because it expresses the state-centred idea that the state may have interests of *its own*, and that what state power is for is not determined solely by society-centred class interests. If seen in conjunction with the instrumental thesis (rather than as an alternative) it suggests that the state must be seen in terms of both the self-interest of state officials and their struggle for self-advancement and the struggle of capitalists to realise their class interests through control of the state.

The concept of the state as a 'system of political domination' (Jessop, 1984, p. 27) may also be seen as a state-centred perspective insofar as it shifts attention to the specific forms of representation and intervention and their effects on the class struggle. Although this approach can involve the claim that the form of state is intrinsically capitalist, it can also, on the contrary, suggest that the state cannot simply be wielded as a neutral instrument and that its specific historically-given form influences the ability of various classes to realise their interests.

The concept of the state as the repressive arm of the bourgeoisie, as discussed above, is identified by Hay as one 'somewhat one-dimensional' view of what state power is for. An arguably more complex approach to defining what the state is for identified by both Hay and Jessop is to treat it as a 'factor of cohesion' within a given society or social formation (Jessop, 1984, p. 16).[13] This approach seems to have some similarity with 'common good' theories of the state since being a factor of cohesion entails regulating conflicting interests to ensure social order. As in the liberal conception, the necessity for the state 'arises out of the contradiction between the interests of an individual ... and the communal interest of all individuals' (Carnoy, 1984, p. 48). However although this function of moderating the conflict between classes and keeping it within the bounds of order can seem to be in the interests of society as a whole, maintaining conditions in which individuals can 'go about their business', in a class society it means in fact maintaining conditions of class domination. As Carnoy puts it, the state 'evolves in order to mediate contradictions between individuals and community, and since the community is dominated by the bourgeoisie, so is the mediation by the state' (1984, p. 48). In other words maintaining order means maintaining *capitalist* order. Although the idea of social cohesion suggests a more complex role for the state than merely coercion it does seem to have a close affinity with the repressive conception since both start from the problem of order in a society potentially torn apart, or, at least, made unstable, by class conflict. An important difference is that as a factor of cohesion the state may be involved, for example, in regulating competitive relations between capitalists as well as the conflict between the two main classes.

A more expansive conception of what state power is for is contained in the idea of the state as an 'ideal collective capitalist'. This approach starts from 'the fact that capital is neither self-reproducing nor capable on its own of securing the conditions for its own reproduction' (Hay, 1996, p. 8; see also Jessop, 2002, p. 18). In other words a capitalist economic structure has certain political preconditions and the function of the state as ideal collective capitalist is to provide these conditions. Such conditions will include the maintenance of order and cohesion, but the approach suggests a wider range of 'needs of capital'.

Some common threads can be drawn together from this brief run-through of apparently diverse approaches. The state is conceived as a set of institutions (rather than a single entity) separated from society as a 'public power'. Despite this complexity the most fundamental feature of the state is that it is a coercive apparatus capable of enforcing rule. This feature is emphasised in the view of the state as the repressive arm of the bourgeoisie, which may be seen as the basic Marxist conception. More expansive conceptions of what the state is for – such as factor of cohesion or ideal collective capitalist – extend, rather than supersede, this basic approach. They share a common starting point in the assertion that capitalism is not a self-reproducing system and is not capable of securing the conditions for its own reproduction. Securing these conditions is, essentially, what the state is for. At the most basic level coercive power, abstracted from relations of production which are based on voluntary exchange, has to be located in a specialised apparatus, the state, and used, when necessary, for the oppression of the proletariat. But the state, as a set of institutions, takes on a wider range of functions corresponding to the needs of capital and/or interests of the capitalist class. The institutional separation is an important feature of the modern state. It is the basis of the critique of the state as an expression of alienated politics. But it also poses as a problem the *connections* between the state and society, between class interests and state power. For example, the idea of the state as a parasitic institution suggests the state may have its own interests. Marxist claims concerning what the state is for need to be supported by plausible accounts of *how* this role is explained. This brings us back to instrumentalism and other approaches in the classic texts.

Jessop, in company with Miliband and Held, identifies the instrumentalist thesis as 'the most common approach' (1977, p. 356). Similarly, Hay refers to it as 'perhaps the most prevalent conception of the state within Marxist theory' (1996, p. 6). Alongside this conception Miliband identifies what he terms a 'secondary view' of the state in

Marx. This is a 'view ... of the state as independent from and superior to all social classes, as being the dominant force in society rather than the instrument of a dominant class' (1965, p. 283) and is found in *The Eighteenth Brumaire*. Miliband sees this analysis of the autonomy of the state as very much a subordinate theme in Marx 'which it is inaccurate to hold up as of similar status with the first' (1965, p. 283). Here we have the misleading contrast between two, apparently contradictory, views of the state in Marx.[14] On the one hand the state is depicted as the instrument of the dominant class, and on the other the state is said to be independent (autonomous) and, indeed, 'superior' to all classes. This basic interpretation of Marx is shared by other writers, although there are some nuances in the presentation of the two views and disagreement as to which is primary (Elster, 1985; Evans, 1975; Held, 1984). According to Held

> There are at least two strands in Marx's account of the relation between the classes and the state ... the first ... stresses that the state ... may take a variety of forms and constitute a source of power which need not be ... under the unambiguous control of the dominant class in the short term. By this account, the state retains a degree of power independent of this class ... [it is] ... 'relatively autonomous'. The second strand ... is without doubt the dominant one ... : the state and its bureaucracy are class instruments ... (1984, pp. 52–3).

We can explore this apparent dualism a little further by considering how Elster makes sense of Marx's views on the state. Elster distinguishes three approaches to the state in Marx: instrumentalism, abdication (or abstention), and class balance theories. The first, instrumentalist, approach may be distinguished from the other two by the state having, in the former case, little or no, and in the latter, substantial, autonomy from the capitalist class. The three approaches to the state in Marx thus offer two different answers to the 'central question' of the relationship between the state and the interests of the dominant class. The instrumentalist view is 'Marx's best known theory of the state' (Elster, 1985, p. 408) and its classic formulation is presented in the *Communist Manifesto*. Elster's basic argument is that after 1848 Marx moved away from this view towards an abdication/ abstention or class balance theory of the state. From the 1850s the view that comes to prominence in Marx's analyses of specific political conjunctures in Europe is that the bourgeoisie abdicate from power (France) or abstain from taking it (England, Germany) because they perceive that their interests are better served if they remain outside politics (Elster, 1985, p. 411).

For example, in *The Eighteenth Brumaire of Louis Bonaparte*, Bonapartism is analysed in terms of 'a voluntary abstention from power by the industrial bourgeoisie ... motivated by a desire to split the attention of the subjugated classes' (Elster, 1985, p. 386). It is also possible to read the analysis of *The Eighteenth Brumaire* in terms of a class balance theory of the state according to which 'the struggle between two opposed classes allows the state to assert itself by divide and conquer' (Elster, 1985, p. 422). What unites both of these views is that they appear to accord a high degree of autonomy to the state *vis-à-vis* the capitalist class. Elster concludes that, far from the instrumentalist view being the dominant one, 'Marx made the autonomy of the state into the cornerstone of his theory' (1985, p. 426). However it seems clear that the abstention/abdication theory is really just a variant of the view of the state as an instrument of the capitalist class. The implication is that the bourgeoisie refrains from direct control of the state only on condition that the state continues to manage the common affairs of the class, and is able to take power (back) into its own hands if this service is not performed. The state as instrument of the capitalist class is wielded in an indirect, or arms-length fashion, and the autonomy or independence of the state is more illusory than real.

The 'class balance' view represents a different case. Here the state seems to enjoy a genuine autonomy from the capitalist class. The suggestion is that conditions of class balance severely curtail the capacity of the capitalist class to exert direct control over the state and thus allow the state to 'assert itself'. This claim evidently shares with the view of the state as a 'parasitic' institution the state-centred idea that the state has its own interests which it may, in propitious circumstances, be able to assert and that it is not, therefore, merely a reflection of external society-centred interests. There is clearly a tension between this notion of autonomy and the reductionist instrumental conception attributed to the *Communist Manifesto*. The two views may be reconciled on the assumption that the state is from time to time autonomous and, at other times, controlled by the capitalist class as its instrument. For example, it might be argued that conditions of class balance are exceptional (Carnoy, 1984, p. 53). Normally, in this view, the capitalist class retains the upper hand in the class struggle and this is reflected in its grasp on political power. Then the analysis of

The Eighteenth Brumaire would just be an exception to the rule of the *Communist Manifesto* (i.e. a secondary view contrasted with the primary view of the *Communist Manifesto*).

The idea of state autonomy can be upgraded by claiming that propitious circumstances for self-assertion by the state (i.e. class balance) are in fact rather more normal than exceptional. Thus Evans suggests that 'the class situation of the French Second Republic may be far more common than the two class model of the Manifesto would indicate' (1975, p. 119). The point is that the analysis of the *Communist Manifesto*, the classic statement of the instrumentalist view, is based on a simplified and one-sided view of the dynamics of the class structure of capitalist societies which overemphasises the tendency toward simplification and polarisation (see Hall, 1977). In his analysis of specific political conjunctures, such as *The Eighteenth Brumaire*, the real complexity of the class structure leads Marx, Elster suggests, away from an instrumental view of the state. Thus Bonapartism may be 'more of a normal than a transitional form' (Evans, 1975, p. 119), so that the state as capitalist instrument becomes a subordinate theme in Marx.

Elster poses the question of autonomy in terms of the relationship between the state and the capitalist class, conceived as a game between two strategic actors. Thus, in this conception, 'the state has explanatory autonomy when (and to the extent that) its structure and policies cannot be explained by the interest of an economically dominant class'. In other words 'the autonomy is defined negatively, as the absence of class-interest explanation' (1985, p. 405).[15] But this is a very narrow conception, ignoring the influence of other classes. The influence of other classes is recognised in the 'class balance' model, but the main point of this model is to show that a more complex and disaggregated class structure may create conditions where it is more difficult for the capitalist class to hold political sway and, consequently, the potential for the state to assert itself is enhanced. Another possibility, in some circumstances, is that some other class or classes are able to influence state power in their own interests. Thus, the state can be autonomous in Elster's sense yet unable to 'assert itself' since its structure and policies may be explained by the interests of other classes or social forces. In this sense negative *autonomy from* (the capitalist class) does not necessarily entail positive *autonomy to*. Most important here is the possibility of effective 'pressure from below'. This is exemplified by the establishment of a 'normal working day' through the enactment of the Ten Hours Bill. This limitation of the working day is famously characterised by Marx as 'the first time that ... the political economy of the middle class succumbed to the political economy of the working class' (1985, p. 11; see Wetherly, 1992). Thus in contrast to the primary-secondary dualism three possible views or models of the state are suggested on the basis of a simple Marxist framework: capitalist rule, working class power, and state autonomy.

These arguments are essentially society-centred in that they focus on the ability of class forces to influence or control the state for their own purposes. They involve a notably weak conception of state autonomy, which is essentially a by-product of the balance of class forces in civil society. Whether exceptional or normal, the state is only able to assert itself in those 'historical instances when no class has enough power to rule through the state' (Carnoy, 1984, p. 53). As for the intrinsic capacity of the state to project power outwards into civil society, these views have nothing to say. This also involves a tendency to counterpose state autonomy to class interest explanation. Thus, for Elster *either* the state is autonomous *or* it is reducible to class interests. The analysis of Bonapartism, whether seen as a normal or transitional (exceptional) form implies an unhelpful dualism insofar as it suggests that in some circumstances the state enjoys genuine autonomy and in others is merely an instrument of the capitalist class. Either-or. However, this is a false dichotomy, for there is a range of 'in-between' positions. These in-between positions can be charted by recognising the capacity of the state to assert itself in virtue of its own capacities and resources, not just as a by-product of particular circumstances of class balance. Thus an instrumental framework is compatible with a conception of the state as a potentially autonomous subject capable of exercising power on its own behalf, combining society-centred and state-centred approaches. This allows us to conceive state power as always a reflection of the various forces, including the capitalist class, working class, state officials and other forces, struggling to assert their interests through control of the state. In this approach the question is not which force or interest controls the state to the exclusion of all others but what is the balance between these forces and, in particular, which carries most weight. The state may be more or less autonomous, more or less controlled by the capitalist class. The idea of the state as an instrument of the capitalist class is not lost but, contrary to the *Communist Manifesto*, this would entail that the bourgeoisie has conquered for itself *predominant* rather than *exclusive* political sway.

The primary and secondary views bring to the fore 'class-theoretical' arguments – focusing on the relationship between the state and class interests. However, there is another side to the theory of the state in

Marx which involves what may be termed a structural (or 'capital-theoretical') approach. This should not be thought of as a rival theory to the instrumental approach but as complementary – indeed, the secondary view is elaborated by a structural argument. The question is not whether state actions are the effect of structure or of agency but the manner in which these two explanatory dimensions are combined. Structural explanation involves roughly the claim that 'social structures' (patterns or systems of social relationships) exhibit their own 'laws of motion', developmental tendencies and effects which are prior to individuals or agents in the explanatory order. Typically the action of agents is explained or conditioned by their location within or in relation to social structure.

In Marxist political economy it is, in particular, the economy which is understood as a structure of this kind. Hence the idea that there are laws or tendencies of capitalist development which originate in the character of the capitalist economy as a structure or system. However Marx's theory of history proposes a model of society which involves two key structures: the 'economic base' and the 'legal and political superstructure'.[16] In elucidating the nature of structural explanation in this theory, there appear to be two distinct theoretical claims which are often compounded. The first is the conceptualisation of the economy as a structure which is prior to individuals in the explanatory order: in this conception 'individuals are dealt with ... only insofar as they are the personifications of economic categories, the bearers of particular class-relations and interests' (Marx, 1976, p. 92). In this approach structure is clearly given priority over agency in the explanation of action – the decisions and actions of capitalists are depicted not as those of choosing agents but as reflections of objective class interests determined by location within a set of class relations. Equally the legal and political superstructure (or, more narrowly, the state system, or parts thereof) may be conceived as a structure in similar terms with its own organisational principles and, indeed, laws of motion (Jessop, 1990, p. 84). Thus state managers or officials may be seen as personifications of political categories, embodiments of objective locations within the state system and corresponding interests. However this conception of base and superstructure as possessing their own distinctive structural or systemic properties does not imply or require, contrary to Jessop, their mutual 'autonomisation or self-closure' (1990, p. 83). The (by no means clean and tidy) institutional separation of the political and economic realms which permits distinctive organisational principles within each (and thus their conceptualisation as structures) is consistent with their interaction and interdependence. The economy is clearly not independent from the state, and no more is the state immune from economic influences. Hence the second type of theoretical claim, which involves a *structural relationship* between the economic and political dimensions of society. We could think of the two interacting systems in terms of an exchange of inputs and outputs which have some influence on how each functions and develops. Clearly the nature and extent of this influence (in both directions) needs to be elucidated. We could, for example, think of the functioning and development of the capitalist economy as being governed primarily by its own internal systemic properties (especially competition between capitalist enterprises and the basic conflict between capitalist class and working class), or as being largely shaped by the exercise of political power through various forms of state economic regulation and control. The first is clearly a more orthodox Marxist conception, but in either case the 'laws of development' of the capitalist economy are better thought of as tendencies, not 'iron laws'. Similarly the form and/or functions of the state may be conceived largely in terms of its own organising principles or as primarily governed by economic influences or constraints of various kinds. In Marxist theory this structural relationship is conceived asymmetrically in favour of the economy – the nature of the economic structure supplies a principle of explanation of the state, more than *vice-versa*.

Although 'structure' and 'agency' are not mutually exclusive explanatory concepts it is possible to set aside for one moment the instrumental conception of the state so that the relationship between the economic base and political superstructure, between economy and state, may be conceived directly in structural terms. On this view the question is not which class controls the state but the constraints faced by the state emanating from the character and dynamics of a capitalist economy. A 'test case' of this approach is where instrumental control of the state by the dominant class or other social force is absent. This is the situation analysed by Marx in *The Eighteenth Brumaire* wherein the state becomes independent of and superior to all social classes (the 'secondary view'). A key finding of this analysis is that, despite the autonomy of Bonaparte's regime from the capitalist class, still 'Bonaparte feels it is his mission to safeguard "bourgeois order". But the strength of this bourgeois order lies in the middle class...' (Marx, quoted in Miliband, 1965, p. 284). Thus even when the state is 'independent' and apparently 'superior' to class forces it 'remains, and cannot in a class society but remain, the protector of an economically and socially dominant class' (Miliband, 1965, p. 285). Similarly Evans suggests that in spite of the asserted autonomy of the state from the capitalist class Bonaparte 'remains the guardian of the bourgeois order' (Evans, 1975, p. 118). Held also notes that even when Marx stresses the independent role of the state the interests of the capitalist class are paramount.

> For the state in a capitalist society, Marx concluded from his study of the Bonapartist regime, cannot escape its dependence upon that society and, above all, upon those who own and control the productive process... Accordingly, Bonaparte could not help but sustain the long-term economic interests of the bourgeoisie (Held, 1984, p. 55).

The idea of 'dependence' supplies a reason, in the absence of capitalist rule, for state action to preserve the 'bourgeois order'. The reason is that such action is necessary for the state itself in the sense that it protects state interests. In this view, state policies support capital accumulation not as an end in itself but as a means to an end, that is as the best way for the state to realise its own interests.

It may appear that the structural argument leaves no room for the idea of the independent state or state autonomy. This is because if the structural context forces the state to pursue policies that favour capital accumulation this effectively shuts out the possibility that state managers face strategic choices. However this conclusion is mistaken for two related reasons. First, the argument is that state policies will favour capital accumulation because this is the best option for state managers to realise their own interests such as, as Block suggests, to stay in power (1987, p. 84). Thus the interests of state managers matter in this argument: it is because of the character of state managers' interests that policy favours accumulation. If the interests of state managers were defined differently then they would act differently within the same structural context. For example it makes a difference to state policies whether state managers act in accordance with a 'public service ethic' or, as Block claims, to maximise their power, prestige and wealth (1987, p. 84). Second, the structural argument need not involve the claim that structural constraints are so powerful that only one outcome is possible and, in fact, such a claim would be highly implausible. This means that the state always has room for manoeuvre. For example Block claims that state managers are 'dependent on the maintenance of some *reasonable* level of economic activity ... since their own continued power rests on a healthy economy' (1987, p. 58). Likewise business confidence is not an on-off variable but is defined by a spectrum within which there may conceivably be a range that is acceptable for state managers. The room for manoeuvre equates to policy discretion and allows the possibility that some policies may even be at odds with business confidence (or the confidence of specific sectors of business) within an overall policy package that maintains business confidence at an acceptable level. And even if we assume, implausibly, that the state must single-mindedly court business confidence as a way of promoting economic health there will always be some element of policy discretion because there will always be more than one possible 'accumulation strategy' (Jessop, 1990, p. 159). Thus the structural argument does not negate the idea that the state has some degree of autonomy, some capacity for choice and independent action, i.e. relative autonomy. As with the instrumental conception of the state the question of state autonomy is not helpfully posed in either-or terms.

A theoretical synthesis?

We have seen that it is misleading to counterpose the instrumental conception of the state to the idea of state autonomy. Rather, a better way of distinguishing two approaches to explaining the role of the state in Marx is in terms of the instrumentalist thesis and the structural constraint thesis. The question of state autonomy may be posed within each of these frames of reference. However it may appear that, viewed in this way, Marx's writings are shot through with ambiguity and tension. Two dimensions of such ambiguity may be perceived. The first is the structure-agency dimension or, in other words, the distinction between class- and capital-theoretical approaches. This ambiguity is encapsulated in Held's apt characterisation of Marx's approach: the state is *both* 'deeply embedded in socio-economic relations *and* linked to particular interests' (1984, p. 52) but no link is made between the working of these two explanatory principles. The second dimension of ambiguity is between a determinist thrust and a recognition that there is scope for independent action by the state, or state autonomy.

To overcome the apparent structure-agency ambiguity the Marxist theory of the state requires a genuine synthesis that elucidates the way in which economic power is both embedded in the structural properties of the system and expressed through class agency, and the relationship between these explanatory dimensions. The apparent ambiguity between economic determinism and state autonomy may be overcome through the principle of causal asymmetry or primacy which states that 'politics' is explained by 'economics' more than *vice-versa*. This allows for the evident truth that state power can and does have significant effects within civil society and yet asserts that over a range of areas that impinge decisively on the reproduction of a capitalist economy state power is subordinate to economic power. Thus the Marxist theory of the state synthesises structure and agency, but this synthesis does not rule out the possibility of some room for manoeuvre by the state, some degree of state autonomy.

This synthesis can be accomplished within the framework of the theory of history and the famous 'base-superstructure' model. In this approach the 'base-superstructure' model is conceived as Marx's general theory of which the strategic actor and structural approaches are specific forms or, better, causal mechanisms. This interpretation opens up the possibility of seeing functional explanation, embodied in the theory of history, as Marx's general theory of the state.[17]

3
The Instrumentalist Thesis – a Restatement

Introduction

The Marxist theory of the state involves economic determination as its principle of explanation. This is a version of a 'society-centred' view of the state that places emphasis on external (located in society) causal influences. Of course, Marxism is not the only version of a society-centred theory as other traditions in state theory, notably pluralism, share this approach.[1] All such theories utilise a conception of the state as institutionally differentiated from 'civil society'. The distinctiveness of Marxism derives from the emphasis it places on causal influences rooted in the nature of the economic structure, coupled with its distinctive characterisation of capitalist relations of production.

Society-centred views are conventionally contrasted with state-centred views that place emphasis on internal causal influences, such as the 'push' of interests originating within the state allied to state capacities or power (Poggi, 1990, pp. 120–5). In this approach the state is conceived as an autonomous subject capable of formulating and pursuing its own interests. However society-centred and state-centred (external and internal) explanations should not be counterposed. Rather, the key question in state theory is to combine these two perspectives so that state power is analysed as an effect of both internal and external determinants. This approach sees the state as, potentially, a subject with its own interests and capacities, but subject to external pressures and influences.

Thus the Marxist theory of the state should not be posed in terms of economic determinism (reductionism) versus state autonomy. The central task of Marxist state theory is to reconcile a theory of economic determination with the potential for state autonomy. This allows for the

27

relative autonomy of the state, that is a degree of autonomy, but asserts the primacy of economic determination. This involves a formula such as, roughly, 'the economy explains not everything but a great deal about politics and the state'.[2]

We have seen that Marx's writing, and much of the contemporary literature, suggests two 'causal mechanisms' that elucidate how economic determination operates, that is how the nature of the economic structure explains the character of the 'legal and political superstructure': instrumentalist and structuralist explanations. These two approaches may be defined provisionally in terms of agency and structure. Thus whereas the instrumentalist thesis seems to rely on 'conscious historical agency to explain state policies' (Barrow, 1993, p. 45) the structuralist approach relies on impersonal structural constraints or imperatives. Because the structuralist approach can involve a form of explanation that makes little or no reference to conscious agency, while the instrumentalist approach seems to involve no necessary reference to social structure, the two approaches are sometimes conceived as alternative strands or approaches within the Marxist state debate. For example Barrow distinguishes 'plain Marxism' (the instrumentalist approach) from 'neo-Marxism' (the structuralist approach). Famously, the Miliband-Poulantzas debate has often, though too simplistically, been characterised in this way (Carnoy, 1984, p. 104).

However, as was argued in the last chapter, there are good reasons to reject this dichotomy (and the sufficiency of either structure or agency as a basis of explanation on its own) in favour of some form of mixed explanation that examines the interrelations between structure and agency. Thus the instrumentalist and structuralist approaches may be seen as two types of explanation which may be combined in the Marxist theory of the state. The approach being advocated here thus rejects two untenable dichotomies, and analyses instead the interrelationship between: economic determination and state autonomy (state-centred and society-centred approaches); and, instrumentalist and structuralist causal mechanisms. Although instrumentalist and structuralist causal mechanisms are elements that combine together to yield a theory of the state, for analytical purposes there is some advantage in separating them out. This will assist in clarifying, and responding to, criticisms that have been made of each approach.

The instrumentalist thesis

Just as a society-centred view of the state is not distinctively Marxist, the same can be said of instrumentalism. Indeed it can be claimed that instrumentalism is at the heart of conventional currents in state theory, such as pluralism and elite theory. It can also be said to be at the heart of mainstream political strategy and action. For example 'parliamentarism' conceives winning a majority in the legislative assembly as securing control of the state and, thus, winning power. In effect it conceives the state as an instrument that can be controlled by a Parliamentary majority. Thus it is logical to begin with instrumentalism in general before going on to distinguish its particular Marxist variant. In fact, as we will see, there is more than one Marxist version of the instrumentalist approach.

At the start of his study of *The State in Capitalist Society* Miliband refers to 'the vast inflation of the state's power and activity in the advanced capitalist societies' in consequence of which 'men' rely increasingly on the state's 'sanction and support' in order to realise their purposes or interests. This means that

> they must ... seek to influence and shape the state's power and purpose, or try and appropriate it altogether. It is for the state's attention, or for its control, that men compete; and it is against the state that beat the waves of social conflict (Miliband, 1969, p. 1).

This statement may be taken as providing a rough definition of the instrumentalist approach.[3] The central claim is that the state, and state power, may be controlled or influenced by external agents or social forces and used to realise their interests, as against rival or conflicting interests. Thus the instrumentalist approach may be characterised as a form of 'influence' theory in which state policies are explained in terms of the interests of the social forces that are successful in influencing or controlling the state's power and purpose. The state is, in other words, an instrument used by agents to realise their purposes.

Miliband's characterisation seems to suggest that it is because of the vast inflation of the state that it has become the focus of a struggle for control. It appears as if it is because the state has become an instrument of a rather powerful kind that there is recognition of the need to control it. However the instrumental conception may apply equally to a 'minimal' as to an 'inflated' state (the state characterised as instrument of the bourgeoisie in the *Communist Manifesto* is, after all, rather closer to the minimal type in historical perspective).[4] And the scope of the state's power and activity might be seen as consequence, rather than cause, of its use as an instrument. In other words, instrumental use of state power to realise specific interests may explain its inflation. Miliband also suggests that 'the waves of social conflict' (i.e. the forces competing for influence or control) are all external to the state, whereas the purposes or interests that the state's power is used to secure may be those generated from inside the state system itself. In Miliband's theory it is precisely the 'state elite' that exercises power, but his emphasis on the links between this and the corporate elite allows little scope for the play of interests generated inside the state. Taking these qualifications into account, three elements are involved in Miliband's definition:

- the state as a particular type (or set) of institution(s) that exercises power;
- the character of external (or internal) social forces or interests that compete to influence or control the state; and,
- the nature of influence or control exerted by these social forces.

The state as a 'power container'

The conception of the state is as a 'power container', that is a key institution that organises power in society. In this approach 'institutions organize power ... by vesting the individuals occupying certain positions with the authority to make decisions about how to deploy the key resources mobilized by that institution' (Barrow, 1993, p. 13). It follows that state power is controlled by individuals who occupy positions of authority within the state system – the state elite (Miliband, 1969, p. 54). The state is 'a phenomenon principally and emphatically located within the sphere of political power' (Poggi, 1990, p. 4). And 'what we should consider as unique to political power, as conceptually intrinsic to it, is control over the means of violence' (Poggi, 1990, p. 5). Thus, in Weberian terms, the state is defined in terms of the means specific to it, or its distinctive form of power. This coercive power is the basis of the state's essential function to make and enforce rules in society, as well as to realise any other ends or purposes that it determines. Or, rather, ends or purposes determined by those agents or forces that control the state. This control can be achieved either by occupying positions of authority within the state, or by exercising influence over those that do.[5]

The conception of the state as an 'instrument' expresses the potential for those who control or influence it to use state power to realise their own purposes. A simplified version (or ideal type) of this conception of the state may be set out using the following assumptions:

• The state is a neutral instrument that can be utilised for any purpose
• The state is a unitary institution with a single 'command centre'
• The state exercises decisive power in society

On the basis of these assumptions individuals 'occupying certain positions' (the state elite) are able to control the key resources mobilised by the state (political power) and by this means exercise decisive power to realise their own purposes (i.e. to rule). For example, Parliamentarism might take this form, where Parliament is seen as the locus of sovereignty so that a Parliamentary majority confers control of the state and thereby the capacity to 'run the country'. Relaxing these simple assumptions does not invalidate the instrumentalist approach, although it does imply a more qualified or modest version.

Weber notes that 'the state cannot be defined in terms of its ends' or purposes, for 'there is scarcely any task that some political association has not taken in hand' (1991, p. 77). This tells us that the tasks undertaken by states in history are highly variable and even open-ended. In other words the state is a flexible kind of instrument that can be adapted to a variety of ends. However this is not the same as saying that the state is a neutral instrument, since it is consistent with what Weber says that particular forms of the state are adapted to some purposes and not others. However, according to Jessop, the instrumentalist account does assume that the state is such a neutral tool 'which is equally accessible in principle to all political forces and can also be used for any feasible governmental purpose' (1990, p. 145). Seen in this way state actions seem to reflect merely the interests of those agents or forces, such as those in civil society, that are successful in influencing or controlling the state at a specific time. The state appears as a kind of transmission belt onto which interests are fed at one end to be converted into appropriate policies emerging at the other end. Jessop objects that

this approach ignores all the effects of state forms on the process of representation and the ways in which the interests of capital can be affected and redefined through changes in the state system and/or through shifts in the balance of political forces within which capitalists must manoeuvre (1990, p. 146).

If interests do not exist independently of the state, and the specific form of state may affect the differential capacities of political forces to exert influence or control and to realise particular purposes, it follows that the state should not be conceived merely as a neutral instrument. However, this is not a reason to reject the instrumentalist approach, only a crude version of it. Indeed in its conventional meaning an instrument is normally better suited to particular users (rather than being equally accessible to all), and adapted to particular purposes (rather than being all-purpose). The state is rather like other instruments in these respects. The objections to the simple instrumentalist thesis show that a more sophisticated understanding of the nature of interests and of the state as an institutionalised form of power resources is needed. But they do not show that it is illegitimate to conceive the state as an instrument that external forces seek to influence or control to their own advantage. Indeed in his criticisms of instrumentalism Jessop is 'not denying that the state can be used to some effect: this is the whole point behind political struggle' (1990, p. 149–50).

One form a more sophisticated version might take is to conceive the state not as a neutral instrument but as possessing 'an in-built, *form-determined* bias that makes it more open to capitalist influences and more readily mobilized for capitalist policies' (Jessop, 1990, p. 148). Jessop sees this notion of 'structural selectivity' as a significant advance on the instrumentalist mode of analysis. This is because it takes the form of state seriously as having some effect. And this is another way of saying that state form has some kind of in-built bias, that it cannot (or is very unlikely to) be neutral. But, far from guaranteeing that state power is functional for capital, Jessop emphasises that 'form problematizes function' (1990, p. 148). Going beyond structural selectivity, Jessop advocates a 'strategic-relational' approach, and the related notion of 'strategic selectivity'. The claimed merit of this approach is that it does not see state power as reducible to the political forces and interests that control it or as an effect merely of state form. Rather it 'stands at the intersection' of these approaches, putting the form of the state 'at the heart of ... analysis' but also directing attention to 'the various forces engaged in struggle' and 'the structural and conjunctural factors' that determine the balance between these forces (1990, p. 149). 'In this sense the "relational" approach ... endorses the notion of "structural selectivity" but does not suggest that its effects always favour one class or set of interests' (1990, p. 149). And the form of the state itself 'depends on the contingent and provisional outcome of struggles to realize more or less specific "state projects" ' (Jessop, 1990, p. 9).

However, despite Jessop's rejection of instrumentalism, this approach looks like a sophisticated version of instrumental theory, rather than an alternative. It builds on the basic instrumentalist insight that the essence of political struggle is, in Miliband's words to 'seek to influence and shape the state's power and purpose, or try and appropriate it altogether' in order to realise specific purposes or interests. There is no incompatibility between instrumentalist theory and recognition that: the state is not a neutral instrument; the bias of the state depends on the relation between state form and strategies for influencing or appropriating state power; and, state form is itself a product of political struggle. Indeed instrumentalist logic suggests that the struggle for state power is one, first (and perhaps foremost), to change or reform the state to advantage particular interests and, second, to use state power to realise these interests. Success in the second will naturally be conditioned by the outcome of the first, but not be dependent on it. That is, those forces for which the given (resulting from past struggles) state form is less accessible may still be successful in exercising influence or control to their own advantage, even though this is more difficult. Conversely those forces for which the state form is more accessible may still be unsuccessful in exercising influence or control. For ex-ample, even if liberal democracy is 'the best possible political shell' for capitalism this doesn't guarantee state actions in favour of capital, and reform resulting from 'pressure from below' is still possible. However it may be that there is a strong tendency for capitalist interests to be favoured.

In the identification of instrumentalist theory with a conception of the state as a neutral instrument, or the neglect of state form, Jessop constructs something of a straw man. Poggi's essentially instrumental theory of the state focuses on the interplay between 'the demand for state action and the supply of state action' (1990, p. 113) or, in other words, 'the pull of interests emanating from the outlying society ... [and] ... the push of interests lodged inside the state itself' (1990, p. 120). Analysing the demand side as comprised of two compo-nents, this framework yields three 'arguments' or types of explanation. The 'invasive state argument' focuses on supply side interests in 'maximising the scope and discretionality of political and administra-tive arrangements, and in increasing the share of society's resources produced and managed by means of those arrangements' (1990, pp. 120–1). On the demand side, the 'serviceable state argument ...

envisages the state as acting obligingly in response to increasing social demands', while the 'partisan state argument' focuses on 'the interested pressures of (in one version) strata disadvantaged by the capitalist order or (in another version) of dominant economic forces which receive the state's assistance in exercising that dominance' (1990, p. 120). Although the emphasis here is on state actions as an expression of interests (i.e. the state is conceived as an instrument) Poggi also draws attention to the effect of the specific form of state. Two features of the state are highlighted: it 'constitutes a functionally differentiated system of society' and is itself 'composed ... of functionally differentiated arrangements, attending to different aspects of the management and exercise of political power' (1990, p. 121). In virtue of this differentiation, at both levels, the state and its various agencies 'tend to become locked into ... [their] ... own specific concerns ..., to become self-referential' (1990, p. 121). Thus the specific form of state reinforces the invasive state tendency and, in consequence, limits or problematises its accessibility to external forces.

Poggi's theory displays an obvious affinity with a Marxist approach, through its demand side emphasis on economically weaker and stronger groups (i.e. working class and bourgeoisie). A Marxist framework can likewise incorporate an analysis of the effect of the form of state on its accessibility to class forces. For example Miliband's essentially instrumentalist account of 'the state in capitalist society' emphasises the same two particular features of this form of state as in Poggi's theory – the existence of the state as a functionally differentiated, *separate entity*, and as a collection of institutions that comprise the *state system* (Miliband, 1969, pp. 49–67). According to Miliband state power lies in a set of institutions 'which make up "the state", and whose interrelationship shapes the form of the state system' (1969, p. 54). Further, state power is 'wielded in its different manifestations by the people who occupy the leading positions in each of these institutions ... These are the people who constitute what may be described as the state elite' (1969, p. 54). The significance of these features of the specific form of the state is that the capitalist class, in seeking to 'influence and shape the state's power and purpose' in its own interests, confronts the state – and the state elite – 'as a distinct and separate entity' (1969, p. 54). In other words, economic power and political power are institutionally differentiated, and the central problem for instrumental theory is to show how and to what extent the former is translated into the latter. Thus, far from treating the state as a neutral instrument that the capitalist class is able simply to lay hold of, instrumentalism cannot avoid the difficulty posed for such control by the specific form of the state. A key aspect of this is that state power is formally in the hands of the government and, in liberal democracy, government is formally accountable to the people as a whole through an electoral system based on political equality. As Luger suggests, this coupling of an economic system based on inequality of resources with a political system based on formal equality makes 'grappling with the issue of power ... particularly complex' (2000, p. 16). For

> while economic resources clearly present a tremendous political advantage to their holders, those with limited economic resources have also succeeded in shaping public policy because power held in one sphere is not automatically or completely translated into the other. Thus it is not axiomatic who will be triumphant in any particular political battle (Luger, 2000, p. 16).

It might be that the 'tremendous advantage' conferred by ownership of economic resources is generally sufficient to allow the capitalist class to translate its economic power into political power. However, the institutional separation of the state and the political equality that are hallmarks of liberal democracy as a specific form of state mean that this translation is never automatic. In this vein Miliband advises that the first step in analysing the accessibility of state power to the capitalist class

> is to note the obvious but fundamental fact that this class is involved in a *relationship* with the state, which cannot be *assumed*, in the political conditions which are typical of advanced capitalism, to be that of principal to agent (1969, p. 54).[6]

The second feature of the liberal democratic form of state – that it is a set of institutions comprising a state system – points up the distinction between government and the state, that the government is only one among this set of institutions. Although the government is formally in charge of the state and thereby provides the basis of its unity, the very separation of government from other functionally differentiated institutions within the state system means that a key question of liberal democracy is how far governments do actually control state power and, relatedly, how and to what extent the unity of the state is secured. This feature of the state has effects on the accessibility of state power to different class and other forces. It suggests that control of Parliament and government does not translate automatically into control of the state, and that, because of this and the institutional complexity of the state, its unity is not pre-given. The form of state seems, again, to make it more difficult for it to be controlled and used as an instrument to realise the interests of an external force, such as the capitalist class. However it does not mean that the state cannot be conceptualised as an instrument, and its complexity and potential fragmentation suggests that instrumental theory must identify the principal channels or mechanisms of influence. The unity of the state is not pre-given, but this does not mean that such unity cannot be politically constituted.

Thus there is no intrinsic or necessary connection between instrumental theory of the state and a conception of the state as a *neutral* instrument. On the contrary instrumentalism provides a coherent explanatory framework for questions such as why particular state forms, and not others, against which beat 'the waves of social conflict', are given. The answer, in general terms, is that they are themselves formed by these waves.

The third assumption of an ideal-type conception of the state as a 'power container' seems to be that the state exercises decisive influence in society.[7] The whole point and interest of conceiving the state as an instrument is that it is an institution (or set of institutions) that does exercise power in society. Thus Miliband's analysis begins by pointing out 'the vast inflation of the state's power and activity in the advanced capitalist societies' in consequence of which 'more than ever before men now live in the shadow of the state' (1969, p. 1). The decisive influence of the state is referred to by Poggi as the 'paramountcy' of political power.

> It can be claimed for political power that it has a functional priority over others, for only in so far as it discharges … [its peculiar] … tasks [(to secure order in the face of external or internal threats)] can individuals go about their business – and that includes the exercise of whatever other form of social power they possess – in a (relatively) peaceable and orderly manner. For this reason it is sometimes claimed that political power is paramount with respect to other forms of social power (1990, p. 9).

These views emphasise that in seeking to influence or control the state's power the stakes are very high. Of course, the state is not the only 'power container', and there are different forms or types of power. Poggi, following Bobbio (1983), distinguishes three forms of social power – economic, ideological (normative) and political (Poggi, 1990, p. 4; also see Mann, 1986; Runciman, 1989). Similarly Barrow argues that 'the individuals who occupy positions of institutional authority in a society control different types of power: economic power, political power, ideological power' (Barrow, 1993, p. 14). This means that the power of the state can only be analysed in the context of these other forms of social power and their institutional embodiments.

This analysis involves describing or mapping the *distribution* of power resources among agents or social forces and thereby revealing the distribution of power in a society – what Barrow refers to as power structure research (Barrow, 1993, p. 13). More than this, power structure research must be concerned with the *relationship* between different forms or types of social power and their institutional embodiments. Poggi describes this relationship as one of rivalry between the three principal forms of social power, or rather between 'the groups which have built one or other of them up as a facility for the pursuit of their own interests' (1990, p. 8). This rivalry is conceived as having

> two overlapping aspects. On the one hand, each power will seek to restrict the autonomous sway of the others ... On the other hand, it will seek to enhance itself by establishing a hold on as great as possible a quantum of the others, by converting itself to some extent into them (1990, p. 8).[8]

Thus an instrumental conception of the state is not concerned merely with the use of the state as an instrument but, more properly, with how the state figures in the intersection or interaction between rival forms of power, each of which is deployed by specific individuals or groups in pursuit of their own interests.[9] An instrumental account of the interaction between state power and forms of power in the outlying society, such as corporate power, has two aspects. The first concerns how far large corporations are able to resist or restrict the sway of state power in order to protect their own interests. The second concerns how far large corporations are able to translate or convert corporate power into state power in order to utilise that power in their own interests (i.e. through 'influence' or 'control'). The first is essentially a negative, and the second a positive, expression of corporate power. (We might, conversely, consider how far the possessors of state power are able to resist the sway of corporate power, or convert state power into corporate power).

It follows that the question of whether the state exercises 'decisive' power in society can only be answered by conceiving power in relational terms. This requires us to consider the other elements in Miliband's definition of instrumentalism: the character of external (or internal) social forces or interests that compete to influence or control the state; and, the nature of influence or control exerted by these social forces.

Social forces and interests

The instrumentalist approach focuses attention on the 'waves of social conflict that beat against the state', that is, the identification of specific agents or social forces and the competition between them to influence the state. Its basic questions are who controls the state? in whose interests? and, what are the means of influence or control? Instrumentalist theories can be distinguished according to the substantive claims they make concerning the distribution of power, or power structure, in society. This boils down to 'the organized control, possession, and ownership of key resources as the basis for exercising power', notably 'wealth, status, force, and knowledge' (Barrow, 1993, p. 13). Barrow emphasises that 'control over these key resources is institutionalized through specific organizations of the economy, society, government, and culture' so that emphasis is placed on those who occupy positions of *institutional authority* (Barrow, 1993, pp. 13–14).[10] On this basis Barrow identifies two types of power structure along a continuum according to whether institutional control of key resources is more widely dispersed (egalitarian) or more concentrated (dominated by a ruling class) (1993, p. 14).

Barrow's approach involves individuals and organisations, and they are related in an apparently simple way. Power resources are institutionalised through specific *organisations*, but ultimately are controlled by *individuals* who occupy positions of authority within these organisations. This may be construed as a simple instrumentalist thesis – individuals control organisations, and thereby power resources, which they use to realise their purposes or interests. Against Barrow's organisational emphasis it may be argued that power may also be exercised by individuals through control of power resources in interpersonal relations. In its most basic meaning power is a relational concept that refers to a social relation between two 'agents'. More specifically, social power 'is an agent's intentional use of causal powers to affect the conduct of other participants in the social relations that connect them together' (Scott, 2001, p. 1). In this basic sense power may be conceived as a chronic feature of social relations whereby individuals' control of power resources (such as knowledge, physical force, or wealth) enables them to influence or control the conduct of other individuals. Yet it seems clear that the most consequential forms of social power involve collective agents such as organisations or groups of various kinds rather than individuals. This means that 'political behaviour' and 'conscious historical agency' should be conceived primarily in terms of individuals occupying positions of authority within organisations or acting together in 'interest groups'. The main actors are groups and institutions rather than individuals as such. This view then justifies Barrow's institutional emphasis. It is exemplified by C. Wright Mills' analysis of *The Power Elite* as comprising individuals holding key positions within three institutional arenas: the military, large corporations, and the executive (Mills, 1959).

Barrow's two types of power structure appear to conflate the distribution of power between institutions and between individuals. Thus where control of power resources is dispersed among *institutions* the power structure is characterised by Barrow as egalitarian, which normally suggests the relevant resources are dispersed among *individuals*. Yet the two do not necessarily correspond since institutional dispersal could be coupled to individual concentration: the many institutions that share power could be controlled by a minority of individuals who (might) constitute an elite or ruling class. Conversely, concentration of resources among institutions could be coupled to dispersed ownership or control of these institutions among individuals. Indeed the anti-Marxist claim that a capitalist, still less ruling, class no longer exists in the advanced societies is commonly based, in part, on precisely this dispersal of ownership of business. Thus Barrow's axioms should be amended to incorporate an individual as well as institutional dimension, so that

the more widely dispersed the institutional control of key resources, *and the more widely dispersed the control of key institutions by individuals*, the more reasonable it becomes to describe a power structure as egalitarian

and

the more concentrated the institutional control of key resources, *and the more concentrated the control of key institutions by individuals*, the more reasonable it becomes to describe a power structure as one dominated by a ruling class.[11]

A further problem of Barrow's approach is that individuals and their purposes appear at the bottom of the explanation in a rather simple way, and organisations as such do not appear to have any effects. The claim that individuals control organisations, and thereby power resources, which they use to realise their purposes or interests ignores the structural or strategic selectivity of institutions. This point applies to other institutional 'power containers' as much as to the state. Specific forms of internal differentiation and rules constrain as well as enable those in positions of authority within institutions to realise their purposes through the deployment of power resources. Further, these positions may generate specific interests that their occupants come to express. We might say that instruments can shape or define their users' identities as well as *vice-versa*. That is, agents, in occupying roles within organisations or institutions, may come to internalise the characteristic identities, modes of calculation and interests of those roles. Institutions are not, again, neutral.[12]

A final problem with Barrow's approach lies in the seeming conflation between the concentration of key power resources and the existence of a ruling class. Concentration of power resources is a necessary but probably not sufficient condition for the existence of a ruling class. There are two, related, ways of thinking about this. The existence of a ruling class may be conceived as an effect of the concentration of power resources, or as a condition. Do individuals/agents exist as a class before they concentrate power resources in their own hands, or is it as a result of the concentration of power resources that a class is formed? Marxist instrumental theory, such as Barrow's or Miliband's, seems to involve both conceptions. The concentration of *economic* power resources constitutes a capitalist class. In other words, the existence of an economically dominant class is primarily an effect of the characteristic concentration of ownership of means of production within the capitalist economic structure. Thus capitalists exist as a class before they concentrate *political* power resources in their own hands. And it is, in some way, in virtue of its control of economic resources that the capitalist class is able to control state power and thereby constitute itself as a *ruling* class. This seems to be the basic structure of the argument, but it requires further elaboration. From the identification of individuals/organisations in whose 'hands' key resources (i.e. means of production) are concentrated further evidence or argument is needed to show that there are significant common interests. Further, to constitute a class as a collective actor, it requires to be shown that there are plausible mechanisms through which such common interests can be articulated and promoted through a willingness to act. Finally, to be a ruling class, plausible mechanisms for the translation of economic into political power are wanted. The first two conditions are clearly inter-related: the will to act will be stronger where interests are perceived to be essential or fundamental, and weaker where interests are non-essential. Where essential interests are at stake the element of volition is reduced: agents more or less have to act to defend or promote such interests.

Class structure and class interests

It is clear that a Marxist instrumental theory of the state relies on an underlying theory of class structure, conceived as a structure of both *power* and *interests*. It is on the basis of this conception of objective interests that instrumentalism can resist the slide to voluntarism and subjectivism.[13] And it is this conception, in the guise of *class interests*, that demarcates Marxism from other variants of an instrumental theory of the state such as pluralism. Classes are defined, of course, by the positions of their members in the economic structure, which is constituted by 'the sum total of relations of production'. And, following Cohen, 'production relations are relations of effective power over persons and productive forces' (1978, p. 63). Class interests express the purpose of the power which production relations embody: fundamentally, the purpose of capitalists to ensure, and of workers to resist, the production of surplus value through exploitation. Thus capitalism is understood as essentially a class society, and the relationship between classes is a relationship of power involving conflicting interests.

To speak of objective class interests is to claim that such interests are structured by the production relations. In other words, these interests can be attributed to capitalists and workers in virtue of their positions in the economic structure. Being objective means that class interests cannot be matters essentially of choice or preference. But since capitalists and workers are agents who do make choices it cannot be assumed that objective interests will automatically translate into subjective interests. Even if the account of objective interests is plausible or true there are many reasons why agents may be mistaken about their true interests. It follows that a claim about objective interests cannot be tested according to whether or not they are recognised by agents.

But the explanatory power of any claim concerning objective interests clearly does depend on this recognition. Objective interests have to be recognised before they can do any explaining.

Cohen argues that a plausible individualised reading of Marx's claim that 'social being ... determines ... consciousness' is that 'the social consciousness of a person is determined by the social being of that person' (1988, p. 43). This means that a person's social consciousness (or beliefs about society) is explained mainly by his economic role, which is his position in the economic structure. These ideas about society are expressions of antagonistic class interests resulting in 'a permanent disposition towards class struggles' which is the proximate cause of social change. Change comes about 'through the agency of human beings, whose actions are inspired by their ideas, but whose ideas are more or less determined by their economic roles' (Cohen, 1988, p. 46). Marx expresses a strong version of this claim in *Capital* where 'individuals are dealt with ... only insofar as they are the personifications of economic categories, the bearers of particular class-relations and interests' (1976, p. 92). Marx goes on to say that this 'standpoint ... can less than any other make the individual responsible for relations whose creature he remains, socially speaking, however much he may subjectively raise himself above them' (1976, p. 92).

This last point suggests that individuals remain as reflexive agents capable of other ways of seeing than the class interests determined by their positions in the economic structure. Yet because individuals can raise themselves above class relations only subjectively and not really, they remain creatures of these relations which they therefore embody. Thus Marx argues that the extension of the working day is due to the coercive force of competition upon each capitalist whatever their subjective views of the matter (1976, ch. 10). Although the individual capitalist can subjectively raise himself above class interests this has no real effect on his conduct. The effect is just as if objective interests are automatically translated into subjective interests.

In this view there are good reasons to believe that a) individuals have objective interests in virtue of the class position that they occupy and that they will b) recognise and c) act on these interests.[14] Interests or purposes are seen as systemic. This means that the capitalist system is governed by the profit motive not primarily as a consequence of individuals choosing this purpose, but that the profit motive of capitalists is primarily a consequence of the fact that this purpose governs the economic system.[15] The argument must be that there is a transparent and essential character to these interests. Capitalists will recognise and act on the profit motive because competition acts as a coercive force necessitating profit as a condition of survival of the firm/capitalist, and survival is an essential or fundamental interest. The same reasoning must apply to workers.

Marx is specifically concerned with economic categories and 'the economic formation of society', not with individuals as they may appear in the realm of politics and the state. The interrelationship of power and interests might be conceived as *internal* to the economic structure, as between essentially economic powers and economic interests. The problem for an instrumental theory of the state is to show how they become operative and effective in the differentiated institutional realm of politics and the state. However it is a small step to argue that fundamental economic interests are carried into the political realm, particularly where these interests cannot be realised through economic action alone. Thus Cohen sees being/consciousness and base/superstructure as distinct but connected pairs. The connection is that individuals participate in the superstructure, which is roughly a set of non-economic institutions, 'with a consciousness grounded in their being', which is their position in the economic structure (1988, pp. 45–6).[16] This is the logic of the instrumental theory of the state. Poggi expresses this logic very clearly (with classes appearing in the guise of economically weaker and stronger groups) to explain the expansion of state activity in the last century.

> Groups at a disadvantage on the capitalist market – chiefly, employees – found, in the widening suffrage and in the related processes of representation and legislation, a means to temper that disadvantage. ... [As] *economic* power belonged to the bourgeoisie ... those in a position of economic inferiority used the quantum of *political* power acquired through electoral participation to widen the scope and increase the penetration of state action, in order to restrict and moderate the impact of that economic inferiority on their total life circumstances (Poggi, 1990, p. 113).

At the same time, and increasingly,

> demands for state action came also from socio-economic groups in possession of economic power, who raised such demands in order to further strengthen their market position, or indeed to allow the market to continue functioning. ... [I]n the course of the century the dependency of private economic forces on positive state action

... became a systemic feature of industrial capitalism (Poggi, 1990, p. 115).

However Marx's argument that individuals/agents are mere 'personifications' of class interests seems to involve a kind of reductionist argument that is widely discredited. Some well known criticisms need to be confronted. First, the concept of agency seems to have been obliterated. Second, the focus on class interests is an abstraction that conceals the real complexity of interests which arises from the fact that position in the economic structure is not a complete description of how individuals are socially situated, or of the roles that they occupy. Third, classes or economically weaker and stronger groups are not the only actors on the political stage so their demands for state action have to compete not only against each other but also against other groups. Fourth, it might be argued that interests are never simple reflections of economic (or other) positions but are always discursively defined and contested.

It seems clear that interests are always discursively represented, that is through language, in thought and speech. This is another way of saying that interests have to be recognised before they can do any explaining. But this is not the same thing as saying that interests are discursively defined, if this means that they are *merely* discursive. This idea is unsustainable insofar as it implies either that the economic structure is not real, or that position in the economic structure has no impact on individuals' interests. But the economic structure is as real and observable as any other social phenomenon, and concrete interest-bearing individuals are always socially situated. The interests clearly cannot be *detached* from the social situation, including position in the economic structure. However, the process of discursive representation of interests clearly opens the space for rival and contested interpretations. It is in this space that ideological or normative power operates. Thus there is clearly more than one way of thinking about the interests of workers and capitalists, a fact that is amply supported by the empirical record of capitalists' and workers' movements. But the space for rival interpretations or discourses is limited ultimately by the need for them to be anchored in the real economic structure, rather than floating free. There are only so many persuasive ways of thinking about the interests of workers and capitalists. And Marx's argument is strengthened by the fact that these interests, defined in a basic way, are quite transparent. Thus, to use Poggi's characterisations again, workers are transparently 'at a disadvantage on the capitalist market' and have an interest in 'temper[ing] that disadvantage', and capitalists who are advantaged have an interest in 'strengthen[ing] their market position'.

It is true that the categories 'worker' and 'capitalist' are not full descriptions of the social situations of individuals or, therefore, of their interests. The basic point here is that the combination of 'economic structure' and 'legal and political superstructure' (or, more loosely, capitalist market and state) does not constitute a whole society or social system. Individuals simultaneously occupy a range of positions within society which may be described using categories such as citizenship, gender, ethnicity, age, family/kinship, nation/region/locality, and so on. These categories denote specific patterns of social relations or social divisions which may structure interests in the same way that positions in the economic structure do. Further, the notion of interests does not do justice to the diversity of individuals' purposes when it is understood, as in the case of workers' and capitalists' interests, essentially in terms of advantage to the individual, or self-interest. For individuals' purposes also encompass 'causes' which cannot be traced directly to their position in society or their own immediate advantage. So individuals may 'personify' a complex set of interests and purposes, not just those related to economic positions. The importance of this is that economic class-interests may be less important or salient, they may be crowded out by the weight of other interests. Thus, just as in the case of assessing the truth of the development thesis, 'a judgement [is required] of the comparative importance of potentially competing ... interests' (Cohen, 1978, p. 15). Workers, it could be argued, might have little interest in tempering the disadvantage they face on the market because, let's say, as women they're rather more interested in tempering the disadvantage they face in relation to men. For example, a woman may have more interest in equalising the sexual division of labour in the household than in supporting the class struggle in the workplace. Or the primary workplace struggle may be defined in terms of challenging vertical occupational segregation rather than improving the condition of all workers. Capitalists, it could be argued, might somewhat relegate their interest in strengthening their market position because it is also their purpose to comply with some idea of 'corporate social responsibility' defined in terms of, say, environmental impact or human rights.

These arguments lead to a consideration of the space for agency. If individuals are conceived as mere personifications of class-interests this seems to leave no room for them to decide about their interests and purposes. (Of course the same consequence for agency arises from seeing individuals as personifying a complex set of interests and purposes, or as personifying a hegemonic discourse). Individuals cannot be agents (in the sense of having the capacity for decision) and be mere personifications of objective interests (in the sense of being the forms in which interests appear). But agents can have objective interests. In this sense it is better to say that agents decide not what their interests are but how they weigh them and what they do about them. Individuals weigh a range of objectively grounded but discursively mediated interests and decide which interests to act upon, when and how. Interests shape but do not completely govern behaviour.

A defence of the Marxist argument from class interests to behaviour can be mounted along the same lines as Cohen's defence of the development thesis. This relies upon coupling the objective character of class-relations and class-interests with human rationality and intelligence. Workers, faced with a situation of disadvantage on the capitalist market which they wish to temper and having intelligence which enables them to devise class-based strategies and forms of collective action will, being also rational, take advantage of the opportunities which intelligence provides, such as seeking to influence or control state power (Cohen, 1978, p. 152 ; Wetherly & Carling, 1992, p. 47).

This argument is susceptible to the noted objection that class-interest might be outweighed by potentially competing interests. It is a fair response to this to assert the fundamental or essential character of class interests. Capitalists have to accumulate to survive, and workers have to act to ensure their disadvantage is lessened (or, at least, not worsened) to safeguard their livelihoods and well-being. This theoretical defence is supported by a broad empirical claim. This is, to paraphrase Cohen again, that if class-interests are accepted as weighty (relative to potentially competing interests) they provide a superior account of key empirical trends of the twentieth century, such as the expansion of state activity analysed by Poggi. It is not just that this expansion can be plausibly shown, in various aspects, to correspond with the class-interests of capitalists and workers. It is also that we can observe the mechanisms linking class-interests to the expansion of state activity in the form of collective actors – parties, movements, groups, organisations, campaigns – representing capital and labour.

The final criticism to be confronted here is that classes are not the only actors on the political stage so their demands for state action have to compete not only against each other but also against other political forces. For 'an analysis of the state ... will include much more than the issue of economic relations and class forces' (Jessop, 1984, p. 221).

Thus the political advantage that economic resources may confer on their holders is not unrivalled, and economic interests will not automatically 'hold sway' in the political struggle but may have to be negotiated, and compromised, with other interests. Jessop proposes that a Marxist analysis of the state 'will be .. adequate to the extent that .. it allows [*inter alia*] not only for the influence of class forces rooted in/or relevant to non-capitalist production relations but also for that of non-class forces' (1984, p. 221). According to Jessop state power is a social relation that reflects the changing 'balance among all forces in a given situation' (1984, p. 225).

The possibility of a general theory

The crucial assertion here is not that there is a multiplicity of forces but that there is, or may be, a *changing balance* among them. The existence of a multiplicity of social or political forces is compatible with either an 'egalitarian' or 'ruling class' power structure, and with either a fixed or fluid distribution of power within either type. However, a Marxist instrumental analysis may take the form of a general theory in which power is fixed both in terms of the type of power structure (i.e. ruling class) and the specific group exercising power (i.e. the capitalist class). This type of theory is not compatible with Jessop's guideline that 'state power ... reflects ... [a] changing balance of social forces' (1984, p. 221). Indeed Jessop argues against the possibility of any such general theory and in favour of 'contingent necessity'. The contingency directly expresses the changing balance among social forces for, considered as causal influences or chains, 'there is no single theory that can predict or determine the manner in which such causal chains converge and/or interact' (1984, p. 212).

It is evident that different instrumental accounts of the state may be premised on different conceptions of both the multiplicity of social/political forces and (the changing or fixed) balance between them. A starting point is provided by Barrow's distinction between 'egalitarian' and 'ruling class' power structures, better conceived as a spectrum or continuum. It is a plausible guideline for an analysis of state power that there is a multiplicity of social and political forces. This merely reflects the diversity and complexity of the whole society or social formation and the corresponding range of interests and purposes. In this limited sense all theories of the state are pluralistic. Ruling class and egalitarian models are not distinguished by one denying and the other acknowledging this multiplicity of forces, but by different estimates of the disposition of power among them. Towards the ruling class end of the spectrum the disposition of power resources is conceived as highly unequal. In this model just a few political forces and interests are in control of key power resources and thereby able to influence or control state power to their own advantage.

As an alternative to the conventional distinction between an 'elite' or 'ruling class' (elite theory or Marxist) model on the one hand and an 'egalitarian' (pluralist) model on the other, three distinctive models can be identified. Contingency theory, including Jessop's 'contingent necessity', argues that no single theory can predict the disposition of power resources and outcome of political struggles, because of the uncertain and changing balance between many social/political forces. Determinate outcomes can only be known through the concrete analysis of specific conjunctures, and it is not possible to generalise from such an analysis because each conjuncture is, in principle, unique. The same disposition might recur but, equally, it might not. In this view no single theory can predict whether the disposition of power will fit the ruling class or egalitarian model, and its location on the spectrum is unstable. More specifically, state power might turn out to be capitalist or non-capitalist in the sense of 'the conditions required for capital accumulation in a given situation' being realised, or not (Jessop, 1984, p. 221).

A general theory of the state, on the contrary, claims that there is a discernible and predictable pattern to power. General theories may be sub-divided into two types. A soft general theory claims that there is an enduring type of power structure – ruling class or egalitarian – but allows for fluidity in the character of the forces and the disposition of power among them within the general type. Thus pluralist theory makes a general claim that the power structure is egalitarian – no single group is dominant across a range of issues – but is consistent with a shifting cast of groups and forces on the political stage. A hard general theory likewise claims that there is an enduring type of power structure, but makes the further claim that there is little variation in the character of forces and the disposition of power among them. The analysis of the state in capitalist society – which claims that the state is, in general, influenced or controlled by the capitalist class – is a theory of this type.

This is fundamentally a question of *power* or, more specifically, the conversion of economic power into political power. It has been argued that there are objective class interests (linked to power), that individuals can be seen in a meaningful sense as 'personifications' of these interests, and that these fundamental interests are carried into the political sphere. The problem, to quote Luger again, is that 'power held in one sphere [i.e. the economic] is not automatically or completely translated into the other' [i.e. the political] (2000, p. 16). This 'translation' evidently turns on the capacity to formulate the interests of capital in general (as opposed to particularistic interests of specific firms or industries), and the capacity to influence or control state power to realise these class interests. Thus a Marxist instrumental theory of state power must show that the key resource controlled by the capitalist class – i.e. capital – does confer an unmatched, though not automatic or complete, capacity to influence or control state power.

The interests of capital in general

There is a gap in the argument so far between the interests of individual capitals, industries or sectors (fractions) and the interests of the class, or the interests of *particular capitals* and the interests of *capital in general*. The former may be pursued to the *neglect* of the latter, and particular interests may even *conflict* with general interests. The basic interest of individual capitals or firms is to secure their own survival, competitiveness and profitability. It may then be supposed that they will not undertake unprofitable activities, such as provision of infrastructure, even though they may be necessary to secure the interests of capital in general and, thus indirectly, their own particular interests. Individual capitals might not undertake unprofitable activities even where they serve their own particular interests directly, such as training of the workforce. In both cases the 'public good' characteristics of these activities permit the rational calculation that individual capitals may benefit without contributing to their provision. More than this, they may not be expected to refrain from profitable activities even where they may undermine or damage general interests of the class, such as artistic or cultural outputs which promote anti-capitalist values. Also relevant here are corrupt or restrictive practices that may undermine the legitimacy of the system (Jessop, 1990, p. 152).[17] These considerations suggest that even if class-wide interests are recognised by individual capitals there may be insufficient incentive to do anything about them. Expressed in conventional terms the problems are those of the free rider and the threat to the commons.

Further, the very egoism of the economic sphere and the competing and/or conflicting interests between firms, industries and sectors may be expected to inhibit the perception of common interests and the prospects for class unity. Rivalry does not tend to engender common purpose. In this context, interests may be primarily defined in terms of the position of individual firms within particular markets or the position of industries and sectors within the macro-economy.[18] If political struggles merely reflect these kinds of interests then the state may become a battleground of particular ends rather than the means of realising the interests of capital in general.

Finally, even if it is recognised that individual capitals share class-wide interests it might be doubted whether these interests will be accurately prescribed. Block rejects 'the idea of a class conscious ruling-class' (1987, p. 52). For capitalists are conscious of their interests as capitalists, but, in general, they are not conscious of what is necessary to reproduce the social order' (1987, p. 54). This does not mean that there is not a discernible dominant business outlook which Block characterises as 'free market ideology'. This is 'an extraordinarily powerful framework for defending ... [capitalists'] ... freedom of action' but is, according to Block, irrational as a way of defining class-wide interests (1987, p. 12). This is because the market order is not self-sufficient. Thus Block's argument suggests that, to the extent that capitalists are capable of developing a shared vision of class-wide interests, this will be myopic. Focused as it is on defending their freedom of action within the market, it fails to see the extra-economic conditions on which the reproduction of the market order depends.

The disjuncture between particular and general interests can also be seen the other way around. 'Capital in general consists in the overall circuit of capital considered apart from the particular, competing capitals through which the circuit is reproduced' (Jessop, 1990, p. 152). Thus the interests of capital in general can be defined in terms of its reproduction, and this means the reproduction of the circuit of capital. Although the overall circuit of capital is reproduced through the circuits of individual capitals and is merely an aggregation of these, it is clear that it does not depend upon any of them in particular. 'For capital in general needs only *some* set of individual capitals whose precise composition can change according to the exigencies of competition and, indeed, it may require the bankruptcy or depreciation of some capitals as a condition of its own survival' (Jessop, 1990, pp. 152–3). This refers to the periodic crises and the requirements to restore conditions for profitable accumulation. But apart from crisis tendencies, capital in general may require the curtailment of certain methods or lines of production which are harmful to the overall circuit. It is clear that the interests of capital in general are not, by definition, the same as the interests of particular capitals, or *vice-versa*.

These considerations tend to suggest the unlikelihood of a ruling class in the sense that position in the economic structure gives rise to a political class struggle to secure the interests of capital in general. They suggest that economic power and interests will be translated into a particularistic political struggle in which large corporations, industries or sectors seek to influence state power to their own advantage. This is the kind of analysis put forward by Luger in his study of the 'U.S. auto industry's political influence' which charts 'its inordinate impact on public policy' (2000, p. 1). Luger's key concept is 'corporate power' and this denotes the 'pervasive influence over public policy' exercised by the large corporation, although this is widened out to 'the contours of political power of an entire industry' (p. 3). Consequently the interests at stake are defined in terms of issues such as vehicle safety, pollution and fuel economy. However there is no space in this analysis for the concept of the interests of capital in general or, therefore, consideration of the relationship between these general interests and the particular interests of the auto industry.

However there are empirical and theoretical reasons to believe that the considerations against the ruling class concept have less force than first appears. Miliband puts forward a general empirical claim that 'men of wealth and property have always been fundamentally united, not at all surprisingly, in the defence of the social order which afforded them their privileges' (1969, p. 47). More specifically, this unity within the dominant class has been based on an

> underlying agreement on the need to preserve and strengthen the private ownership and control of the largest part of society's resources, and ... on the need to enhance to the highest possible point the profits which accrue from that ownership and control (p. 47).

In this way, Miliband claims, 'the rich have always been far more "class conscious" than the poor' and, by inference, the capitalist class more than the working class (1969, p. 47). That this degree of class consciousness, claimed as an empirical generalisation, is 'not at all surprising' may be argued on the lines that, although competition divides, there is a deep congruence of interest on which the fundamental unity of the capitalist class is based.

The interests of capital in general can go against the interests of particular capitals because 'capital in general', that is the circuit of capital as a whole, is indifferent to the particular capitals that comprise it. Indeed, it is part of the normal reproduction of the circuit through competition and through recurrent crises that some firms will be eliminated through bankruptcy or takeover. But the chronic risk of closure faced by all firms as a result of the system is quite consistent with commitment to the maintenance of the system. Through the normal exigencies of competition only a minority of firms will face closure or takeover, and the most vulnerable firms will naturally tend to be the weakest not only economically but also politically. In any case to avert closure these firms will normally claim some protection from the normal rules of competition, such as state financial assistance, rather than express opposition to the competitive system as such. But they are likely to be opposed by stronger competitor capitals whose interests are served by their closure. Even in a crisis most firms survive and consequently support actions to restore conditions for renewed accumulation including, again, restructuring involving closure of weaker capitals. Thus the interests of most firms remain tied to preserving the system of private property and reproducing the circuit of capital.

More generally, it can be seen that each particular capital has an interest in preserving the system of private property, and therefore capital in general, since each capital owes its existence to the system of which it is a part. But the system of private property cannot be preserved without preserving the existence of rival capitals. Thus competition is inherent in the system of private property on which the process of accumulation by individual capitals rests. The freedom of each individual capitalist to go about his business, which is what the system of private property in capitalism amounts to, is also the freedom of other capitalists to compete in the same line of business. Thus competition is double-edged. Seen as a threat, it is a price worth paying for the system of private property. But competition is also an opportunity that the system of private property creates.

It might be objected that private property does not entail competition since it may take the form of monopoly. Indeed, it may be argued not only that there is a tendency towards monopoly within capitalism but that this is in the interests of individual capitals who acquire monopoly power. However monopoly is inconsistent with the system of capitalist private property since it goes against the ability of other capitals to operate freely. It is not only, or even mainly, the interests of consumers that are damaged by monopoly but also those of all other capitals who are potential rivals. Here we see again the double-edged nature of competition. The interest of the monopolist in evading the threat of competition is outweighed by the interests of the many potential rivals in the freedom to compete.

Thus it is misleading to claim that competition creates a divergence of interest between particular capitals and capital in general. This is because the negative side of competition, as threat, needs to be set against its positive side, as opportunity. On its negative side competition is a price worth paying for the existence of private property, and on its positive side the freedom of each individual capitalist to go about his business goes against monopoly and restrictions on competition. The upshot of these arguments is that individual capitals have a fundamental class interest in preserving the system of private property. It is plausible to suppose that individual capitals do not act as isolated units indifferent to the wider system but recognise the intimate connection between their own prospects and those of the system as a whole. Preserving the system of private property is a necessary and transparent condition for the reproduction of each individual circuit of capital. Thus class consciousness arises from the economic role or position in the economic structure that each capitalist occupies – 'being determines consciousness'.

Preserving the system of capitalist private property (including, as suggested, preserving competitive relations between capitals) is clearly a fundamental aspect of the interests of capital in general and the reproduction of the circuit of capital. This is because it is tantamount to preserving the system of production relations – the economic roles of capitalist and worker – that comprise the economic structure. However a legal system of property relations is not the only external condition or 'system need' of the circuit of capital. Block's argument is relevant here. If class consciousness is restricted to a defence just of private property the fundamental unity of the capitalist class that Miliband asserts might be based on commitment to an irrational free market ideology. Of course, against Block it can be suggested that no great leap in the intellectual and imaginative capacities of capitalists is required for other external conditions (such as the provision of infrastructure or the reproduction of labour power) to be recognised also as class interests. However it is true that not all such conditions are as transparent as property relations, and this suggests that some plausible mechanisms are required to support the ruling class thesis.

According to Block the inability of capitalists to develop an authentic class consciousness necessitates a move beyond instrumental theory to an analysis of 'the processes within the state that mediate between business influence and policy outcomes' (1987, p. 13). In place of the idea of a class conscious ruling-class Block suggests that of a 'division of labour between those who accumulate capital and those who manage the state apparatus' (1987, p. 54). The alleged irrationality of the capitalist class does not matter if they have no hand in managing the state. But why should those who manage the state do so in the interests of those who accumulate capital, if not because they are pressured to do so by the influence or control exerted by the latter? We will examine Block's structural answer to this question later. But first we will examine, against Block, how it could be that the capitalist class is capable of articulating its authentic interests and rational policies.

The position of individual capitalists is a necessary but not sufficient condition for the development of class consciousness. What else is needed to constitute sufficient conditions? A preliminary move is to question what the terms 'class consciousness' and the 'unity' or 'coherence' of the capitalist class require for the purpose of an instrumental view of the state. The answer to that is *sufficient* class consciousness and *sufficient* class unity. This is certainly less (and probably considerably less) than *complete* class consciousness and unity, however that unrealistic condition might be defined. The instrumental theory requires an account of how class interests may be represented by a part or fraction of the class (e.g. 'dominant coalition' or 'hegemonic fraction'), and through particular institutional or organisational forms (e.g. political parties, pressure groups, employer associations, think tanks) or informal social networks. As already indicated, the mechanics of the representation of interests are closely bound up with their pursuit and, hence, the mechanics of the exercise of power. In other terms, an instrumental theory requires an account of how *leadership* is exercised within the class and, more generally, within the wider society.

If basic class interests are, as we have claimed, transparent, the process of representation is not so much about defining what they are as how they can be realised. Class interests define ends or purposes, such as preservation of capitalist private property, but realising such ends requires policies or strategies, and the latter clearly do not follow automatically from the former. There is more than one effective way (though only a limited number of ways) of stabilising capitalist production relations, and some ineffective ways (as the irrationality of free-market ideology attests). What is more this is a complex purpose, an umbrella term covering a range (though, again, a limited number) of specific 'needs of capital'.[19] The key test of instrumental theory is not the consciousness and unity of the whole class, but whether there are agents/agencies capable of formulating class-based strategies to secure the needs of capital, and exerting influence or control in respect of key state policies or actions (not the state as a whole).[20] It should be added to this, however, that a plausible instrumental account also needs to show how the state is able to insulate itself from particularistic and economically irrelevant or harmful demands from individual capitals or elements of the class. In other words 'it seems that the state must resist too ready an access to particular capitalist interests if its policies are to promote the reproduction of capital as a whole' (Jessop, 1990, p. 146).

The interests of the capitalist class at the most general level consist in the securing of capitalist production relations, the reproduction of the circuit of capital, and (since the circuit is not merely reproduced on the same scale) accumulation. Successful accumulation requires a strategy – an 'accumulation strategy' – and it follows that a successful accumulation strategy represents the interests of capital.[21] But since there is more than one possible accumulation strategy and, correspondingly, no single 'predetermined pattern of accumulation that capital must follow', Jessop argues that there is more than one way of conceiving of the interests of capital (1990, p. 152). The interests of capital are whatever they are defined to be within the prevailing accumulation strategy, but they could have been defined differently. According to Jessop the interests of capital

> are not wholly pre-given and must be articulated in, and through, specific accumulation strategies which establish a *contingent* community of interest among particular capitals. For this reason the interests of particular capitals and capital in general will vary according to the specific accumulation strategy that is being pursued ... (1990, p. 159).[22]

In a similar vein Jessop has argued that

> it is a commonplace nowadays in Marxist theory that class determination (i.e., location in the relations of production) entails little for class position (i.e., stance adopted in class struggle). ... Instead we must recognise that the specific interpretations of these relations offered in various class schemata and ideologies ... are integral but independent elements in the formation of class forces (1984, p. 242).

Accumulation strategies are specific interpretations of class interests. They might vary, for example, in terms of particular fractions or sectors of capital that they advantage or disadvantage and thus in the communities of interest they create. It is certainly true that this approach establishes a somewhat contingent relationship between class determination and the specific interpretation of class interests (class position). This type of argument suits Jessop's purpose in moving away from economic determinism or reductionism. For it becomes inadmissible to 'treat the means of representation as essentially neutral transmission belts of objective, pre-given interests which simply relay these interests into a different field of action' (1990, p. 160). Yet Jessop does not deny an objective material basis of class interests, so it becomes crucial to know to what extent class interests are pre-given. 'Not wholly' is consistent with the answer to that question being either 'large' or 'small'. His purpose is

> not to argue that the relations of production have no impact on class formation ... For they involve differential patterns of association and interaction and impose definite limits on the success of particular class projects, strategies, and tactics (1984, p. 242).

Thus it is just as implausible to argue that there are no inauthentic strategies (because the production relations impose no limits on them) as that there is only one authentic strategy (because it is reducible to location in the relations of production). The definite limits on the success of particular strategies, including accumulation strategies, derive from the fact that, as Jessop recognises,

> the reproduction of the value-form [i.e. the circuit of capital] depends on certain general external conditions of existence which provide the framework within which the law of value operates (1990, p. 153).[23]

These conditions constitute parameters within which successful accumulation strategies must operate. In other words, accumulation strategies, apart from their differences and peculiarities, must be functionally equivalent ways of securing the needs of capital.[24] This justifies us in saying, against Jessop, that what class determination entails for class position is fundamental.[25] This is a not a matter of whether the external conditions of accumulation explain a great deal of the detail of particular accumulation strategies, for there is likely to be much detail that escapes explanation in this way. It is a matter of those conditions or needs of capital explaining certain fundamental attributes of accumulation strategies. It is only these attributes that the Marxist theory of history is required to explain, for it is these only that are included in the superstructure.[26]

Accumulation strategies have to be worked out and implemented by agents, so the concept can illuminate how leadership is exercised within the class. Accumulation strategies may operate at many levels, from individual firms, through industries and sectors, to global strategies that operate at the level of capital in general. The concept of a global strategy may itself operate at a variety of spatial levels, from that of the nation-state through regions to the global economy. It seems clear that for micro-level (firm, industry) accumulation strategies to be successful they must operate within parameters set by macro-level (national, global) strategies. It also seems clear that the agents and institutions involved in the articulation and implementation of accumulation strategies will vary at these different levels.

At the micro-level we could analyse the strategies pursued by individual firms and various forms of collaboration between firms (collusion, partnerships, networks). These will include both horizontal (between competitors) and vertical (between firms at different stages of the supply chain) relationships. Capitalist associations, such as those representing particular trades or industries or representing capital in general at local/regional levels (e.g. Chambers of Commerce) might also be important. We should also examine the potential for trade unions at firm or industry level to play a collaborative role. Finally the role played by non-capitalist institutions, particularly state agencies, would have to be analysed. This will include not only local/regional layers of government but also local agencies and forms of intervention emanating from the state at national or supra-national level. Prominent among these agencies and interventions will be those concerned with business/economic development and regeneration, and educational/research establishments.

At the macro level individual firms will still be important, particularly large national firms and multi-national corporations, insofar as these deploy instrumental resources that allow them to bargain with nation-states and influence global strategies. By the same token capitalist (and worker) associations representing particular industries or sub-national regions will still play a role. But the capacity to formulate the interests of capital in general presupposes agents and institutions with a national and supra-national/global outlook and reach. This seems to suggest that prominent among these will be peak associations of capital and (ambivalently) labour, nation-states, and inter-governmental or supra-national institutions and forms of decision-making.

However, though a successful 'global' accumulation strategy must operate within the parameters of the needs of capital, this leaves scope for competing strategies that will take accumulation on different paths and, in consequence, involve different balances of advantage and disadvantage within the capitalist class. This makes it unlikely that a peak organisation representing capital as a whole can ever manage to represent the interests of all fractions. Jessop suggests that 'to succeed, ... [an accumulation strategy or growth] model must unify the different moments in the circuit of capital ... under the hegemony of one fraction' (1990, pp. 198–9). Thus a successful accumulation strategy will privilege the interests of one particular fraction of capital but must also involve the exercise of hegemony. According to Jessop 'a strategy can be truly "hegemonic" only where it is accepted by the subordinate economic classes as well as by non-hegemonic fractions and classes in the power-bloc' (1990, p. 201). Acceptance can, in principle, be secured through coercion or consent, or some combination of these. Coercion may be required in relation to any class or fraction that feels disadvantaged or whose existence is threatened by a particular accumulation strategy and may, therefore, put up resistance (e.g. particular firms or industries facing decline or closure). But reliance on large-scale coercion can never be the basis for a stable accumulation strategy. Hegemony implies some form or degree of consent – ranging from passive acquiescence to willing agreement. This in turn implies that a successful accumulation strategy must, while favouring the interests of a particular fraction, also articulate the interests of other fractions and classes. In relation to the capitalist class as a whole a crucial factor here is that the accumulation strategy secures the needs of capital and, in this fundamental sense, represents the interests of capital in general. As Jessop notes,

> insofar as a combination of 'economic-corporate' concessions, marginalization and repression can secure the acquiescence of the subordinate classes, the crucial factor in the success of accumulation strategies remains the integration of the circuit of capital and hence

the consolidation of support within the dominant fractions and classes (1990, p. 201).

But the integration of the circuit of capital and the charting of a particular path of accumulation presupposes that the external conditions of accumulation, or needs of capital, are secured. Securing the needs of capital is a necessary condition for a viable accumulation strategy, and a necessary, though perhaps not sufficient, condition for it to be hegemonic. Although particular firms and industries may be losers it is probably also necessary that the strategy involves a broad-based model for growth across industries and sectors. However the very interconnectedness of the multiple individual circuits of capital that constitute the accumulation process make this condition fairly easy to satisfy. For example the Fordist accumulation strategy, while advantaging particular mass production industries such as automobile production, also facilitated a broad-based and sustained process of economic growth.[27]

A hegemonic fraction requires agents and/or institutions to represent it. It seems easier to see how a sufficient degree of unity and coherence can be achieved at the level of a class fraction rather than the class as a whole, but it still needs to be politically constituted. There seem to be three obvious categories for this:

1. Capitalists who are members of the dominant/hegemonic (or seeking-to-be dominant/hegemonic) fraction,
2. Other agents and/or institutions in civil society who are not members of the dominant fraction,
3. Agents and/or institutions within the state system.

Representation of the interests of the dominant fraction through articulation of an accumulation strategy might conceivably be achieved by any of these categories, singly or in combination. In addition, the categories themselves, particularly the second and third, contain diverse elements. Jessop casts doubt on the capacity of members of the dominant fraction itself to articulate their own interests through particular capitals or capitalist associations. This is due, for example, to

the potential non-identity of the interests of particular capitals and capital in general ... [and] ... the organizational and managerial dilemmas confronting capitalist associations ... in promoting anything beyond the interests that particular capitals happen to have in common for the moment ... (1990, p. 167).

Thus capitalists themselves cannot rise above a particularistic outlook. Therefore

> it is quite reasonable to expect other agencies to be the key forces in the elaboration of accumulation strategies. The 'organic intellectuals' of capital could well be found among financial journalists, engineers, academics, bureaucrats, party politicians, private 'think-tank' specialists or trade union leaders (Jessop, 1990, p. 167).

In another formulation

> it is typically the role of organic intellectuals (such as financial journalists, politicians, philosophers, engineers and sociologists) to elaborate hegemonic projects rather than members of the economically dominant class or class fraction (1990, p. 214).

Jessop's enumeration of 'organic intellectuals' includes agents and/or institutions both in civil society (e.g. financial journalists, engineers, private 'think-tank' specialists, trade union leaders) and within the state system (academics, bureaucrats, party politicians).[28] Specifically excluded, however, are members of the capitalist class. Whereas the first formulation leaves open the possibility that members of the dominant fraction may be involved (though not as 'key forces') in the elaboration of an accumulation strategy, the second suggests that they play no part since it is organic intellectuals *rather than* capitalists who undertake this role. However this fails to take account of mechanisms and tendencies towards cohesion and class consciousness within the capitalist class.

Jessop suggests that organic intellectuals operate against a background of a fragmented capitalist class unable to formulate its own interests. If you like, the organic intellectuals solve the problem of unity that members of the capitalist class cannot solve for themselves by being able to stand back from particularistic demands. However this dislocation brings other problems. While organic intellectuals have the capacity to *formulate* an accumulation strategy it is less clear that they have the capacity to *implement* it successfully. For although the category of organic intellectuals includes some agents in positions of institutional authority (especially within the state system) it might be doubted whether, taken together, they exercise adequate power. The strength of the traditional Marxist instrumental view is, after all, that class interests are backed up by the power resources controlled by the capitalist class. Related to this, it is not clear how the organic intellectuals are able to secure the hegemony of a particular accumulation strategy within the capitalist class, especially since there are always alternatives that would involve different balances of advantage and disadvantage.

If there are, contrary to Jessop, mechanisms for cohesion within the capitalist class these problems would be alleviated. For it would permit a relative degree of unity around, and backing for, a specific accumulation strategy. The most important mechanism may be interlocking directorates which tend to mitigate the fragmentation of the capitalist class into competing firms and industries (Mintz, 1989; Stokman et al., 1984; Schwartz, 1987; Barrow, 1993). Interlocking directors constitute a network spanning different companies and industries, so their outlook is not tied to particularistic demands. It is not claimed that there is, or could be, one all-embracing network or 'financial group'. Indeed there is potential for rivalry among a number of such groups, and this could be conceived analogously to the rivalry between accumulation strategies. However the key claim is that 'interlocking directors are much more likely than other elements of the corporate elite to be the agents of classwide interests' (Barrow, 1993, p. 19). Interlocking directorates may take the place played in Jessop's theory by fractions of capital, but with two key differences. Interlocking directorates have a wider span than specific fractions, and they provide a mechanism for cohesion and the formulation of class-wide interests.

Added to these strictly economic linkages, the perception of class-wide interests (i.e. class consciousness) may be 'reinforced by a variety of noneconomic status linkages, cultural affiliations, and social interactions' (Barrow, 1993, p. 22). In other words the economic networks constituted by interlocking directorates are supplemented by social networks which cement an 'upper class'. It is not claimed that these networks, economic and social, overcome divisions or conflicts within the class but that they do provide the basis for relative unity. Similarly a perception of class-wide interests does not amount to the formulation of an accumulation strategy, but it arguably provides a supportive context for such a strategy. Thus in this view, contrary to Jessop, organic intellectuals operate against the backdrop of a relatively coherent and class conscious capitalist class.

If economic and social networks provide a mechanism for the formulation of class interests it is plausible to suppose that there will be conscious attempts to project these interests within the political domain and, specifically, to influence the political agenda and policy formulation process. In its simplest form instrumental theory would examine the relationship between the corporate elite and the state elite, such that the former is the originator of class-interests-as-policy-demands which are translated into requisite policies by the state elite.[29] Though this relationship remains crucial, the concept of 'organic intellectuals' allows a more complex form of instrumentalism. For state managers are part of a wider category of organic intellectuals whose role is, in effect, to mediate this relationship, and to convert class-wide interests articulated by financial groups into a viable accumulation strategy. The range of possible accumulation strategies establishes a somewhat contingent relationship between class interests and policy outputs, but organic intellectuals remain nevertheless, in Jessop's term, 'spokesmen' of the capitalist class. And, as we have argued, all viable accumulation strategies must operate within the parameters of the needs of capital, so contingency operates in a framework of necessity. The category of organic intellectuals, including key actors within the state system, does not obviate the need for capitalist interests to be projected into the political domain. Just as, looked at the other way around, the tendencies to unity and class-consciousness within the capitalist class do not obviate the need for organic intellectuals to formulate specific accumulation strategies. Thus it is important to analyse the nature of the relationship involved. How are organic intellectuals connected to the capitalist class?

An accumulation strategy always, and perhaps mainly, involves a programme of state action. It does so because, as we have seen, all viable accumulation strategies must secure external or extra-economic conditions of the value-form and the accumulation process, and because any particular path of accumulation will invoke the need for some kind of state support or direction. In other words, an accumulation strategy necessarily involves the exercise of state power. Jessop defines state power as a 'form-determined condensation of the balance of forces' (1990, p. 269) and asserts that 'the power of the state is the power of the forces acting in and through the state' (1990, p. 270). In other words the state system merely 'mediates' this power. Insofar as we can say that, in acting in and through the state, these forces are *harnessing* or *using* the state this is tantamount to an instrumental view. This is, as we have seen, not inconsistent with the important emphasis placed by Jessop on state power being form-determined, which means that the state is structurally or strategically selective rather than neutral. The organic intellectuals that articulate the interests of capital must be included in the overall balance of forces. Thus Jessop says that 'these forces include state managers as well as class forces, gender groups as well as regional interests, and so forth' (1990, p. 270). But to treat state power as a condensation of the balance among these forces and to treat state managers or 'officialdom' in the same category as other forces is misleading. The category 'state managers' denotes a structure of positions or roles within the state and the identities of the particular individuals occupying those positions. It is of course true that state managers, in both these aspects, reflect the balance of political forces since both the structure of positions and the occupancy of those positions is the focus of political struggle. However, the point about state managers is that they actually exercise state power through occupancy of positions of authority within the state system seen as a power container. These positions allow them to make decisions about the deployment of power resources institutionalised by that system (within form-determined parameters and constraints). Thus Jessop ignores or elides a crucial distinction between agents and forces *within* the state and those *external* to it.[30] When Jessop says that 'the state as such has no power' (1990, p. 269) this appears true in the sense that 'it is merely an institutional ensemble'. But it is misleading because these institutions comprise roles which are occupied by agents who make (constrained) decisions concerning the deployment of power resources, and it follows that these agents do have power. In this vein Miliband observes that

> while there are many men who have power outside the state system and whose power greatly affects it, they are not the actual reposito- ries of state power; and ... it is necessary to treat the state elite, which does wield state power, as a distinct and separate entity (1969, p. 54).

State power

Thus in analysing the relationship between organic intellectuals and capital, and the role of the former in articulating the interests of capital through the formulation and implementation of an accumulation strat- egy, it is the role played by agents within the state system (politicians and 'officialdom') that requires particular analysis. We need to analyse the connections between organic intellectuals within the state and those located in civil society (e.g. journalists, private think-tanks), and the connections with the capitalist class whose interests they serve. These connections have to establish a sufficient degree of unity or cohesion between what seem to be essentially separate categories – members of the capitalist class on the one hand, and organic intellectuals, including state managers, on the other. Why should these intellectuals serve the interests of the dominant class/class fraction?

There are broadly two sets of answers to this within an instrumental framework. First this separation can be denied, or at least blurred, on the basis that members of the capitalist class are directly involved in the exercise of political power and the policy planning process and/or that capitalists and organic intellectuals belong to the same class and thus share the same interests. Second, a range of mechanisms, direct and indirect, may be adduced to show how, even though there is separation, the interests and/or actions of organic intellectuals are pulled into line with those of capital. The first set of arguments focus on the social composition of state managers or the 'state elite'. If it is the case that (some proportion of) these people are capitalists or that they are members of the same class, then a direct and powerful mechanism of control of the state by the capitalist class would be shown.

'Colonisation' involves occupation of key positions notably within the state system (but, in principle, other institutional power containers too) by members of the capitalist class. This seems to be the most direct means of controlling state power in the interests of the capitalist class. The state elite becomes tendentially merely an extension of the corporate elite. In this connection Miliband points to the entry of businessmen into government, and 'their growing colonisation of the upper reaches of the administrative part of … [the state] … system' (1969, p. 57). The colonisation thesis seems to depend on capture of the key command positions within the state system, and on the assumption that capitalists entering the state system do so with the purpose of securing class interests. Both of these conditions are problematic. In connection with the first, there may be some question as to which the key command positions are and what would be sufficient colonisation to ensure the operational unity of the state adequate to secure the interests of capital in general. In any case the empirical evidence appears rather weak insofar as there is wide variation in the social background of state managers and, as Miliband acknowledges, capitalists 'have never constituted … more than a relatively small minority of the state elite as a whole' (1969, p. 59). In connection with the purposes of businessmen entering the state system, Miliband claims that even though they

> may not think of themselves as representatives of business in general or even less of their own industries or firms in particular ... businessmen involved in government and administration are not very likely ... to find much merit in policies which appear to run counter to what they conceive to be the interests of business ... since they are ... most likely to believe such policies to be inimical to the 'national interest' (1969, p. 58).

In fact Miliband puts more emphasis on systematic pressures within the state system to favour capitalist interests than on these interests having to be carried into the state system by colonising capitalists. What is more, Miliband suggests that they do not typically bring with them so much a coherent political programme, still less a viable accumulation strategy, than a general perception of the interests of business. For these reasons – limited penetration and limited class consciousness – the colonisation thesis does not provide the single, or even principal, mechanism for translating class interests into policy outcomes. This is not to say that this mechanism is not important – Barrow claims that 'their occupation of ... key positions in the [state] apparatus enables ... [capitalists] ... to exercise decisive influence over public policy' (1993, p. 27). Still, there is more to instrumentalism than colonisation.

Colonisation is closely related to the phenomenon of overlapping membership between corporate and state elites. This refers to the movement of personnel between the worlds of business and public policy, not only capitalists entering the state system but politicians and officials entering business. So much so that Miliband claims 'the world of administration and the world of large-scale enterprise are now increasingly linked in terms of an almost interchanging personnel' (1969, p. 125). There is little doubt that this interchange serves to reinforce the influence of capitalist interests in policy-making. For example, Luger points to the way the automobile industry 'hire[s] top-level former government officials to ensure access to policymakers' and 'to make its case most effectively' (2000, p. 184).

In addition to actual colonisation of the state system, and perhaps more important, is the direct involvement of members of the capitalist class in the policy formation process. The concept of a 'corporate policy-planning network' (Barrow, 1993, p. 33) shows that it

would be a false dichotomy to think of capitalists as either colonising the state system or as exerting pressure and influence from
outside the state apparatus (as either 'in' or 'out'). For the corporate
policy-planning network is a Marxist version of the pluralist concept
of a policy network or policy community, and shows that capital
enjoys privileged 'insider' status within the policy formulation
process.[31] Contrary to Jessop's suggestion that it is organic intellectuals rather than members of the corporate elite who formulate accumulation strategies, the policy-planning network constitutes a
mechanism for the development of class consciousness and for
the direct engagement of capitalists with organic intellectuals in the
policy process (Barrow, 1993, p. 33).

The corporate policy-planning network is important in instrumentalist theory because it provides a powerful linking mechanism
between the corporate elite and organic intellectuals in civil society
and in the state system. According to Barrow, policy-planning
networks bring together major private associations or 'power elite
planning organizations' financed through corporate contributions
with overlapping memberships drawn from the financial groups
(interlocking directorates) and upper class.

> The objective of these organizations is to bring together leading
> members of the capitalist class from the entire country to discuss
> general problems of concern to all members. Thus, planning organi-
> zations identify the long-term interests of the capitalist class in
> regard to issues of general import (Barrow, 1993, p. 33).

The 'capitalist inner circle' is joined by intellectuals 'usually drawn
from ... major universities, foundations, and privately financed
research institutes or think-tanks' who may be attracted by various
inducements. 'Likewise, high-ranking state managers and emerging
legislators are often invited into the planning network, where they are
trained and socialized to become the spokespersons, allies, and future
executive leaders of the power elite' (Barrow, 1993, pp. 35–7).

In addition to colonisation of the state apparatus, interchange
of personnel between capital and the state, and the relationships
maintained through the corporate policy-planning network, it can
be argued that capitalists and organic intellectuals are united by
shared class interests. In the strict sense of position in the economic
structure 'organic intellectuals' are clearly not members of the capitalist class. Most of these individuals will be dependent for their

livelihood on a wage/salary, though they might not be subordinate producers and so, on that score, are certainly not proletarians.[32] However Miliband makes a distinction between a capitalist class and a larger dominant class. Not all capitalists are included in the dominant class, which incorporates the 'corporate elite' – 'people who wield corporate power by virtue of their control of major industrial, commercial, and financial firms' (1989, p. 20) – and 'people who control, and who may also own, a large number of medium-sized firms' and make up part of 'what is often called the upper middle class, or the middle class' (1989, p. 21). Excluded are 'a large number of people who own and run small businesses' who make up part of 'a substantial petty bourgeoisie or "lower middle class" ' (1989, p. 21). But in addition to the two capitalist segments of the dominant class Miliband identifies the 'state elite' and a professional part of the middle class. The 'corporate elite' and the 'state elite' comprise the 'power elite' at the apex of the class pyramid. The non-capitalist part of the middle class comprises

> a large professional class of lawyers, accountants, middle-rank civil servants and military personnel, men and women in senior posts in higher education and in other spheres of professional life – in short, the people who occupy the upper levels of the 'credentialized' part of the population (1989, p. 21).

These people are '"notables", "influentials", "opinion leaders" '(1989, p. 21) or, in other words, intellectuals. Thus Miliband includes the category of organic intellectuals (in the state elite and the professional middle class) within the dominant class. The criteria used by Miliband in making this designation are source of income, level of income, and degree of power. Although the non-capitalist elements of the dominant class do not derive their incomes from profit (or not mainly so) their high incomes and the degree of power, influence and responsibility they exercise are sufficient to place them in the same class. According to Miliband a 'very basic material set of interests ... in terms of property, privilege, position, and power' (1989, p. 34) is the fundamental basis for the cohesion of the power elite and dominant class.

> Here, by definition, are the people who have done very well out of the existing social order and who, quite naturally, have every intention of continuing to do very well out of it, for themselves and their offspring (Miliband, 1989, p. 34).

The reference here to the determination and capacity of members of the middle class to pass on privilege to their offspring is important because it alludes to the way class interests are shaped by the social origins and socialisation of these privileged individuals.[33] Thus class interests are not just the views that people may rationally be expected to hold given their position in the class structure, but also have wider sociological explanations. An important aspect of this may be social milieu. The highest paid individuals in these occupational categories may be said to constitute part of a privileged stratum of the social order and to 'move in the same circles' as members of the capitalist class. In this way material interests may be reinforced by participation, alongside members of the corporate elite and the capitalist segment of the middle class, in the social networks that help to cement an upper class. Thus, quite apart from the extent of any colonisation, interchange or networking of personnel, common class interests explain 'the underlying cohesion which binds capital and the state' or what Miliband also refers to as 'a partnership between corporate power and state power' (1989, pp. 32–3).[34]

The argument for cohesion based on shared material interests is closely related to argument in terms of the ideological dispositions of organic intellectuals and the state elite. This distinction may seem difficult to maintain. This is because ideology is sometimes seen as more-or-less a reflection of class interests. If it is distinct then explanation is required of how ideology is created and sustained, and how it works. One answer to this is to say that ideology as a form of power is exercised through control of the means of communication and persuasion. But then there would appear to be circularity in using ideology to explain the beliefs of members of the dominant class, since control of the means of communication and persuasion is in the hands of this very class.[35]

Ideology can, of course work in both these ways: it can have a material basis and be generalised through society via deliberate mechanisms of communication and persuasion. Organic intellectuals in civil society and within the state might serve capitalist interests in part due to ideological convictions stemming from material interests and in part because capitalist ideology is hegemonic within the wider society.[36] The existence of a dominant or hegemonic ideology may be useful to explain the class allegiance of lower order intellectuals, whose allegiance to the existing social order could not otherwise be readily explained by their having 'done very well' out of it.

According to Miliband the social composition of the state elite does create a 'strong presumption ... as to its general outlook, ideological dispositions and political bias' (1969, p. 68). This seems to suggest that ideological dispositions are, at root, material interests. But Miliband also suggests that commitment to the existing social order is not 'simply a matter of cynical self-interest' (1989, p. 34). In other words that commitment is not simply a rational judgement but may be 'a profound belief that "free enterprise" is the essential foundation of prosperity, progress, freedom, democracy, and so forth, and that it is also therefore synonymous with the "national interest"' (1989, p. 34). To the extent that the ideological inclinations of state managers and other organic intellectuals are explained in terms of ideology as a form of power this brings into play a second strand of instrumental explanation. For the instrumental account of the state would involve not only direct control of the state via colonisation, interchange of personnel, policy planning networks and material interests, but also indirect control via instrumental use of the means of communication and persuasion.

A third strand is based on the control of the means of economic activity and the associated array of instrumental resources and mechanisms which may be used to bring pressure and influence to bear on politicians and state managers. In general terms what is at stake here is the claim that ownership of wealth or capital can be converted into power, 'that wealth and income (i.e., capital) are always a potentially generalizable source of power in capitalist society. Capital is convertible to other forms of power to a degree that is not true of social status, political influence or knowledge' (Barrow, 1993, p. 15). Indeed, the point is that money can be converted into these and other forms of power. More specifically, control of capital converts into influence over politicians and state mangers through what may be referred to as the special interest process. Luger cites an array of specific mechanisms which account, in part, for the political influence of the American automobile industry. These include

- Use of in-house lobbyists and public relations staffs (often located in Washington), and external lobbyists and public relations firms
- Contacts between top managers and high level government officials
- Collective representation of firms by trade associations, and connection to the broader business community e.g. through the US Chamber of Commerce
- Organisation of coalitions to take on specific industry-wide issues, and participation in corporate-wide coalitions to influence nonindustry specific policy issues

- Advertising to shape public opinion (ostensibly to influence consumer choices but also shaping perceptions of the place of automobiles in the wider society and political culture)
- Election campaign contributions
  (Luger, 2000, pp. 183–4).[37]

Perhaps more important than these forms of pressure group politics is the power afforded by control of the means of economic activity to reward, and therefore encourage, favourable policies through willingness to invest. And the other side of this coin is of course that control over investment is a potent source of the power to oppose and resist unfavourable policies. Thus the threat to withhold investment or relocate overseas can be used as a weapon in political struggle.[38]

The instrumental account of the state can thus draw on three analytical strands relating to the three main sources of domination. Control of the means of state administration and coercion (through colonisation, interchange of personnel, policy networks, class interests/ideological dispositions) is supplemented by the instrumental use of control of the means of communication and persuasion and the means of economic activity. These strands of argument explain how the interests of capital in general are reflected in the exercise of state power. They rely on tendencies to class consciousness within a dominant class that controls the main sources of domination. A crucial role is played by organic intellectuals who, though members of the dominant class, are able to stand back from particularistic interests/demands and formulate the interests of capital in general in the shape of a specific accumulation strategy. The relative independence of organic intellectuals from the capitalist class makes it possible to formulate the interests of capital in general.[39] But, given competing accumulation strategies, this leaves unanswered how a particular strategy becomes dominant or hegemonic. It seems tempting to suggest that intellectuals tie their colours to the mast of whichever fraction happens to be dominant, but that would put the cart before the horse. For the dominant fraction owes its position to the accumulation strategy. The question is: how do organic intellectuals come to articulate a particular accumulation strategy that advantages a specific fraction, and not a possible alternative? Part of the answer might be whichever fraction is most successful in making itself heard and exerting influence.[40] Another part might be that organic intellectuals tend to formulate an accumulation strategy according to which path of accumulation will be most successful given such considerations as difficulties faced by the current strategy, the balance of class forces, and the form of state.

This chapter has set out a range of arguments to support a Marxist instrumentalist view of the state. More specifically, these arguments support an instrumental account of the capitalist state, consistent with the theory of history. It is possible, of course, to develop a Marxist account that places more emphasis on the capacity of the working class to secure reform through pressure from below. The theory of history does not preclude such 'space for reform', only so long as reforms are compatible with the maintenance and reproduction of capitalist production relations. The theory is only concerned with the superstructural aspects of the state, and so only with state policies or actions that secure the needs of capital. One mechanism through which such policies are explained is the kind of instrumental account of state power set out here. However the instrumental view does not stand alone: what we are after is some form of 'mixed explanation' that examines the interaction between structure and agency. That is the purpose of the next chapter.

4
Structure and Agency in State Theory

Introduction

The instrumentalist theory of the state is strongly associated with explanation in terms of the role of agency,[1] and agency is sometimes counter-posed to structure.[2] However we have seen that the role of agency in the instrumental view of the state, far from being counter-posed, is linked in a number of ways to the structural context of behaviour. In setting out an instrumental view of the state agential factors cannot provide plausible explanations on their own. This reflects a more general point that, far from seeing 'agency' and 'structure' in terms of a dichotomy, it is necessary to elucidate the interrelationship between them. In this chapter we will make explicit the structural dimension of the instrumentalist view, and show how structural explanation can contribute to a fuller explanation of the state within a Marxist perspective.

Agency and structure aren't all there is

The structure-agency question or debate is clearly of fundamental importance within social science, going as it does to the heart of what it means to provide an adequate explanation of social phenomena (Hay, 2002, pp. 93–4). On the face of it, 'structure' and 'agency' seem to exhaust the possible ways in which explanation can be offered.

> Essentially, what we are concerned with here is the relationship between ... political actors ... and the environment in which they find themselves; in short, with the extent to which political conduct shapes and is shaped by political context (Hay, 2002, p. 89).

Thus it seems that explanation can make appeal only to 'political actors' or to 'the environment' (or some combination of these) and to nothing else. It has become a commonplace view within social science that adequate explanation must somehow combine structure and agency, that purely 'structuralist' or 'intentionalist' explanations are not tenable.[3] As Hay suggests, political conduct (agency) in some sense is 'shaped by' but also 'shapes' political context (structure). In fact, there are three ways of conceiving the agency-structure relationship: reduction, opposition, and a dialectical approach. In a reductionist approach the distinction between structure and agency is denied so that everything is, according to taste, either structure or agency. For example, methodological individualism claims that

> all social phenomena – their structure and their change – are in principle explicable in ways that only involve individuals – their properties, their goals, their beliefs and their actions (Elster, 1985, p. 122).

Thus what may appear as social structures are in principle always reducible to (i.e. really comprised of) individual agents.[4] Against this, methodological collectivism makes the reverse claim, that what may appear as the properties of individuals are in principle always reducible to (i.e. really comprised of) the effects of social structures.[5] However this is a false dichotomy. Methodological individualism may be rejected without dispensing with agency – for it can be denied that *only* individuals are involved. We might say instead that individuals are necessary but not sufficient. The insufficiency of methodological individualist (or intentionalist) explanation is precisely the neglect of context. If individuals are necessary then it follows by the same token that methodological collectivist explanation, as defined by Elster, must also be rejected. If this is accepted then structure and agency must somehow be combined.[6]

In the second way of conceiving the agency-structure relationship, structure and agency are essentially separate and, in some sense, operate independently or autonomously.[7] Although this opposition, or dualism, may be compatible with purely agential or purely structural explanation, it is most likely to yield mixed explanations in which agential and structural factors are combined. Thus social phenomena are explained as the combined effect of structural and agential factors treated separately. This, then, involves an external relationship between structure and agency.

In the dialectical approach a distinction between agency and structure is maintained but the relationship is one of duality where 'structure and agency both influence each other' (Hay, 2002, p. 116). In distinction to the second approach neither structure nor agency can exist independently of the other yet, in distinction to the first, neither is reducible to the other.[8] This approach is already suggested in the earlier statement from Hay: political conduct *shapes and is shaped by* political context. Here the relationship between structure and agency is internal – they are seen as mutually constitutive.

Perhaps the key dilemma in the structure-agency debate is revealed in the contrast between the second and third approaches: how to maintain a distinction between structure and agency while allowing, what seems obviously true, that they influence each other. The weakness of the second approach seems to be that it denies this mutual influence since structure and agency are essentially separate. Yet recognising the mutual influence can seem to undermine the very distinction between structure and agency since each is constituted by the other. In short, the distinction can 'harden' into separation, and mutual constitution can 'soften' into reduction.

Before proceeding any further with discussion of these approaches, some definitions of agency and structure are required. Clearly, what the relationship is between agency and structure and whether they exhaust social science explanation depends on what these terms mean. Here are some definitions:

> Agency refers to individual or group abilities (intentional or otherwise) to affect their environment. Structure usually refers to context; to the material conditions which define the range of actions available to actors (McAnulla, 2002, p. 271).

> *Structure* basically means context and refers to the setting within which social, political and economic events occur and acquire meaning. ... [A] notion of structure ... refer[s] to the ordered nature of social and political relations ... *Agency* refers to action, in our case to political *conduct*. It can be defined, simply, as the ability or capacity of an actor to act consciously and, in so doing, to attempt to realise his or her intentions. ... [T]he notion of agency implies ... a sense of free will, choice or autonomy – that the actor could have behaved differently ... (Hay, 2002, p. 94).

Structures or 'structural forms' may be defined as 'institutions', so that the structure-agency question may be expressed in terms of the role of institutions as independent variables in causal chains and, specifically, 'the causal connections between institutions and individual behaviour' (Jessop, 2001, p. 1221). Jessop summarises the conventional definition of institutions as 'social practices that are regularly and continuously repeated, that are linked to defined roles and social relations, that are sanctioned and maintained by social norms, and that have a major significance in the social structure' (2001, p. 1220).[9]

According to Cohen a structure consists of a set of roles, and a set of relations is a set of roles *vis-à-vis* one another.[10] The paradigmatic case is the economic structure of a society which is defined in terms of its production relations. Thus in capitalism the fundamental roles/relations are those of/between capitalists and workers (1978, pp. 28–37; 1988, pp. 37–50).

It is plausible to define agency in terms of a sense of free will, as proposed by Hay. Free will is often counterposed to the notion of determinism and, from this, it might be thought that the agency-structure debate is related to the fundamental issue of determinism versus free will (McAnulla, 2002, p. 272). It is true that these questions are related, but it is a mistake to equate them, and this is because structure (or structural explanation) is not equivalent to determinism.

If we take determinism simply to be the idea that we are 'products of our environment' (McAnulla, 2002, p. 272), the point is that 'environment' (or context, or setting) is not synonymous with structure. That is because 'context' may be taken to include both material or physical as well as social elements.[11] And, within the social, we should say that context includes social structures but also includes non-structural (or extra-structural) dimensions. This distinction is important because the way structures explain conduct, or what it is they explain about conduct, may be different to the causal influences coming from other aspects of the environment.[12] This can be seen from the work of proponents of structure as well as their critics. For example, Archer distinguishes structure and culture, and conceives a causal relationship between culture and agency which is analogous to that between structure and agency (Archer, 1995; McAnulla, 2002). Thus action takes place within a structural *and* cultural context and is conditioned by both. Archer's emphasis on culture is of course roughly comparable to the claims of many other writers that 'ideology', or the set of norms prevalent in a society, may exert a powerful influence on conduct. The key point for present purposes is that, for Archer, ideology is not a 'structure'. In a similar vein, Jessop suggests that the institutional (or structural) turn can be fruitfully complemented by a 'discursive turn', on the basis that institutions are not all that matters (2001, pp. 1225 and 1231). On the other side of the debate, King rejects Archer's concept of structure in favour of revealing the microfoundations comprised 'only of individuals and their social relations' (1999, p. 199). But this doesn't mean dispensing with context altogether. Indeed the interpretive tradition, as defended by King, claims

> that nothing meaningful can be said about individual practices or understandings independently of the social and historic contexts in which those individuals are situated. In other words, that nothing meaningful can be said without situating individuals in their social networks with other individuals (1999, p. 219).

In this view dispensing with the notion of structure does not mean failing to recognise that individuals are constrained by the social context in which they operate. King's claim, against any structural argument, is that 'the social context .. can, logically, only be other individuals' (1999, p. 220). Thus context and constraint are not synonymous with structure. 'We are constrained by other people (most of whom we do not and will never know) not by structure but that does not make the constraint any less real' (King, 1999, p. 223).[13]

Determinism may, of course, also include a biological or psychological (at any rate, individual as opposed to social) component. Thus the 'enemy' of agency as free will is not just the extent to which we are products of our environment, but also the extent to which we are products of our own human nature. Although the capacity for agency must itself be reckoned as an aspect of human nature, that nature plausibly also includes some fixed elements, such as instincts or needs, that exert causal powers in relation to conduct. For example, the idea that agency consists in 'the ability or capacity of an actor to act consciously ... to realise his or her intentions' (Hay, 2002, p. 94) must be qualified by the possibility that some intentions are rooted in the actor's human nature and not freely chosen. Most, if not all, social theories contain more-or-less explicit theories of human nature that ground their explanatory claims. Marxism contains a 'philosophical anthropology' according to which humans are by nature 'creative beings, who are only truly themselves when they are developing and exercising their productive faculties' (Cohen, 1988, p. 156). Cohen argues that 'historical materialism does not depend on the Marxist view of human nature' (1988, p. 157), although he does not fully consider whether it creates problems for the theory. Yet historical materialism does itself depend on a (Marxist) theory of human nature, even if it is not what is normally taken as the standard account. The theory of history is, according to Cohen's reading, grounded in an account which cites two facts of human nature – that 'men' are rational and intelligent. These are added to a purported fact about the historical situation – scarcity – to provide support for the development thesis. Scarcity, though, may seem like a fact about human nature masquerading as a fact about the environment since the important claim for the theory is that people have a trans-historical desire to reduce or mitigate scarcity. That people are not prepared to subsist at relatively low levels of productivity when opportunities to attain higher productivity present themselves looks very much like a fact about human nature.[14]

If Hay is right to define agency in terms of free will, then it cannot refer to action or conduct. The tendency to conflate agency and action is a source of confusion within the agency-structure debate. It is better to say that agency as free will is part of the explanation of conduct, alongside environmental influences (including social structures) and the influence of human nature. Conduct or behaviour is fundamentally what is to be explained, and therefore to define agency in terms of conduct is to conflate explanandum with (partial) explanans.[15]

These conceptual clarifications seem to support the second approach to the agency-structure relation: structure and agency are essentially separate and, in some sense, operate independently. This does not mean that they are empirically separate and independent, for the causal powers of agency cannot be observed outside of a structural context, and *vice-versa*. Conduct will always be the effect of the interplay between structure and agency but, despite this, the analytical distinction must be maintained.[16] These considerations suggest a multi-dimensional explanation of action, behaviour or conduct. The principal causal influences may be presented as follows:

1) Causal influences which stem form characteristics of the physical or material environment
2) Causal influences which operate at the level of social context (external factors). These can be broken down into:
   a) social structures
   b) non- (or extra-) structural aspects
3) Causal influences which operate at the level of the individual actor. These can be broken down into:
   a) fixed elements of human nature
   b) the capacity for agency as free will

This rudimentary classification shows that structural and agential factors do not exhaust the explanation of conduct. It is clear that these categories require further refinement, particularly the concept of social structure. At this point, though, it will be instructive to examine some recent discussions of the structure-agency question, focusing on the influential strategic-relational approach advocated by Hay and Jessop.

The strategic-relational approach

Some of the key claims are presented by Hay as follows:

1) The distinction between structure and agency is ... a purely analytical one. ...
2) [Therefore] structure and agency must be present simultaneously in any given situation ...
3) Stated most simply ... neither agents nor structures are real, since neither has an existence in isolation from the other
    3(a) their existence is relational (structure and agency are mutually constitutive) and
    3(b) [their existence is] dialectical (their interaction is not reducible to the sum of structural and agential factors treated separately) (2002, p. 127).[17]

Statements 1) and 3) amount to the same claim – the structure-agency distinction is purely analytical because they are not real. Hay also states that 'structure and agency, though theoretically separable are completely interwoven' (1995, p. 200). 'From our vantage point they do not exist as themselves but through their relational interaction' (Hay, 2002, p. 127). 1) and 3) entail, but are not necessary for, 2). For belief that agency never operates outside of a structural context is also compatible with an ontological distinction – two things can be really separate but always present together. 3(a) stipulates that the relational interaction of structure and agency is such that they are 'mutually constitutive'. Saying that the relation is dialectical 3(b) doesn't seem to add anything to the claim that it is relational 3(a) (that structure and agency cannot be summed as separate causal influences is already given in the statement that they are mutually constitutive). The distinctiveness of the strategic relational approach evidently turns on the sense in which structure and agency are said to be 'mutually constitutive'.

Hay (1995, 2002), drawing on the work of Jessop (1990, 1996) seeks to clarify this sense in contrast with the dialectical approach of

Giddens in which it might also be said that structure and agency are mutually constitutive (Hay, 2002, pp. 118–9). According to Hay, structuration theory (Giddens, 1984) and the strategic-relational approach both put forward a dialectical view of structure and agency (1995, p. 193) in which they are internally related. 'Dialectical', as we have seen, doesn't seem to mean much more than 'relational' or 'mutually constitutive', as opposed to separable, or a duality as opposed to a dualism. One way in which Hay distinguishes these views is his contention that structuration theory offers an 'insider' or agency-centred account whereas the strategic-relational approach offers an 'outsider' or structure-centred approach. What Hay means by this is that Giddens redefines structure in such a way (i.e. as 'rules and resources') as to move it away from its conventional sense (as context) and bring it close to the notion of agency. Rules and resources are used or deployed by agents in action, and structure is instantiated in action. But, for Hay, this brings structure and agency too close, for 'there would seem to be little distance to bridge theoretically between them' (2002, p. 121). In fact 'Giddens thus develops a form of sophisticated intentionalism' (Hay, 1995, p. 198). And, in consequence, the agency-structure problem remains, for context reappears in the form of 'system' in Giddens' theory. In contrast Hay contends that the strategic-relational approach has

> a more structuralist starting point, positing the existence of layers of structure which condition agency and which define the range of potential strategies that might be deployed by agents ... in attempting to realise their intentions. ... [T]his ... is an 'outsider', or structure-centred account of the relationship between structure and agency (1995, p. 199).

The strategic-relational approach has 'a somewhat different conception of the dialectic' (1995, p. 200), such that structure and agency are not two sides of the same coin (Giddens) but 'the two metals in the alloy from which the coin is moulded' (1995, p. 200; 2002, p. 127). This means that whereas you can see one side or other of the coin (structuration) you can only see the product of their fusion in the alloy and never either of the components (strategic-relational approach). It is, then, a more thorough-going process of mutual constitution. This is a striking metaphor, but it is not yet clear that the strategic-relational approach is substantially different from Giddens' theory.[18] Whereas Giddens defines structure as rules and resources, the strategic-relational approach retains the orthodox sense of structure as context. Agency and structure are formulated in terms of strategy in a strategic terrain. The context, or terrain, is always strategically selective in the sense that it favours some strategies and/or purposes over others. This bias affects the relative chances of success of different (individual or collective) actors, and their strategic capacity involves utilising their knowledge of the context of action in order to maximise their chances of success. Further, the struggles that take place on this uneven terrain may alter its contours so that strategic selectivity is always path dependent, which means that it is shaped by and inherited from past conduct and struggles. This conception of the structure-agency dialectic is strikingly similar to Giddens' – structure appears as both the medium and the outcome of action, shaping and shaped by conduct. Hay, following Jessop, claims that the dialectic is different because the basic concepts – structure and agency – have been transformed through a complicated double movement bringing each concept into the definition of the other. In this way they become 'mutually implicated', each in the other, producing a 'strategically selective context' (where there was mere structure) and a 'strategic actor' (where there was mere agent) (2002, p. 128). But, however the concepts are turned around, in the end we are still left with an 'actor' within a 'context'. Jessop claims that

> a genuine duality can be created by dialectically relativizing ... both analytical categories. In this context social structure can be studied in 'strategic-relational' terms as involving *structurally inscribed strategic selectivity*; and action can likewise be analysed in terms of its performance by agents with *strategically calculating structural orientation* (1996, p. 124; see also Jessop, 2001, p. 1223).

Thus 'dialectically relativising' means conceiving structure relative to action, and *vice-versa*: structure has always to be seen in terms of its selectivity in relation to specific agents and strategies, and action is always oriented to specific structural contexts.[19] In this approach 'structures ... *have no meaning* outside the context of specific agents pursuing specific strategies' (Jessop, 1996, p. 126, emphasis added) since structural constraints are only (more or less) constraining of specific strategies. It might equally be said that agency has no meaning outside of specific structural contexts.[20] It certainly looks as though the emphasis on 'strategy' might be the key innovation, though Jessop acknowledges that 'a strategic-relational approach ... cannot be exhausted by concepts of strategy. Instead it aims to transform other concepts by articulating them with strategic concepts' (1990, p. 263).[21] Yet it is not clear that this articulation amounts to very much in the case of agency since this is already conventionally defined in strategic terms. Thus the agent with *strategically calculating structural orientation* looks very much like the reflexive agent of Giddens' theory. This is shown by Jessop's own definition of such agents as 'reflexive, capable of reformulating within limits their own identities and interests, and able to engage in strategic calculation about their current situation' (1996, p. 124).

The strategic reformulation of structure expressed in the concept of strategic selectivity is more interesting, and an advance on the theory of structuration. Even here though it might be argued that Giddens' concept of structure is at least consistent with this understanding since the particular disposition of rules and resources is bound to have an effect on the relative chances of different actors realising their intentions through specific strategies. Although Hay is critical of Giddens' concept of structure for moving too close to agency, it can be argued, on the contrary, that Giddens' approach has the advantage of a precise concept of structure against the loose and undifferentiated idea of context in Hay's discussion of the strategic-relational approach. Jessop recognises that institutions aren't all that matter and, thereby, makes a distinction between 'structure' and 'context'. He notes that there is 'wide variation in how institutions are defined' (2001, p. 1213) and, therefore, that definition is the first step in 'taking an institutional turn' (2001, p. 1221). Yet no such definition is provided by Jessop.

The insight that structural constraints must always be understood relative to specific actors and strategies is a crucial one. It means, as Jessop argues, that contextual elements that are experienced as constraints by one agent or set of agents may be experienced as opportunities for others. Or, equally, a constraining element in relation to one strategy may be permissive of, or open to transformation by, other strategies. Jessop formulates this distinction in terms of 'structural' moments (elements in a situation that cannot be modified) and 'conjunctural' moments (elements that can be modified). The point is that what is structural or conjunctural depends on the specific agent and strategy in question. An important aspect of this is that 'the structurally inscribed strategic selectivities of institutions are always and inevitably spatiotemporal' so that 'some practices and strategies are privileged and others made more difficult to realize according to how they "match" the temporal and spatial patterns inscribed in the structures in question' (Jessop, 2001, p. 1227). This approach also implies, given that agents are reflexive, able to learn from experience and modify their strategies, that a 'structural constraint for a given agent ... could become a conjunctural opportunity' if the appropriate strategy is adopted. Indeed, Jessop goes so far as to assert that 'any constraint could be rendered inoperable through competent actors' choice of longer-term and/or spatially more appropriate strategies' (1996, p. 126).

Strategic selectivity means that institutions are 'path-shaping', that *'institutions select behaviours'* (Jessop, 2001, p. 1236). They do so in the sense that individual and/or collective actors must select appropriate strategies in the face of the bias or selectivity of institutions. This depends on their being knowledgeable and rational, able to learn from previous experience and history and then devise the most effective strategies. But it also depends on two other important factors: the goals, purposes or interests of the actors, and their power or capacity to implement a viable strategy. And both of these have a lot to do with an aspect of structure that Jessop neglects, that is, the structural locations or positions of the actors. In Jessop's theory actors are disconnected from structural locations, and identities and interests thus appear largely as aspects of agency. Thus the capacity for

> reflection ... about the strategic selectivities inscribed within structures ... can (but need not) extend to self-reflection about the identities and interests that orient their strategies. For individuals ... can be reflexive, can reformulate within limits their own identities, can engage in strategic calculation about the 'objective' interests that flow from these alternative identities in particular conjunctures (Jessop, 2001, p. 1224).

The 'limits' presumably include the shaping of identities and interests by the positions occupied by actors within structures, but because Jessop is silent on this he suggests a more 'voluntarist' approach in which identities are largely (re)formulated by individuals. However it is plausible to assume that the identities and interests that shape strategies oriented to the structural selectivities actors face are influenced by the relative advantage or disadvantage of those actors within the structures in question. On this basis disadvantaged groups (e.g. classes, but also including non-class social groups) are more likely to engage in structure-modifying, and advantaged groups in structure-preserving, strategies. The relative powers or capacities of advantaged and disadvantaged groups to realise their strategic interests may then provide an important explanation for structural continuity or change. Thus group conflict is an exemplar of a 'structural contradiction', which is one of the reasons Jessop gives for the tendential nature of 'structured coherence' or stability (2001, p. 1225).[22]

There are, then, three large weaknesses in the strategic-relational approach. First, there is the tendency, noted earlier, to conflate agency and conduct, so that any sense of agency as free will is lost.[23] The second problem, in common with Giddens, is that structure is conceived essentially as a medium or terrain of action, to the neglect of the ways in which structure conditions action. In particular, within this terrain actors may occupy specific positions and perform specific roles that generate particular interests. In this sense, despite Hay's contention that the strategic-relational approach is structure-centred, it is arguable that both approaches offer sophisticated intentionalism. Third, Jessop seems to suggest that whether actors can transform social structures just depends on the appropriate strategy. But some structures are going to be more intractable than others and this awareness needs to be built into the strategic-relational approach. There is no inconsistency between recognising that structural constraints are always relative to specific actors and strategies, and recognising that some constraints are stronger, and others weaker, relative to all conceivable actors and strategies. We need to know what contributes to structural strength and, similarly, to structural continuity.

The structural constraint thesis

A structural, or structuralist, explanation of the state sees the economic structure as a principle of explanation or explanans. It claims, roughly, that the nature of the economic structure explains something about the character of the state. This rough claim can be refined. Accordingly 'structural explanation' is used here to refer to all explanations in which structure exercises a causal effect or power, in which sense 'instrumentalist' explanations are structural. The term 'structuralist explanation' is used in the more precise sense of explanation in terms of the structural interconnection between (or coupling of) the economy and the state. Typically this involves a notion of 'structural constraint' or its equivalent.[24] More specifically, the explanation need make no reference to the question of who rules, and that is because the structural constraint will still exercise its constraining effect regardless of who is in charge of the state.[25] Structuralist explanation is distinguished by the *causal mechanism* it invokes, not by the effect(s) brought about by the mechanism. This is to disagree with Barrow who claims, following Mandel (1978), that 'the structuralist thesis ... is that the function of the state is to protect and reproduce the social structure of capitalist societies ... insofar as this is not achieved by the automatic processes of the economy' (1993, p. 51). The structuralist thesis may well explain this function, but so may the instrumentalist thesis. The structuralist thesis is distinguished by *how* this is explained.

According to structuralist explanation 'the state tends to promote ... capital accumulation regardless of the particular governing elite' because policy-makers are 'prisoners' of the market (Barrow, 1993, pp. 61–2). Miliband's 'instrumentalist' view of the state does, of course, rely very heavily on the character of the particular governing elite in terms of its social composition, yet this view shades into a structuralist explanation in which the state elite are, in effect, prisoners of the capitalist system. A commitment to maintaining and defending the capitalist system is explained by the upper and middle class origins of the state elite and the ideological dispositions that are shaped by these origins. This may be construed straightforwardly in terms of class interest – state managers administer to the needs of the system in the interests of a particular class to which, through their own privileged origins and life-styles, they belong or are attached. However Miliband argues that policy-makers 'do not at all see their commitment to capitalist enterprise as involving any element of class partiality' (1969, p. 72). They may, on the contrary, sincerely believe that this commitment is consistent with, even a precondition of, serving the national interest or common good. But, going further than this, even if commitment to the national interest is the prime motivation and there is no particular commitment to capitalist enterprise as a matter of political belief or values, there will still have to be a commitment to such enterprise as a matter of practical policy. This is where the structuralist argument comes into play. For governments aiming to promote the national interest will find that

> this naturally includes a sound, healthy, thriving economic system; and such a desirable state of affairs depends in turn on the prosperity of capitalist enterprise. Thus ... the governments of capitalist countries have generally found that their larger national purposes required the servicing of capitalist interests (Miliband, 1969, pp. 83–4).[26]

Thus whereas in the instrumentalist approach the point is precisely that it is the purpose of the state elite, because of its social composition, to serve the needs of capitalist enterprise, in the structuralist approach it doesn't matter if this is not the purpose. Even if the state elite had other origins and ideological dispositions than Miliband's instrumentalist argument claims and, consequently, other purposes, this 'should not obscure the fact that, *in the service of these purposes*, they [are] the dedicated servants of their business and investing classes' (Miliband, 1969, p. 84).[27]

The concept of 'structural constraints' is a relatively minor theme in *The State in Capitalist Society* compared to the emphasis on the composition and ideological dispositions of the state elite. However in later writing structural constraints are given more emphasis, as one of 'three distinct answers' to the question why the state should be thought to be the instrument of a ruling class (Miliband, 1977, p. 68).[28] The answer, in a strong version of the structuralist thesis, is that

> *given its insertion in the capitalist mode of production*, it cannot be anything else. ... [T]he nature of the state is ... determined by the nature and requirements of the mode of production. There are 'structural constraints' which no government ... can ignore or evade. A capitalist economy has its own 'rationality' to which any government and state must ... submit (Miliband, 1977, p. 72)

The instrumentalist/structuralist distinction can be formulated in terms of means and ends. The instrumentalist thesis relies on an account of the *ends* of policy-makers, or those that influence them, in virtue of who they are. The servicing of capitalist interests is an end in itself. The structuralist thesis relies on the claim that serving the 'business and investing classes' is the indispensable *means* of securing whatever ends policy-makers have. It is clear that the explanatory power of the structuralist thesis depends on the specification of this means-ends relationship. In other words it depends on the force of the notion of *requirement* in the claim that 'national' purposes require the servicing of capitalist interests. This involves two elements, or questions:

1) what does the servicing of capitalist interests entail, i.e. how are capitalist interests defined?

At the most general level this is defined by Miliband in terms of the 'prosperity of capitalist enterprise', i.e. profitability. But the second question is

2) how far, and in what ways, do 'national purposes' require the prosperity of capitalist enterprise?

The question in 1), the definition of capitalist interests, has relevance beyond structuralist explanation since the instrumentalist thesis also requires such a definition. Therefore we will not deal with it fully here. However some points are relevant. First, of course, the structuralist thesis entails that state actions are consequential for capitalist interests, that is, what the state does or does not do will impact on the prosperity of capitalist enterprise. The claim that the state serves capitalist interests (as a means to other ends) entails that capitalist interests stand 'in want' of such service. We will take this statement to mean that 'bases need superstructures' in the sense that there are certain functional requirements of capitalist enterprise, or 'system needs', that state actions satisfy.[29] However it should be noted that the statement need not be taken in this way. It could be taken to mean that, though the economy is self-sufficient (has no system needs or external conditions of existence), state actions are consequential in enhancing (or inhibiting) its performance.[30] Of course, even if there are system needs, as we will argue, state actions may also be understood in this latter sense too.

Second, the claim that the state serves capitalist interests does not entail that there is only one way, or one best way, of doing so.[31] This argument applies whether interests are defined in terms of functional requirements and/or enhanced performance. The requirement for state managers to serve capitalist interests (in order to realise their own purposes) might not be a requirement for optimisation. For these reasons, the structuralist thesis is not incompatible with the ideas of strategy and strategic choice. For example, putting this question of strategic choice in simple terms, Miliband points to the alternative strategies of those 'who stood for a large measure of state intervention in economic and social life, and those who believed in a lesser degree of intervention' (1969, p. 71). Although important issues are at stake in this 'quarrel between strong interventionists and their opponents', it is ultimately merely a choice between 'different conceptions of how to run the *same* economic and social system' (Miliband, 1969, pp. 71 and 72). In Bob Jessop's work this idea of strategic choice is expressed in terms of alternative accumulation strategies, each defining a specific economic 'growth model' and each advantaging certain capitalist interests at the expense of others. Far from their being a single best or adequate strategy, in any situation 'there will typically be several economic strategies which could be pursued' (Jessop, 1990, p. 200; see also 2002, p. 30).

This consideration of strategy clearly bears closely on the question in 2): how far, and in what ways, do 'national purposes' require the prosperity of capitalist enterprise? How constraining, that is, are 'structural constraints'? This is certainly 'a difficult question' (Miliband, 1977, p. 73). The strong version of the structuralist thesis cited above claims that all governments must submit to the 'rationality' of the capitalist economy and none, therefore, can evade these constraints. Miliband rejects this conception as a form of 'hyperstructuralist trap' in favour of some notion of 'freedom of choice and manoeuvre' (or relative autonomy), but this doesn't get very close to knowing how constraining the structural constraints are.

The idea of 'structural constraint' refers to a kind of causal power or effect which the capitalist economy (or economic structure) exercises in relation to the state system in virtue of their structural coupling or interconnection. This causal power is manifest in a) limitations in regard to what the state is *able to do*, and b) requirements or imperatives in regard to what the state *must do*. Structural constraints will be more constraining the more

1) the strategic capacities of the state are a function of capital accumulation/the prosperity of capitalist enterprise, and
2) the prosperity of capitalist enterprise is a function of state action[32]

Limitations in regard to what the state is *able to do* follow from 1) because, in some sense, the capital accumulation process limits the feasible set of state actions, and the greater the prosperity of capitalist enterprise, the greater the strategic capacities of the state. Requirements or imperatives in regard to what the state *must do* follow from 2) (in conjunction with 1)). For the state is constrained to undertake actions that will support capitalist enterprise in order to support its own strategic capacities. We can see that the structuralist thesis may involve mutual constraint (or mutual compatibility, dependence) between the prosperity of capitalist enterprise and state action/capacity – each depends on the other. 1) says that, in general, the prosperity of capitalist enterprise is favourable for the capacity of the state to realise its purposes, whatever those purposes are. Thus, in order to realise their purposes it will, in general, be rational for state managers to promote the prosperity of capitalist enterprise (i.e. to serve capitalist interests) insofar as they are able to through formulating and implementing pro-capitalist policies (and refraining from policies that will harm capitalist interests). 2) says that state action may indeed promote the prosperity of capitalist enterprise. 1) and 2) taken together say that the prosperity of capitalist enterprise cannot be secured through market mechanisms alone but depends on certain forms of state action, and it is rational for state managers to implement these actions because they thereby tend to enhance their own capacity to realise the purposes of the state, whatever they happen to be. So, the more the prosperity of capitalist enterprise depends on state action and the more state capacities are enhanced by the prosperity of capitalist enterprise, the more constraining are the structural constraints.[33]

In order to assess the truth of 1) we need to consider the purposes of governments or the state. It will clearly not do, here, to say that these are to serve capitalist interests since the whole point of the structuralist thesis is that such servicing may be explained even if policy-makers have other purposes. Just as Jessop argues that structural constraints only have meaning in relation to specific strategies, the claim that capital accumulation/the prosperity of capitalist enterprise constrains state capacities and actions only has meaning in relation to specific purposes. Thus it should not be assumed, *a priori*, that all state capacities and actions are constrained by capital accumulation, nor that those that are constrained are equally so. Nevertheless, it can be argued that the state faces structural constraints of a very general kind related to the nature of a capitalist economy and the capital accumulation process, that is, constraints that affect it across the board. A relationship of constraint

> occurs wherever control over resources and opportunities allows some agents to set the conditions under which others must act. ... Whether intentionally or not, subaltern agents act under manipulated conditions of action and they must take account of the inducements that are offered and the anticipated reactions of their principals. To constrain is to severely limit the options that are available to rational calculators, bringing about a mutual adjustment or concordance of interests. Subalterns concur in actions that accord with the ... interests of a constraining principal because it is in their own interest to do so. Constraint ... [involves] limiting ... the courses of action that [are perceived as] feasible and desirable (Scott, 2001, p. 72).

This definition of constraint involves a relation between agents – a principal and subaltern – but can be adapted to the case of structural constraint. In effect structure takes the place of a principal. In the constraint which capital accumulation exercises over the state there is no principal with interests or intentions. For although capital accumulation comprises the decisions and actions of individual capitals or firms it is not reducible to them. The ... investment decisions of individual business enterprises ... have their effects on state policies principally through their macroeconomic consequences. ... [Thus] states ... respond to the constraints that are imposed by the macroeconomic processes on which they depend (Scott, 2001, p. 89).

These macroeconomic processes (capital accumulation) set the conditions under which state managers act, severely limiting the feasible and desirable options available to them as rational calculators. This involves adjusting policies according to what works within the parameters of capital accumulation and the anticipated reactions of capitalist enterprises. The constraints imposed by macroeconomic processes can be analysed in terms of inputs and outputs, and also in terms of quantitative and qualitative aspects. State capacities and actions depend on a flow of inputs, particularly financial resources and public support, and the ability to secure these inputs depends, directly and indirectly, on capital accumulation. The state derives its revenue principally from taxation, and the flow of taxation depends on output and incomes mainly generated in the private sector of the economy (i.e. through capital accumulation). This fiscal dependency is the most direct way in which the state is dependent on the performance of the macroeconomy and the prosperity of capitalist enterprise (Bridges, 1973; Block, 1987; Gough & Farnsworth, 2000). This is, of course, a very general form of constraint because state activities across the board are financed largely or entirely through taxation. All governments operate under a fiscal constraint and must therefore make decisions about the allocation of public expenditure according to political purposes and priorities, but the greater the flow of tax revenues the looser the budget constraint. Within this quantitative resource constraint the question of government purposes and priorities appears to be essentially a political one, that is, a choice determined by specifically political criteria. However, judgements as to feasibility and desirability are also constrained by the capitalist economy, in roughly two ways. Feasible outcomes tend to be assessed in terms of 'solutions' to problems that are achievable or will 'work' within the parameters of a capitalist economy, which are, in Miliband's phrase, compatible with the 'rationality' of the system. This is true particularly in the fields of economic and social policy that impinge upon macroeconomic processes and performance. But, more than this, the dependence on capital accumulation to generate tax revenues creates a strong incentive for rational decision-makers to prioritise policies that support accumulation (and to rule out policies that may be damaging to economic performance).

Capital accumulation is thus both a source of restriction and a maximand and explains, respectively, both the limits of reform and the pro-capitalist bias of governments. For example, a poverty reduction programme will be constrained by the limits of what is achievable within a capitalist economy. Such limits may stem from the structural causes of poverty, the tendency for market processes to widen inequalities, and the damage that taxation policies may do to incentives and thereby to economic performance. But insofar as it is rational (desirable) for policy-makers to promote capital accumulation this may induce them to introduce policies that tend to increase poverty and inequality, such as promoting flexible labour markets and reducing taxes on the rich.

The state is required to maintain public support or legitimacy, and the links between legitimacy and capital accumulation reinforce the constraints imposed by the latter on the state. The first link is that economic performance is an issue of high political salience because voters tend to attribute responsibility for employment and prosperity to policy-makers and to place the economy high up on the list of political issues. The second link is that legitimacy also depends on the state's capacity to meet a range of citizen demands and concerns largely through public spending programmes, and this capacity in turn depends on tax revenues. Thus the state is dependent on capital accumulation for key inputs (revenue, legitimacy), and this dependence creates a strong incentive for rational decision-makers to select policies (outputs) that will support (or at least not threaten) accumulation. State managers select pro-capitalist policies because it is in their own interest to do so, in order to maintain or increase tax revenue and public support. In other words capital accumulation constrains both what the state is able to do (through its influence on the flow of inputs) and what it must do (through its influence on the selection of outputs).

Block and 'business confidence'

In contrast to Miliband, Block is critical of instrumentalist claims and attaches more weight to a 'structural argument'. In doing so he is more explicit than Miliband regarding the nature of the structural mechanisms involved, and his argument centres on the concept of 'business confidence'. One of the central pillars of the instrumentalist thesis rejected by Block is the possibility of a class-conscious ruling class. On the contrary, Block claims that the dominant class is not capable of formulating its own general or long-term interests, its principal outlook being defined in terms of an irrational belief in a free market ideology. This ideology is irrational precisely because the market is not capable by itself of securing all the necessary conditions for its own operation and reproduction – capitalism cannot operate as a free market. Hence, if the state were an instrument in the hands of the capitalist class the consequences would be disastrous from the point of view of that class. In place of the concept of the state as an instrument, Block characterises the relationship between business and state managers as a 'division of labour between those who accumulate capital and those who manage the state apparatus' (1987, p. 54).

This division of labour could be explained as a deliberate policy on the part of the capitalist class, that is, as an abstention from power. However Block rejects this kind of argument because it relies on a class-conscious ruling class to formulate such a policy. This is really just 'a slightly more sophisticated version of instrumentalism' (Block, 1987, p. 53). The point of Block's argument is that 'the state must have more autonomy from direct capitalist control than the instrumentalist view would allow' (1987, p. 53). It does so because the instrumentalist assumptions that support such control do not hold. For example, there are divisions within the business community and policy reflects a competitive political process involving other groups.

In Block's view, then, the mechanisms of instrumental control or influence are weak (though not absent) and this turns out to be a good thing from the point of view of capitalist interests because the state requires greater autonomy than would be consistent with their being strong. But, despite this autonomy, that 'state managers are strongly discouraged from pursuing anticapitalist policies' (1987, p. 52) depends on a structural argument. 'Those who manage the state apparatus ... are forced to concern themselves to a greater degree with the reproduction of the social order because their continued power rests on the maintenance of political and economic order' (Block,1987, p. 54). Thus Block's argument relies on an account of the self-interest of state managers and the reproduction of the social order as means to an end. There is a strong incentive for rational decision-makers to select policies (outputs) that will support (or at least not threaten) accumulation because it is in their own self-interest.

The major structural mechanism (or explanation) identified by Block is that the continued power of state managers rests on a 'healthy economy'. It does so because of the links between economic performance and tax revenue and legitimacy. A healthy economy depends on willingness to invest (capital accumulation), and this depends on 'business confidence' (Block, 1987, p. 59). Thus the structural constraint under which state managers operate boils down to the need to maintain business confidence. In other words the decisions of state managers are controlled by the anticipated reactions of capitalists in terms of their investment decisions. Policies that undermine business confidence are irrational from the point of view of the interests of state managers because they will, in turn, undermine state revenue and legitimacy.

The concept of a division of labour between capitalists and state managers is not intended to suggest a complete separation, or the simple absence of capitalists from the public sphere and political engagement. And although the mechanisms of instrumental control of the state by the capitalist class are weak they are incorporated into Block's account as 'subsidiary structural mechanisms'. The importance of these mechanisms is that, though too weak to afford the capitalist class effective control of policy-making, they are strong enough to influence the general direction of policy through their impact on the climate of thought and opinion. In other words, 'the overall effect of this proliferation of influence channels is to make those who run the state more likely to reject modes of thought and behaviour that conflict with the logic of capitalism' (Block, 1987, p. 57). This discouragement of anti-capitalist policies is reinforced by 'bourgeois cultural hegemony' (1987, p. 57). Thus the major impetus behind the formulation of policies that serve the interests of the capitalist class comes from the rational calculation of self-interest on the part of policy-makers. But this rationalism is reinforced by a climate of opinion, shaped by political pressures and the dominant culture, that make anti-capitalist policies unthinkable.

Block's theory seems to depend on a delicate balance in terms of the influence exerted through instrumental channels – just enough to shape the direction of policy, but not enough to take control and send it disastrously off-course. Or, just enough 'voice' to command attention in terms of policy priorities, but not enough to issue commands in terms of policy decisions. In fact, given the emphasis on the rational self-interest of policy-makers, Block's theory of the capitalist state could cope with weaker influence channels but would be undermined were they stronger. This is certainly a source of tension in Block's theory, for he does acknowledge that the control of wealth is convertible into political power (1987, p. 86). The obvious problem that capitalists may use this power to oppose and resist reforms that are functional for capitalism is tackled by invoking working class struggle and exceptional periods. Thus Block argues that 'the major impetus for the extension of the state's role has come from the working class and from the managers of the state apparatus, whose own powers expand with a growing state' (1987, p. 64). The irrational capitalists are outweighed, it seems, by the combined interests and influence of the workers and state managers. But this move just introduces further tensions which Block doesn't really recognise. Some working class demands are functional for capital and/or can be implemented in such a way as to bring them into line with the reproduction of capitalism, but this is clearly not true in all cases. Similarly even if it is generally rational for state managers to support accumulation in the interest of expanding their own powers, sometimes that interest in expanding the role of the state will conflict with capitalist interests. It is not only in exceptional or crisis periods (e.g. war, depression) that state managers enjoy autonomy, but Block claims that in such periods their freedom of action is increased and so major reforms can be implemented. However the need for reform may be a routine requirement of the system in normal periods, and periods of crisis, such as depressions, may create strong pressures for retrenchment rather than the further progress of reform.

The importance of these questions for Block's theory is that however rational it is for state managers to serve the interests of the capitalist class they have to be able to carry through such policies, and that depends critically on the balance of political forces offering support and resistance. Given the inability of the capitalist class to recognise its own class interests there is a profound tension between the politics of support and the politics of rational self-interest that policy-makers have to manage in Block's theory. However the most important source of tension in Block's theory is between his concept of business confidence and the notion of ruling class consciousness. Block dismisses the latter notion and therefore defines business confidence as very different. Business confidence is 'rooted in the narrow self-interest of the individual capitalist who is worried about profit' and 'does not make subtle evaluations as to whether a regime is serving the long term interests of capital' (Block, 1987, p. 59). Being pre-occupied with making profit is, of course, the role of the capitalist in the division of labour. But the theory relies on two questionable assumptions: that capitalists respond only to market signals, and that there is no trade-off facing state managers between short-term profitability and long-term class interests. Although business confidence is not defined in terms of ruling-class consciousness it cannot be divorced from the political ideas and beliefs of capitalists. This is because capitalists are not purely economic actors, responding solely to market signals and incentives. They also have political views and, on Block's own argument, the dominant business outlook is a free market ideology. This means, expressed simply, a belief that reducing the tax and regulatory 'burden' on business is desirable for the prosperity of capitalist enterprise. But capitalists cannot be, as political actors, supporters of free markets and, as economic actors, unperturbed by taxes and regulations in the state of their business confidence. In other words, policies that involve increases in taxation and/or regulation are bound to damage business confidence given an irrational commitment to free market ideology. The difficulty for state managers is that short-term profitability is directly affected by tax and regulatory changes, and there is a trade-off between the long-term interests of capital and the short-term interests of capitalists. For example state managers have to raise taxes now in order to invest in a programme of public spending that will yield long-term benefits for capital. It may be true that capitalists do not make 'subtle evaluations as to whether a regime is serving the long term interests of capital', but they do respond to its immediate implications for profitability. And it is precisely due to a lack of class-consciousness that this response is likely to manifest itself as a decline in business confidence.

The 'structural power' of capital

For Block the major structural mechanism relates to the control over investment decisions by capitalists and the link between the willingness to invest and business confidence. Gough and Farnsworth analyse five sources of the 'structural power' of capital, highlighting control over investment as 'perhaps the most important form' (2000, p. 92). However it can be argued that two of the five sources ('control over investment' and '"exit" and international capital mobility') explicate control over investment as the basic form of 'structural power'. The other three sources ('power over labour', 'state revenue dependency' and 'ideological control') are really manifestations of this basic form. The structural power of capital is defined as 'the ability of capital to influence policy without having to apply direct pressure on governments through its agents – the power of "exit" rather than "voice"' (Gough & Farnsworth, 2000, p. 77). In this approach the instrumentalist channels of influence are recognised and the 'two forms of power' are seen as 'intertwined', but Gough and Farnsworth focus on structural power alone.

The exit-voice coupling cannot really be sustained as an alternative form of expression to the structure-agency coupling because 'exit' can also be seen as a strategy of an agent. The archetypal case of exit linked to the control of investment is the withdrawing or withholding of investment, shown in an interruption or scaling down of the circuit of capital.

> Where 'investment strikes' are threatened within the political realm in order to influence the actions of both state and labour, the use of the threat is always action-based, though the power on which the threat is based may be structural (Gough & Farnsworth, 2000, pp. 77–8).

In this formulation, 'exit' is not a phenomenon of structure alone but of structure and agency combined. This is an example of the 'intertwining' of structural power and agency power in that agency (the threat/strategy of exit) has a structural basis or foundation (the disposition of control over investment).[34] Thus, capitalists are able to threaten investment strikes because of the control of investment which they exercise in virtue of their position and role within the economic structure. Both structure and agency are necessary, but only in their combination sufficient to account for the phenomenon of exit. The same can be said of voice, since the threat or carrying out of an investment strike is not simply a phenomenon of agency or action. This is because 'voice' expresses the structural disposition of control over investment and the interests of capitalists in virtue of their structural position.[35] However there is a striking difference between Gough and Farnsworth's characterisation of the threat of an investment strike as a political act and Block's mechanism of investment being withheld as a result of a decline in business confidence. In the first case the investment strike is a channel of influence or pressure on the state consistent with the instrumentalist approach. Whereas in the second case the withholding of investment is accounted for in non-instrumentalist terms as the result of a decline of business confidence that is related to the impersonal logic or rationality of the economic system. In other words the example given by Gough and Farnsworth of an investment strike does not comply with their abstract definition of structural power as not relying on direct pressure being exerted by agents, whereas something like Block's analysis does exhibit compliance.[36]

The structural power of capital is rooted in control over investment, exerted through dependence on investment decisions, and manifest in the constraining of action by its anticipated effects on the willingness to invest (Gough & Farnsworth, 2000, p. 83). Control over investment is a source of power because investment decisions are highly consequential for society as a whole: they 'have public and long-lasting consequences … for all' (Przeworski & Wallerstein, 1988, p. 12, quoted in Gough and Farnsworth, 2000, p. 83). The notion of 'dependence' captures this high-consequence character of investment decisions: it means that investment contributes for all to the realisation of interests or achievement of 'well-being'. And this means that 'all social groups are constrained in the pursuit of their material interests by the effect of their actions on the willingness of owners of capital to invest' (Przeworski & Wallerstein, in Gough and Farnsworth, 2000, p. 83). This applies especially, but not exclusively, to the state and policy-makers.

Given dependence on investment, it is irrational to pursue actions that discourage investment, that is, that encourage 'exit'. It follows that the structural power of capital is determined not just by the dependence of all social groups on investment, but also by the sensitivity of investment decisions to adverse actions or conditions. This sensitivity will depend not only on the resilience of the capital accumulation process but also on the available 'exit options'. The willingness to invest depends on the profitability of investment. The resilience of capital accumulation refers to the flexibility and adaptability of the capitalist system and its capacity to sustain profitability in the context of adverse conditions or external shocks. The weaker this adaptability, the stronger the structural constraints. Faced with declining profitability the willingness to invest depends on the exit options available. 'Exit' can involve withdrawing money from the circuit of capital altogether but routinely it involves the redirection of investment into more profitable uses. This can involve the movement of investment between firms/industries/sectors and/or between regions. Hence the structural power of capital is dependent in part on its spatial and sectoral mobility.[37] Thus, Gough and Farnsworth argue that this mobility is an asymmetrical source of power of capital over labour (2000, pp. 85–6). This means that the constraint workers are under not to damage profitability because of the negative impact this may have on the willingness to invest is strengthened by the option of redirecting investment to another plant or firm or to another location.[38] Increased possibilities for exit also enhance the structural power of capital in relation to the state, and this is an important effect of 'globalisation' involving international capital mobility (Gough & Farnsworth, 2000, pp. 83–6). Each state is increasingly constrained to secure conditions for profitable accumulation to attract inward investment and deter capital flight. 'This transformation ... is eroding the relative structural powers of the state and tipping the balance of power decisively in favour of capital' (Gough & Farnsworth, 2000, p. 84).[39]

The structural power of capital in relation to the state is exerted through state revenue dependency. In other words, as in Block's analysis, the key argument is that 'the state sector necessarily relies on the capitalist sector for its revenues'. Because of this, as Offe and Ronge argue, the promotion of 'those conditions most conducive to accumulation' arises from 'an institutional self-interest of the state' (1982, pp. 135–47, quoted in Gough & Farnsworth, 2000, p. 86). Gough and Farnsworth also see 'ideological control' as a source or form of the structural power of capital. This is structural because it doesn't depend on deliberate attempts at ideological dominance through control of the means of communication and persuasion as analysed by Miliband. Rather, 'the dependence of society and state on capital profitability and accumulation acts as a gravitational tug on the "volitions" of the population' (Gough & Farnsworth, 2000, pp. 86–7). However this is different to the mechanism of constraint whereby workers and policy-makers adjust their conduct to take account of the anticipated reactions of capitalist investors. For here actors do not just adjust to but 'internalise' the logic or rationality of the system.

A feature of Gough and Farnsworth's presentation of the structural power of capital is that dependence extends beyond the state and policy-makers and embraces all social groups including workers and citizens. In a democratic polity the self-interest of policy-makers can also be expressed as the indirect dependence of citizens on capital accumulation. The structural power of capital can be seen as operating through the two principal institutional mechanisms for determining 'who gets what, where and when' in society: the economy and the state. Individual command over resources (in the widest sense, including personal income and access to public goods) depends on economic decisions (and thus position in the economic structure, particularly the labour market) and political decisions (thus status as citizens). In both cases citizens/workers are constrained as individual and collective actors by their dependence on capital accumulation and the willingness to invest.

The structural power of capital may be conceived as a specific instance of a more general idea of structural power and therefore not the only form. Since the capital relation or the economic structure is not the only structural element within a society there may be other instances of structural power or constraint. If so, the structural power of capital would have to be examined in the context of these other instances. Thus Gough and Farnsworth argue that 'the structural power of a specific set of institutions, such as economic institutions, is always relative to the power of other institutions' (2000, p. 80). The structural power of capital might be analysed in relation to labour and the superstructure.

Gough and Farnsworth refer to the structural power of capital in two senses: the *internal* power of capital over labour within the economic structure, and the *external* power of capital over the state beyond the economic structure. In the first case structural power simply expresses the character of the economic structure as a set of production relations which are relations of effective power. In the second case structural power expresses the constraint that the economic structure as a set of production relations imposes on the state.[40] Within the capital-labour relation labour is not powerless but there is a power imbalance in favour of capital.[41] Furthermore the balance is somewhat variable and unstable, and can shift one way or the other. The power of 'labour' is based on workers 'owning' their own labour power, and this power can be increased relative to the power of capital through combination of workers in trade unions. Or, in other words, in this way workers can reduce their subordination to capital within the economic structure (Cohen, 1978, p. 70). Gough and Farnsworth characterise trade unionism as the exercise of agency power and argue that 'both sides can exercise agency power but only capital disposes of structural power' (2000, p. 81). However this seems incorrect since the basis of workers' power is their position within the economic structure and the ownership of labour power that this position entails. This is structural power in the same sense that the power of capital over means of production is structural. The economic structure involves a relationship of mutual dependence between capital and labour or, in other words, a relationship of mutual power. And each side not only exercises agency power in virtue of their respective ownership positions, but each must anticipate the reactions of the other as a consequence of interests and the logic of the system in which they interact. Just as labour is constrained by 'business confidence', so capital is constrained by what might be termed 'labour confidence'. The important point remains that there is imbalance in the relationship of mutual power, and this stems very largely from the greater dependence of labour on capital than *vice-versa*. Put simply, workers are effectively forced to sell their labour power to a capitalist and cannot exit. It is because workers, unlike capitalists, have no effective choice that it is usual to speak of business confidence but not labour confidence. Yet, though capitalists are assured of a supply of labour they still have to ensure the expenditure of effort in the labour process in order to produce surplus value. Thus, since capitalists must 'anticipate ... [workers'] ... intentions and their likely actions and act in relation to these' (Scott, 2001, p. 4) they face structural constraint or power within the production relations.

It is also misleading to argue that only capital 'disposes' of structural power in relation to the state. The structural constraint or power confronted by the state is inherent in the relationship between the state and the capital relation or economic structure. This is not just a question of its relationship to capital understood as one side of the capital-labour relation. Thus, the idea of labour confidence is relevant here too. Just as state actions are constrained by the need to maintain business confidence and the willingness to invest, the health of the economy on which the state depends also requires the performance of labour. To some extent state managers must therefore act in relation to the intentions/interests and anticipated reactions of workers in order to secure a healthy economy.[42] Here again there is an imbalance of power in that business confidence and the willingness to invest is a stronger or more pressing constraint. And although the state may need to respond to the interests of labour within the economic structure, the interests of the capitalist class remain paramount since the reproduction of the economic structure reproduces the subordination and exploitation of labour.

In the relationship between capital and the state it is obvious that power does not flow only in one direction, from capital to the state: capital also confronts state power. The point is that there is mutual dependence, or interdependence, between capital and the state: the state is dependent on capital, but at the same time capital is dependent on the state. This raises the question whether capitalists are constrained by this dependence in the same way that policy-makers are constrained in their actions by state revenue dependence. Are not capitalists prisoners of the state, just as policy-makers are seen as prisoners of the market? In fact it is clear that, although there is mutual dependence between the state and capital the mutual constraint which arises from this is asymmetric. For although both sides benefit from the 'exchange' – the state gets revenue and capital gets class-based policies – it is in the main the state that has to adjust to the interests and anticipated reactions of capital, rather than *vice-versa*. The state has to formulate and implement policies favourable to capital, whereas capitalists are not required to do anything other than what they would in any case do, that is, accumulate. Of course, capitalists have to pay taxes, and it might be argued that this reveals the power of the state over capital. For the point is that firms have no choice about the payment of taxes, and the capacity of the state to raise taxes rests ultimately on its coercive power. But for all the power of the state that is evident here, the more basic point is that tax revenues are still dependent on the health of the economy. For all that the state can forcibly extract tax revenues from the capitalist sector it can only do so on a sustained basis within limits set by the rate of capital accumulation. Values have to be produced before they can be distributed.

The constraint faced by policy-makers in virtue of their dependence on a flow of revenue/resources generated in the capitalist sector needs to be viewed in the context of other structural constraints related to the form of the state itself, of which two will be briefly considered. First, constraints arising from the structural properties of systems of representation, especially the competitive electoral system of democratic polities. Second, the structural properties of the international system of states. The importance of recognising the multiple-structured context is that these may pull decisions of policy-makers in different directions. The responsiveness of policy-makers to the needs of capital may be reinforced, it has been argued, by the need to maintain public support or legitimacy. Thus if legitimacy is strongly dependent on economic performance the implication is that the constraints of the electoral system are congruent with economic constraints. For in acting to support accumulation in order to boost state revenue politicians will simultaneously boost their re-election chances. Against this the electoral cycle may induce short-termism in economic policy as policy-makers seek to engineer a 'feel-good' factor by stimulating the economy in a pre-election period irrespective of long-term requirements for capital accumulation. Another important structural context is the international system of states, which may be characterised in terms of military and economic competition between self-interested states. It can be argued that this competitive system reinforces economic constraints on policy-makers as economic strength is a key to success in the international arena. However, again, it is possible to see structural constraints pulling in different directions. For example, governments may devote resources to military expenditures at the expense of civilian projects (e.g. infrastructure) that contribute to the accumulation function of the state. The importance of these, briefly considered, arguments is that what is a rational course for policy-makers is shaped by the interaction of their own self-interests with a multiplicity of structural constraints, and these may pull in different directions. Thus the claim that the state may be understood primarily as a capitalist state must show either that non-economic structural constraints are congruent with economic ones, or that the former are weak relative to the latter.

The idea that state managers have their own interests, coupled with the multiplicity of structural contexts, shows that the constraint of the state by capital should be understood as creating a strategic dilemma for policy-makers. The dilemma arises from the fact that serving the interests of capitalists is not an end in itself but a means to an end. The question of the interests or purposes of state managers can be put aside from a structural point of view since the basic claim is that a flow of revenue/resources is required for any purposes of the state and these resources must be obtained from the capitalist sector.[43] The argument also does not need to assume that state managers are maximisers, for a 'good enough' or 'satisficing' approach to revenue still involves dependence on the capitalist sector. Policy-makers want to increase state revenue for diverse purposes (ends), and this requires capital accumulation (means). But the dilemma is that boosting accumulation may require limiting taxation (as an unproductive burden or drain on surplus value) and prioritising spending on programmes that are functional for capital. Thus structural constraints do not simply bring policy-makers into line with the needs of capital. Rather, rational decision-makers are required to calculate how best to balance immediate or short-term interests against securing the necessary means to realise interests in the long-term. Capitalists face a similar dilemma for, although payment of taxes is not a decision, they do have to decide between acquiescence and resistance to taxation. Of course if, in an extreme version of Block's analysis, capitalists were free market fundamentalists they would oppose all taxes on business, but this would be irrational. The idea of a dilemma suggests that capitalists are rational calculators who see the necessity of tax in their own self-interest. They too have to calculate how best to balance immediate or short-term profit with securing the long-term interests of capital.

Structure, agency and the state

The aim of this final section is to draw together the principal arguments concerning the relationship between 'instrumental' and 'structural' arguments, and between 'structure' and 'agency', in the Marxist theory of the state. More specifically, to show how 'instrumental' and 'structural' arguments can be used to elaborate the claim that the nature of the economic structure explains the character of the legal and political superstructure. In this historical materialist claim the nature of the economic structure is the explanans (or independent variable) and the character of the superstructure is the explanandum (or dependent variable). It is clear from this that the types of explanation that connect the superstructure to the base are by definition 'structural' since they must refer to the nature of the economic structure. For this reason the standard instrumental-structural distinction is misleading – as we have seen, structure not only creeps into but looms large in so-called instrumental explanation. Hence we have characterised the instrumentalist thesis as a species of structural explanation, distinguished from structuralist explanation in terms of structural interconnection and structural constraint. A related distinction, following Scott (2001), is between pressure and constraint, both of which have a structural basis. In these terms the conventional instrumentalist approach emphasises the role of pressure and the structuralist approach emphasises constraint, though it is important to see their interrelation.[44]

Marxism is a theory of economic determination. According to this theory the nature of the economic structure explains a range of non-economic phenomena. This does not mean that all non-economic phenomena are explained by the economic structure, and nor does it mean that the economic structure operates alone as a sufficient principle of explanation. Some non-economic phenomena escape economic explanation, and economic explanation normally operates in combination with other causal influences. But Marxism singles out economic-structural explanation because of its causal power. In other words for Marxism, though a multiplicity of causal chains is recognised, economic explanation is a fundamental determinant or strong tendency.[45] Within Marxism the theory of history makes the specific claim that a range of non-economic phenomena are *functionally* explained by the nature of the economic structure. These are only those non-economic phenomena that are economically relevant in the sense that they meet functional requirements of the structure. Only these phenomena are included in the 'superstructure', and their explanation is that bases need superstructures. This 'restricted' historical materialism may be distinguished from Marxist sociology, which embraces some wider claims of economic determination.[46]

The state is not synonymous in the theory of history with the 'superstructure', although the description of the latter as 'legal and political' suggests that it may be largely comprised of state institutions. However there may be some aspects of the state that are non-superstructural, and some elements of the superstructure may be non-state. Only those parts of the state that are functionally explained by the nature of the economic structure are included in the super-structure. There may be economic, but not historical materialist, explanation of other parts of the state, these explanations coming within the ambit of Marxist sociology. And there may be some parts of the state that escape economic explanation. Thus to the extent that Marxism offers explanation of the state this explanation is structural, that is, economic-structural. This does not mean, again, that other causal influences do not operate, but Marxism claims that these are secondary compared to the primary explanatory power of the economic structure. Among these other causal influences is agency, so agency does not come within the ambit of the theory but is treated as an 'exogenous variable'. Agency properly refers to 'the capacity of an actor to act' but not, as Hay also says, to 'action' or 'conduct' itself (Hay, 2002, p. 94). The capacity to act, and not to be a slave of the environment, 'implies a sense of free will, choice or autonomy – that the actor could have behaved differently'. Structure explains conduct but not in an 'ultimately determinant sense' (Hay, 2002, p. 94) for there is a space or gap in the explanation that is occupied by agency. Likewise, agency explains conduct but operates within structural para-meters or constraints. Thus structure and agency combine to explain conduct. For example, structural constraints limit the feasible set of actions available to actors to realise their interests and/or assign differ-ent risks and rewards to different actions. Further, the positions occu-pied by actors within structures may shape their interests. But agency, the capacity to make choices and to act, means that actors can reflexively monitor the consequences of past conduct and the struc-tural constraints facing them in order to decide a course of action. In general terms there is always some scope for agency, and agency as choice constitutes an essentially unpredictable element. How much scope there is for agency cannot be answered in general terms since it depends on the specification of the explanandum, or what it is that is being explained. Different kinds of structure will have a sometimes strong, and sometimes weak, explanatory power in different cases. But 'the greater the influence of structure, the more predictable political behaviour is assumed to be' (Hay, 2002, p. 94). Or, the more determinant the structural explanation. In the specific case of the Marxist claim that the nature of the economic structure explains the character of the superstructure, the influence of structure is indeed great.

'Instrumental' and 'structuralist' arguments can be brought together in a range of related causal mechanisms. These mechanisms elaborate the claim that the economic structure functionally explains the superstructure. The conventional 'instrumental' approach focuses on the instrumental use of power resources controlled by the capitalist class in order to influence and/or control state power. These instrumental resources consist ultimately in control over investment (means of production) and, more generally, wealth. The control of investment confers decisive power on capitalists because investment decisions are high-consequence for all members of society, including state managers. The importance of wealth is that money is 'convertible' into forms of power and influence such as campaign contributions. But control of wealth and investment are linked to other channels of power, especially connections between capitalists and other members of an upper class, and the social prominence and authority that go with economic position. The instrumental approach emphasises the political conduct of members of the capitalist class and their participation in the exercise of political power. This can be inside the state system through colonisation of the executive and/or through upper class origins of members of the state elite. In the case of colonisation capitalists may be said to exercise power in the form of 'command' through occupying positions in the state system that confer legitimacy (Scott, 2001, p. 20). From outside capitalists influence state power through what Scott refers to as 'pressure', for example through a range of activities under the label 'lobbying and public relations', or through investment strikes.[47] The internal-external distinction is not clear-cut, as shown by the existence of networked connections between capitalists and the state elite such as social interactions and participation in policy planning. But the distinction is important in bringing out the extent of separation or cohesion between Miliband's two elements of the power elite. Although command and pressure can be combined, it may be that the lesser the involvement in command the greater the requirement to apply pressure. The instrumental approach is a structural explanation in the fundamental sense that the instrumental resources of wealth and control of investment are in the hands of capitalists in virtue of the positions they occupy within the economic structure. Furthermore the interests of capitalists are shaped by the roles they perform in the economic structure and carried over into political struggles. In other words the origins of both the power resources and the interests they are used to serve are structural. Thus structure profoundly shapes the conduct that is the focus of the instrumental approach.

The instrumental approach relies on the presence of capitalists in the public sphere. A second, related, approach focuses on the exercise of power through effective constraint even without the participation of capitalists in politics and the state. The distinction between holding and exercising power is important here. Because capitalists have the capacity to intervene in politics, and apply pressure through the instrumental use of power resources, state managers have to anticipate and take account of the likely reactions of capitalists to policy decisions. State managers, not wanting to provoke a negative reaction from business, are under pressure to pursue pro-business policies, without capitalists having to do anything. Policy-makers will be loathe to incite the public and vocal opposition of the business community, and wary of the capacity of business to apply effective pressure for policy change through the public sphere and behind the scenes. In extreme, this pressure may take the form of the threat of an investment strike. The implicit or explicit threat of action may be enough to bring policy-makers into line. This approach is really a refinement of instrumentalism because it relies on the political consciousness and willingness to engage in political action of the capitalist class. Although power may be exercised through the threat of pressure, this may be more effective if it is reinforced from time to time by actual pressure.

Although an investment strike may be used as a deliberate political act to bring pressure on policy-makers, there are severe limitations on such acts. This is because investment decisions are primarily driven by competition and profit, not by political considerations. Competition is the key driver since firms must invest in order to survive in competitive markets through improvements in efficiency. And firms must make profits as a source of internal finance for investment. Thus, capital accumulation has to be understood primarily in terms of the 'rationality' or 'logic' of the capitalist economy (economic structure), and it is because of this logic that policy-makers face compelling structural constraints. For failure to ensure favourable conditions of accumulation will lead to an 'automatic' withholding of investment. 'Automatic' in the sense that it doesn't involve any political consciousness or action by capitalists, only their routine responses as economic actors to 'market signals'. It is, of course the positions occupied by capitalists within the economic structure, and the interests that are attached to these positions, that determines these responses. And structural constraints also operate through the interests of state managers. State revenues depend on the health of the capitalist sector. Thus state managers pursue policies that serve capitalist interests because the health of the economy requires them, and because by improving the health of the economy state managers serve their own interests.

The effect of structural constraints is to bring about an adjustment of the interests of state managers to the functional requirements or needs of the economy. For state managers capital accumulation is not an end in itself (since state managers are outside the circuit of capital and do not earn profits) but a means to an end (since state revenue depends on incomes generated by the circuit of capital). This suggests that state managers do not serve the capitalist class willingly but only because, and to the extent that, they have to, that is, only to the extent that such service is 'good enough'. However they will be more willing to the extent that dependence on capital accumulation leads state managers to 'internalise' the logic of the system. Constraint is a mechanism whereby an actor is induced to do something she would not otherwise have done. When constraints are internalised this becomes what the actor would choose to do. Thus state managers may become habituated to serving the interests of the capitalist class.

In all these mechanisms the nature of the economic structure explains powers, interests, constraints and the actions of agents. The economic structure is conceived as having its own logic or rationality. It comprises a set of production relations, and these are characterised as relations of effective control or power over economic resources – means of production and labour power. Positions in the economic structure may be defined in terms of roles with definite interests attached to their performance.[48] Thus the decision to invest by capitalists must be understood in terms of their role and interests, that is, as 'capital personified'. It is the same system logic that constrains policy-makers in virtue of their dependence on capital for revenue. And it is the role of capitalists in the economic structure with its attendant powers and interests that explains the instrumental operation of pressure within the political system and the public sphere. But economic and political actors remain agents with the capacity to calculate and choose a course of action. Agents have, that is, room for manoeuvre – they are not merely 'prisoners' of the economic structure, and structure does not explain conduct in an 'ultimately determining sense'.[49] Cohen distinguishes between occupying and performing a role and, although performance may normally conform to the prescribed role, this allows for some discrepancy or gap. It is, so to speak, in that gap that agency operates (in unpredictable ways).[50] For example, though accumulation is driven by profit and competition, this does not mean that capitalists have no choice between alternative possible corporate strategies, or that they are singleminded profit-maximisers. Equally, the presence of capitalists in the political sphere is not a mere reflection of economic roles and interests. Finally, structural constraints do not simply determine policy decisions but create dilemmas for state managers calculating how best to pursue their own interests (or respond to other pressures) within these constraints. However the Marxist contention is that the scope for agency is limited and the influence of structure is strong.

Although the mechanisms we have considered may be set out as analytically distinct, in practice they are interrelated and mutually reinforcing. This suggests that although no single mechanism can fully explain superstructural phenomena, taken together they provide strong support for the explanatory primacy of the economic structure. For example, Luger suggests that 'state dependence is an essential policy consideration, not a force that automatically shapes specific state actions to the benefit of business' (2000, p. 28). Thus structural constraint may not be sufficient to explain the needed state actions. Therefore 'it is important to analyze precisely how business takes advantage of its privileged position, and how the combination of the political behaviour of business and its structural position shape public policy' (2000, p. 28).

Arguments for the explanatory power of structure rest implicitly on an assumption of the enduring nature of structure and its resistance to change. For example policy-makers, and other actors, are prisoners of the market because of the difficulties they face in trying to effect structural change. There are four factors that may contribute to the durability of structure, and the economic structure exemplifies these. The factors are: 1. the strength of its internal dynamic; 2. the scope for actors to innovate or withdraw; 3. the existence of mechanisms designed to reinforce or sustain the existing structure; and, 4. the importance of the structure for the realisation of actors' interests or well-being. Despite its crisis tendencies, capital accumulation exhibits a high degree of flexibility and robustness that enables it to 'continue operating, if necessary through spontaneous, adaptive self-reorganisation, in a wide range of circumstances ... [and] ... to resolve or manage its internal contradictions, paradoxes and dilemmas' (Jessop, 2002, p. 26).[51] Capitalism has, in other words, a strong internal dynamic. Seeming to qualify this is the fact that capitalism depends on external conditions of accumulation secured through political action – it is not a self-sufficient or self-reproducing system. However the remaining points show that state managers have little choice in securing these conditions. They must do so because the state depends on the economic structure for its own revenue and, indirectly, because economic reproduction is critical for all members of society (4). Capitalism also generates its own mechanisms for defending the existing system because in concentrating economic resources it also concentrates power resources. Thus capitalism produces its own ruling class or 'guardians' with a vested interest and power to defend the system (3). Finally, although capitalism depends on political action to stabilise and sustain it, withdrawing support is not really an option. Short of a wholesale transformation of capitalism state managers find it difficult to create and sustain alternative production relations within capitalism. From the perspective of state managers capitalism is the only game in town (2).

5
Base and Superstructure

Introduction

According to the theory of history, the character of the legal and political superstructure is explained by the nature of the economic structure.[1] This is a claim of economic determination. But it is, according to Cohen, a restricted claim: the superstructure only includes those non-economic phenomena that are 'economically relevant' in the sense of being functional for the economic structure. This means, roughly, only those phenomena that are necessary to stabilise an otherwise unstable structure. Only these phenomena are functionally explained by the nature of the economic structure and so come within the ambit of the theory of history. In the Preface the superstructure is characterised by Marx as 'legal and political', and this suggests that the state looms large in its composition, although it does not follow that the entire state system is included in the superstructure. The theory of history in this restricted form is distinguished by Cohen from Marxist sociology which may make wider claims of economic determination, some of which might be functional in character.

In order to know the content of the superstructure we need to clarify 'the nature of the economic structure'. It is of the nature of the economic structure that it is, by itself, unstable and, therefore, needs to be stabilised. It is this nature that is explanatory of the character of the superstructure. Thus to say that superstructural items are functionally explained by the base is to claim that their occurrence is explained by their having this stabilising effect. It is the disposition of the economic structure to be stabilised by these items (which is a statement about its nature) that explains why they occur. Thus one way of delimiting the superstructure is to identify legal and political phenomena that perform the function of stabilising the base. However we would need to avoid conflating function statements with functional explanations: It does not follow from 'A is functional for B' that 'A is functionally explained by B'. The functional explanation may be justified by an empirical generalisation that 'whenever A would be functional for B, A occurs', and/or by elucidating a plausible mechanism connecting the functional item to the functional requirement.

To count as performing a function for the base, legal and political phenomena must meet a genuine 'functional requirement': in other words they must be necessary for the stabilisation of the economic structure. This is the sense in which bases need superstructures: bases have functional requirements which superstructures come into being to fulfil. Thus we can delimit the superstructure by starting at the base level, by identifying the functional requirements of the economic structure. What are the sources of instability of the economic structure? And then, what 'things' (e.g. institutions, policies, decisions, behaviours) need to happen in order to secure the stability of the economic structure? In order to understand the 'needs of capital' it is necessary go beyond Cohen's narrow definition of the economic structure.

The nature of the economic structure

In defining the concept of economic structure in the Preface, Marx says that it is constituted by 'the sum total of ... relations of production'. Following this guidance, Cohen stipulates that 'production relations alone serve to constitute the economic structure' (1978, p. 28). It follows that it is the nature of these relations which has explanatory force *vis-à-vis* the character of the superstructure. These are social relations in the peculiar sense of being relations of power or effective control, and the terms of production relations, the things which are connected by them, are persons and productive forces. Thus 'production relations are relations of effective power over persons and productive forces' (Cohen, 1978, p. 63).

This conceptualisation is highly abstract. It tells us what characteristics social relations of production always display (connectedness of persons and productive forces through relations of effective control) but does not tell us the precise form or pattern of effective control – what might be called the precise structural form. At this high level of abstraction the most general explanatory claims are made, such as that 'the character of some non-economic institutions is explained by the nature of the economic structure'.[2] The claim is not made in relation to a specific structural form – say, capitalism – but as a general assertion of the causal primacy of the 'economic' *vis-à-vis* (some part of) what is non-economic in all class societies, and thus encapsulates the theoretical ambition of Marx's theory of history. Furthermore the explanation of the non-economic by the economic might be conceived as being always of the same type – as in Cohen's functional construal of the theory of history. It is important not to lose sight of this large claim when the focus is on a particular social type. Nevertheless the particular character of non-economic institutions will differ according to the particular form of the prevailing economic structure (thus with the change of economic structure the entire immense superstructure is transformed) and the particular mechanisms through which economic determination is effected might also differ. If it is true this general claim should, of course, be instantiated in analyses of particular structural forms such as capitalism.[3]

Although Cohen defines production relations as relations of ownership (effective control) by persons of productive forces or *persons* it is always the control of the *labour power* (a productive force) of such persons which is the real significance of such relations. Thus production relations can be defined as: relations of ownership (or effective control or power) by persons of, or over, productive forces which comprise, principally, labour power and means of production (instruments and materials).

Hence Cohen classifies sets of production relations or structural forms according to the ownership positions of the 'immediate producers' with respect to 'his labour power' and 'the means of production he uses' (1978, p. 65 *et seq.*). For example in an idealised characterisation of capitalist relations of production proletarians own all of their labour power and none of the means of production they use (we will note a qualification of this description shortly). Conversely capitalists own none of the labour power of the immediate producers and all of the means of production they use (Cohen, 1978, p. 65). Cohen's position can be summarised as follows:

1. It is the nature of the economic structure which is explanatory of the superstructure.
2. The economic structure is constituted by social relations of production alone.
3. Social relations of production are relations of 'ownership' (or effective control) by persons of productive forces (labour power and means of production).

Additionally:

4. 'Basic is not a set of processes but a set of relations ... The point has some importance, since the fact that certain relations obtain explains phenomena in a different fashion from the fact that certain processes occur' (Cohen, 1978, p. 31) and Marxism's explanatory theses have a 'structural cast' (ibid.): it is relations that explain, not processes.

This amounts to a rather narrow concept of the nature of the economic structure: it comprises solely relations (as distinct from processes) and these are relations of ownership (effective control) only. This conception may be adequate for Cohen's purpose of mounting an explanation of rights in terms of the basic powers that they match, but appears too narrow to support explanation of the 'entire immense superstructure'. In other words, there are good reasons to think that the superstructure is not confined to a legal structure of rights. This is because the capitalist structure of power over productive forces is necessary but not sufficient to ensure their development. The forces of production can only be developed in any type of society through the *process of production*. Each distinctive economic structure gives rise to a characteristic production process. In capitalism this is the circuit of capital and the process of capital accumulation. Thus in order for capitalism to develop the forces of production it is the process of capital's circuit and accumulation that must be stabilised, not just the positions or roles of capitalists and proletarians.[4] Let us then examine the nature of the economic structure more broadly conceived. This entails the incorporation of relations other than 'ownership' and allowing that process is part of the nature of the economic structure.

The ownership position of proletarians tends to constitute labour power as a commodity. For, having ownership or effective control of their labour power, proletarians are free to dispose of it in their own way, yet, lacking ownership of means and production, apparently have no choice but to sell this labour power to a capitalist who does own means of production. Thus

the essential feature of capitalism is the existence of labour power as a commodity. A necessary condition for this is the separation of labour from ownership or claim to the means of production (Fine, 1975, p. 41).[5]

However it is not always true that the proletarian owns no means of production (Cohen, 1978, p. 70): non-ownership of means of production is not a necessary condition of proletarian status. Cohen says of the descriptions of the ownership positions of immediate producers (slave, serf, proletarian, independent producer) that they are idealised. A proletarian may own some means of production yet still be proletarian because, for example, although his means of production make it technically possible for him to produce independently he cannot compete with capitalist production (Cohen, 1978, p. 72) which means that 'he cannot use ... [these means of production] ... to support himself save by contracting with a capitalist'. Thus the structure of ownership of proletarians and capitalists with respect to productive forces seems to entail a *relationship of exchange.*[6] It is this need to sell his labour power to a capitalist rather than his lack of means of production that defines the proletarian condition. Further, the proletarian is defined not simply by having to sell his labour power but by his thereby entering a relationship of 'subordination to a capitalist' (ibid.). The linkage between relations of ownership, exchange and authority is summarised by Cohen as follows:

lacking means of production, [the proletarian] ... can ensure his survival only by contracting with a capitalist whose bargaining position enables him to impose terms which effect the worker's subordination (1978, p. 70).

However the elements of contracting and subordination may be seen as providing a fuller characterisation of capitalist production relations and so ought, in effect, to be incorporated into the *concept* of the economic structure. In this more expansive conception exchange coupled to subordination, in addition to mere ownership, become the defining features of capitalist relations of production and thereby figure in explanation of the superstructure. In other words Cohen's conception of production relations as relations of ownership by persons of productive forces should be seen as a starting point and extended to incorporate relations of exchange and relations of authority which follow from the basic ownership positions. In outline we can say that capitalist production relations are characterised by:

1. relations of *ownership* or formal control by persons of productive forces, which give rise to

2. relations of *exchange* between proletarians and capitalists (as buyers and sellers in the labour market), which entail
3. relations of *authority* between proletarians and capitalists (as employers and employees in the production or labour process).

The relations of exchange and authority are inherently contested and conflictual, as 'commodification turns both the labour market and labour process into sites of class struggle between capital and workers' (Jessop, 2002, p. 15). For example, the terms of the contract, notably the wage rate, will depend upon the bargaining positions of each side, which will in turn depend on factors such as the supply and demand for different types of labour and the organisational strength of capitalists and workers. Thus trade unions may improve the bargaining position of workers and so alleviate to some extent their subordination. This may even be thought of as a reduction of proletarian status (Cohen,1978, p. 70).

Within capitalist relations of production, however, the bargaining position achieved by proletarians through unionisation is structurally constrained by the requirement of capital not just to hire but to exploit labour power (Miliband, 1984, p. 55; Coates, 1980), i.e. to make a profit. The sale of labour power concedes to a capitalist the right to its use and places the proletarian in a position of subordination within a relation of authority. Cohen says that the ascription of subordinate status is warranted by three facts of the proletarian condition: proletarians produce for capitalists, are subject to their authority within the production process, and tend to be poorer than the latter (1978, p. 69). However it might be argued that the second aspect, authority, is the most important because it is this above all that makes exploitation possible.[7] Thus Marx famously contrasts the labour market, '... a very Eden of the innate rights of man ... the exclusive realm of Freedom, Equality, Property and Bentham', with the labour process in which 'the money-owner now strides in front as a capitalist; the possessor of labour-power follows as his worker' (1976, p. 280).

Here we have a relationship of authority, of domination-subordination. The capitalist buys labour power in order to use it and, having bought it, becomes, for the duration, the owner of this commodity with an interest in maximising its use-value. The question of 'ownership' or effective control of labour power now looks rather different to the way it did from the vantage point of the relations of production narrowly conceived, from outside the sphere of production so to speak. *Within* production the ownership position of the proletarian is that he owns none of the productive forces he uses – neither the means of production nor his 'own' labour power. In fact, although by act of purchase the capitalist obtains formal ownership of the labour power of the proletarian and the latter relinquishes the same by act of sale, the reality of control is the focus of a process of struggle and contestation between capitalist(s) and proletarians. This contrast between the formal freedom and equality of exchange and the unfreedom of production is a familiar one but it is important to emphasise here because it is missing from Cohen's 'legalistic' conception of the social relations of production.

Let us summarise at this point. Cohen's conception of economic structure, it is being argued, is inadequate insofar as it utilises a 'legalistic' conception of the social relations of production characterised in terms of 'ownership'. Relationships of exchange and authority engendered by the ownership positions of proletarians and capitalists need to be incorporated into the concept of the capitalist economic structure, as part of its nature, and so assigned a potential explanatory role *vis-à-vis* the superstructure.

Against this, Cohen draws a distinction between structure and process which are, in turn, bases for 'distinct sorts of explanation' (1978, p. 87). We may be able to explain some non-economic phenomena by reference to economic processes to which the structure is subject but, on the basis of Cohen's argument, these would not be historical materialist explanations.[8] For, to repeat, the superstructure is explained by the nature of the structure, the structure is constituted by relations alone, and relations are not the same things as processes. However the exclusion of process from explanation of the superstructure weakens the theory of history by restricting its explanatory power. The kind of superstructural phenomena that Cohen is particularly interested in – legal rights that match basic powers – might be capable of explanation just on the basis of reference to the nature of the economic structure. But it is not clear that such phenomena are adequate to stabilise the productivity-enhancing character of the economic structure. This is because the structure develops the productive forces through the process of production (i.e. the circuit of capital and accumulation) in which it is implicated, but in order for the structure to perform its historical function this process also needs to be stabilised. Although we cannot, strictly, define the concept of economic structure to incorporate process, this suggests that the character of the legal and political superstructure is explained by the nature of the economy or economic system, incorporating structure and process.[9] We might say that the nature of the economic system involves elements of 'structure' and 'structured process'. Schematically

Structure ⇨ Structured Process

On the other hand processes, of exchange and production, which originate in structure, may, in turn, modify this structure. Thus

Process ⇨ Structural Change.

We will say more about the phenomenon of structural change shortly. For the moment we emphasise, in distinction from Cohen, that the processual aspects of the economy exercise important determining influences on the character of the superstructure.

The circuit of capital

The economy as structured process, embracing the elements of exchange and production we have discussed, is captured by the analysis of the circuit of capital. The circuit of capital describes the process whereby surplus value is appropriated from the immediate producers (exploitation) under the specific conditions of capitalist relations of production. In other words the circuit describes capital as 'self expanding value' (Fine, 1975, p. 47): the rationale of the circuit is to enlarge the sum of money capital which the capitalist invests at the beginning. This augmentation of money capital, or surplus value (profit) 'thrown off' by the circuit (Fine, ibid.), equates to the surplus product appropriated from the immediate (subordinate) producers through the extraction of surplus labour.[10] But in capitalism self-expanding value is linked to the 'self-valorisation of capital' as 'capital expands through the profitable reinvestment of past profits' (Jessop, 2002, p. 15). In other words the self-expansion of value within the circuit feeds the enlargement of the circuit through the recurrent reinvestment of profit. In capitalism, as

> in all (class) modes of production, for exploitation to take place, two conditions must be met. First, the productivity of labour must exceed the minimum level necessary to maintain life and necessary health and the reproduction of the population ... Second, one class must own and control at least a part of the means of production and thereby be in a position to claim the product of the surplus labour (Gough, 1979, p. 18).

In other words there must be a surplus product and one class must be able, by virtue of its 'ownership' position with respect to means of production (and labour power), to successfully claim this surplus. These, then, are basic conditions which capitalism shares with all previous antagonistic modes. A prior condition in capitalism is the availability on the labour market of labour power as a (fictitious) commodity. We can add to this that capitalist relations of production arise, according to Marx's theory of history, when and because the productivity of labour has risen to a level at which a 'moderately high surplus' (Cohen, 1978, p. 198) can be produced.

It is important to note that these conditions only make exploitation possible: two considerations show that they are necessary but not sufficient conditions for exploitation to take place. First, a surplus has actually to be produced: productive power or potential, in short the productivity of labour, has to be realised. Ownership of means of production and labour power is important here insofar as it constitutes the structural basis of a relationship of domination-subordination – of the subordination of the immediate producers – in the process of production. Nevertheless the effort/productivity of labour is determined by the outcome of the struggle over the control of the labour process within production itself. Second, the degree of exploitation depends on the share of output successfully claimed by the immediate producers: in other words, within capitalism, the value of the wage. This bears upon the value of labour power and its 'historical and moral dimension'. But whatever the value of labour power at any moment, the wage will be determined by the bargaining position of proletarians as sellers of labour power *vis-à-vis* the capitalist, that is, in the relationship of exchange with capital. More fully,

> the magnitude of the rate of surplus value is directly determined by three factors: the length of the working day, the quantity of commodities entering into the real wage, and the productiveness of labour. The first establishes the total time to be divided between necessary and surplus labour, and the second and third together determine how much of this time is to be counted as necessary labour ... The rate of surplus value may be raised either by an extension of the working day, or by a lowering of the real wage, or by an increase in the productiveness of labour, or, finally, by some combination of the three movements (Sweezy, 1942, pp. 64–5).

Equally, the rate of surplus value may be lowered by contrary movements. The point is that each factor, and each movement, is contested: the rate of surplus value is determined through class struggle. The appropriation of surplus value, exploitation, thus depends on the ability of the capitalist to secure and sustain a favourable combination of the three factors.[11] At the same time the rate of surplus value must not be of such a magnitude that the reproduction of labour power, and thus the sustainability of exploitation, is threatened. This might result from excessive lengthening of the working day,[12] a lowering of the real wage below subsistence, excessive intensity of labour, or some combination of the three. In sum, Sweezy's three factors concern the possibility of exploitation, but for a sustained appropriation of surplus the rate of surplus value must neither fall to zero or be increased to a level which involves over exploitation of labour power. This analysis is important because it points to potential sources of instability within the economic structure – and to some requirements for stability. These requirements might be important in explanation of the superstructure, as exemplified by the functional explanation of the Factory Acts.

The simple analysis of the circuit of capital provides the basis for a full abstract characterisation of the (dynamic) nature of the capitalist economic structure. The circuit describes a cycle of 'buying in order to sell' and may be represented schematically by the following sequence (Campbell, 1981; Brewer, 1984; Catephores, 1989).

$$M \quad \Rightarrow \quad C \quad \Rightarrow \quad C^1 \quad \Rightarrow \quad M^1$$

where
M = money capital
C = commodities (labour power + means of production)
$C^1 = C + c$ (c = surplus product, i.e. $C^1 > C$)
$M^1 = M + m$ (m = surplus value, i.e. $M^1 > M$)

In this depiction the circuit starts and finishes with money and in the process the sum of money is enlarged. The circuit as a whole comprises three distinct stages: exchange (M-C), then production (C-C^1), then exchange again (C^1-M^1). From the capitalist's point of view this circuit comprises buying – producing – selling (hence 'buying in order to sell'). The capitalist starts with a sum of money and, let us say, a stock of means of production and raw materials but needs labour power to set the instruments to work on the materials. He meets in the market propertyless proletarians with labour power to sell and the two parties contract to their mutual advantage (M-C). The capitalist thus acquires the right to use the labour power of the proletarians with the aim of extracting surplus labour (C-C^1). Finally the capitalist sells the commodities that result from production and thereby recoups not only his original outlay but enlarges his money capital (C^1-M^1).

Relations of 'Ownership' ⇨ Relations of Exchange (M-C) ⇨
Relations of Authority (C-C^1) ⇨ Relations of Exchange (C^1-M^1).

It can be seen that relations of 'ownership' constitute the starting point or foundation for this circuit and that the first two stages comprise the relations of exchange and authority discussed earlier. We now encounter a third stage, which completes the circuit, constituted by the sale of commodities in order to realise the profit embodied in them. The capitalist as seller has to meet buyers who are willing to purchase these commodities at their full values. Thus the magnitude of surplus value (m) (profit) generated by the circuit depends on conditions in each of its three stages:

Value of the wage	} (M->C)	}	}
Length of working day	} (M->C)	} Rate	}
		} of	}Rate
		} Exploitation	}of
Productiveness of labour	} (C->C^1)	}	}Profit
			}
Realisation conditions	} (C^1->M^1)		}

Through the circuit

> industrial capital changes successively into its three forms: money capital (M), productive capital (P), and commodity capital (C^1) ... money capital acts as a means of purchasing labour power, productive capital acts as a means of producing surplus value, and commodity capital acts as the depository of surplus value (Fine, 1975, p. 47).[13]

In fact, of course, the circuit does not, in general, end with the return of an enlarged sum of money to the capitalist but is renewed, and this time on an expanded scale as capital is *accumulated*. Accumulation occurs 'via capitalist saving out of surplus value and its investment in additional constant and variable capital' (Howard and

King, 1975, p. 183). Thus capital is inherently expansionary, not only in the sense that the circuit of capital involves the self-expansion of value but also in the sense that the circuit itself is perpetually enlarged through the re-investment of surplus value (profit). Although profit-as-income provides an incentive for capitalists to save and invest, the decisive element driving the accumulation process is not greed but the fear of competition. Competition

> is fought by the cheapening of commodities through reducing their value, that is to say the labour time necessary for their production. This is achieved by technological advance, ... and this requires accumulation of capital (Fine, 1975, p. 34).

This brings out very clearly the connection between the capitalist 'way of producing' and the development of the productive forces. Competition between capitals is, then, a fundamental process in which the economic structure is implicated and a second source, alongside the capital-labour relation, of capitalism's restless tendency to develop the forces of production. It may follow that the function of the superstructure is, in part, to stabilise this competitive process and its productivity-enhancing tendency.

The process of accumulation is, according to Marx and the mainstream Marxist tradition, inherently crisis-ridden, and crises are certainly a regular feature of the history of capitalist economies. Crises occur 'whenever the social accumulation of capital is interrupted' (Fine, 1975, p. 51), and they result, at the most general level of explanation, from threats to profitability which arise in the accumulation process.[14] There is, of course, much controversy within Marxism as to the causal mechanisms involved in the generation of periodic crises, and the plausibility of 'possibility theories' or 'necessity theories' (Shaikh, 1991, p. 161). Marx's theory of the necessity or inevitability of economic crisis is usually based on the law of the tendency of the rate of profit to fall (Fine, 1975, p. 51). The existence of such a tendency, though, remains a matter of dispute, and there are strong arguments to suggest that the law is invalid (Howard and King, 1975, p. 207). However the necessity of periodic crises may still be related to general features of the capitalist economy, notably the 'essential contradiction in the commodity form between its exchange- and use-value aspects' (Jessop, 2002, p. 16). Possibility theories of crisis include: over-accumulation in relation to the supply of labour power/wage squeeze, disproportionality, and underconsumption/stagnation (Fine, 1975;

Howard & King, 1975; Campbell, 1981; Shaikh, 1991). These theories point to systemic tendencies and causes and may suggest that although a crisis-free path of accumulation is conceivable it is unlikely.

Periodic crises evidently constitute a major form of instability characteristic of capitalist economies. In interrupting the social accumulation of capital, crises also evidently disrupt the development and/or use of the productive forces. For these reasons it may be thought that the function of the superstructure to 'stabilise' the economic structure includes the prevention or, at least, management and amelioration of crises. However two different meanings of 'stabilisation' are in play in the idea of 'economic stabilisation' in reference to: a) economic policy designed to even out the business cycle, and b) 'stabilisation of the economic structure by the superstructure'. In the first case the meaning is 'to minimise or eradicate fluctuations' (in the level of economic activity), whereas in the second it is 'to establish necessary conditions of existence' (of the economic structure). Crises are interruptions of the social accumulation of capital, yet they do not fundamentally threaten accumulation. This is because, on the contrary, periodic crises are inherent features of the normal path of accumulation, and have a 'role in reintegrating the circuit of capital as a basis for renewed expansion' (Jessop, 2002, p. 16). This point also shows that although crises do disrupt the development and/or use of the productive forces in the short-run, they are normal features of the accumulation process through which capitalist production relations act as forms of development of the forces in the long-run. Capitalism can only develop the productive forces from a small surplus to the threshold of a massive surplus through its characteristic crisis-ridden path of accumulation.

The perpetual renewal of the circuit reproduces, and, because the circuit is enlarged through accumulation, extends, capitalist production relations.[15] Thus at the end of one circuit, which is the beginning of the next, the ownership positions of capitalist and proletarians are as they were at the start: the capitalist has a (larger) sum of money with which to purchase means of production and labour power, and proletarians, having spent their wages on consumption goods, depend for their continued livelihood on the sale of labour power for a further period. The circuit of capital may be conceived, as we have described it, in terms of an individual capitalist or capitalist firm. However

as the individual capitalist accumulates, what is true of him is true of capital as a whole. This is reflected in the social accumulation of capital, the reproduction of capital and its relations of production on an expanded scale (Fine, 1975, p. 36).

'Class interests' and 'needs of capital'

It is in the nature of the economic structure that it needs stabilising, and it is this need that functionally explains the character of the legal and political superstructure. But we have seen that if the production relations are to function as forms of development of the productive forces it is not just the structure in this strict sense that needs to be stabilised but the process of self-valorisation of capital. Therefore the need for stabilisation can be expressed in terms of the 'needs of capital', and these then provide the basis or principle of explanation of the superstructure.

The idea of the 'needs of capital' involves two general statements about the character of a capitalist economy: first, that it has its own distinctive logic and dynamic but, second, that it is not capable of self-reproduction. The 'needs of capital' are those extra-economic conditions that are required for the logic of the system as a process of self-valorisation of capital to operate. They are, expressed succinctly, 'those essential requirements which must be met in order for capitalism to continue' (Burden & Campbell, 1985, p. 1). In slightly more expansive terms, Jessop states that 'the so-called economic base clearly has crucial extra-economic conditions of existence, for example, in law and the state. This makes its own operation dependent on how far and in what respects these conditions are secured' (1990, p. 81), and Jessop also refers to the 'extra-economic preconditions of accumulation' (1990, p. 85). For example, the ownership positions of proletarians and capitalists engender relations of exchange and authority and the self-expansion of capital within its circuit through the unfolding logic of capitalism. But this logic depends on the reproduction of labour power as a fictitious commodity outside the circuit of capital.

To say that a capitalist economy has its own logic means that it is not fundamentally explained by the subjective preferences of capitalists and proletarians – by the greed of the capitalist for example – but by their standing within objective relations of production. The ownership positions of capitalists and proletarians compel the sale/purchase of labour power and competition compels firms to accumulate.[16] The competition-accumulation dynamic is the key to understanding the 'laws of motion' of the economic sphere – its development and *change* through time. This is not just a question of

quantitative change – of expansion of productive power, enlargement of the circuit, extension of commodification, and spatial
expansion of capitalist production relations – but also, and more
significantly, of developmental tendencies involving qualitative
change (Sweezy, 1942, p. 94; Howard and King, 1975, p. 181). Accumulation involves reproduction of the economic structure – as the
ownership positions of capitalists and proletarians at the end of each
circuit are as they were at the start – but also change within it; that
is, structural change. In order to understand how a structure might
exhibit both continuity and change, Cohen's distinctions between
three varieties of economic change are helpful. Cohen distinguishes
structure-preserving change, type-preserving changes in the structure
that preserve the social form, and changes of social form (Cohen,
1978, p. 85). We may say that 'the structure changes when the set
of production relations is altered, yet the same *type* of economic
structure persists as long as the same production relations remain
dominant' (Cohen, 1978, p. 85). The continuity of type consists
essentially in the ownership relations – capitalists and proletarians –
and the self-expansion of value through the circuit of capital. Two
related examples are the periodisation of capitalism and technical
change. The analysis of the periodisation of the capitalist economic
structure, that is its progression through characteristic 'stages of
development' – classically *laissez-faire* – monopoly – state monopoly
(Fine and Harris, 1979) – involves a conception of type-preserving
structural change. This progression is largely grounded in tendencies
towards increasing concentration and centralisation of capital as
fundamental 'laws' of capitalist development inherent in the capital
accumulation process.

A second example of change within the structure, upon which 'the
Marxian view lays primary stress' (Sweezy, 1942, p. 94), is the constant
revolutionising of the methods of production. According to Marx 'the
tendency inherent in capitalism [is] for technical change to be biased
towards labour-saving (capital-using) innovations' (Howard and King,
1975, p. 196). Such technical change is type-preserving of the economic structure, which remains capitalist, but nevertheless is the basis
of significant changes in the way that structure functions. 'Marx's
theory of technical change is in fact the key to important "contradictions" in the accumulation process' (Howard and King, 1975, p. 182).
Here we have an example of the 'feedback loop' discussed earlier:

Structure   ⇨   Structured Process   ⇨   Structural Change

The change in the structure will in turn have effects on the processes which that structure engenders. Thus the labour-saving bias of technical change is a key element in Marx's analysis of the creation of a reserve army of labour which exerts downward pressure on the wage level (Sweezy, 1942, pp. 87–92). Changes in methods of production also increase the productive power of labour and may enhance capitalists' control over the labour process. Hence technical change may contribute to the extraction of surplus labour through its effects on the capital-labour relation in the spheres of both exchange and production. In this case type-preserving changes in the structure may eventuate in a change of social form. For, according to the theory of history, productivity-enhancing technical change will expand the surplus product up to the point where it has become massive and so created the material conditions for a transition to socialism.

The 'laws of motion' of the economic sphere – its development and qualitative (type-preserving) change through time – have implications for explanation of the character of the superstructure. For change in the economic structure, consistent with fundamental continuity (of type), may generate new needs of capital. For example, explanation of the evolution of welfare states in advanced capitalist societies may be based on an analysis of how 'the course of capital accumulation continuously generates new "needs" or "requirements" in the area of social policy ... [that is] requirements of the capitalist mode of production at a particular stage of its development' (Gough, 1979, p. 32). Thus, in explanation of the superstructure with reference to the economic structure at different stages of development, we will expect to find elements of explanatory continuity (as a structure of the same type explains the superstructure in some of the same ways) and explanatory variance (as the superstructure is explained in some sense differently by a changed structure).

There appears to be a tension between this emphasis on the structural properties of the economy – having its own logic and dynamic apart from the intentions of economic agents – and the recognition that the structured processes – of exchange and domination – are inherently processes of class struggle based on conflicting class interests. Taking account of class struggle seems to imply that the process of capital accumulation is relatively open-ended, for its course will be shaped by the strategies of different classes or class fractions and the balance between them. For example the actual path of technical change will depend in part on the ability of workers to resist labour-saving innovations. There is then a tension between an account of capitalist development in terms of the unfolding of a determinate or closed logic and the unfolding of an indeterminate or open-ended struggle. This tension can be expressed in terms of a distinction between the form and content of class struggle.

> This struggle (the struggle to maintain or restore the conditions of accumulation) is subject to certain formal constraints and goals which can be derived logically from the nature of surplus value production. The outcome of the struggle, however, cannot be derived from its form, but can only be analysed in terms of the concrete contents of the struggle (Holloway & Picciotto, 1978, pp. 27–8).

If the development of capitalism generates new needs and the path of this development is relatively open-ended, it follows that the needs of capital are themselves somewhat indeterminate. They will depend in part on which of the possible paths of accumulation is followed, and this will depend on the concrete contents of the class struggle. However the path of accumulation and capitalist development is only relatively open since there is a limited number of viable accumulation strategies. And each strategy/path of accumulation is, of course, type-preserving, which means that there are fundamental and enduring needs of capital which have to be met for capitalism to continue along any of its paths. It is these needs with which the theory of history is primarily concerned.

'Needs' (of capital) and (class) 'interests' are inherent in the nature of the economic structure, and therefore explanation of the character of the legal and political superstructure requires a clear understanding of their relationship. Needs and interests both centre on the set of roles comprised by production relations, for example capitalists and proletarians. The needs of capital are conditions that must be met to reproduce these roles and the associated process of production. Class interests are fundamentally the interests that occupants of these roles have in their preservation or transformation. For example structural powers, for their stability, need to be matched by superstructural rights and, it follows, power-holders (i.e. capitalists) have an interest in securing these needs/rights. Those who capitalists exercise power over (i.e. proletarians) seem to have an interest in transforming these rights as part of their struggle against subordination. This example exemplifies an objectivist understanding of class interests as more-or-less 'corresponding' to positions in the economic structure. Thus, schematically:

Class Position   ⟹   Class Interests   ⟹   Class Conflict

The conflicting interests centre on the capital-labour relation and the appropriation of surplus labour or exploitation. As Miliband expresses it

> conflict essentially stems from the determination of the dominant classes to extract as much work as possible from the subject classes, and, conversely, from the attempts of these classes to change the terms and conditions of their subjection, or to end it altogether. In relation to capitalism ... [this involves] ... the imperative necessity for the owners and controllers of capital to extract the largest possible amount of surplus value from the labour force; and ... the latter's attempts either to reduce that amount, or to bring the system to an end (1977, pp. 19–20).

This passage defines the basic interests of the two fundamental classes of the capitalist mode of production. The basic interest of capitalists, the owners and controllers of the means of production, is the extraction and realisation of surplus value and thereby the enlargement of the sum of money capital which they advance at the 'beginning' of the circuit ($M \to C \to C^1 \to M^1$). Thus the basic interest of the capitalist corresponds with the completion of the circuit, that is, with capital as a process of the self-expansion of value (hence Marx's depiction of the capitalist as 'capital personified'). However, beyond this, the interest of the capitalist class lies in the continual renewal of the circuit: thus 'its true interests presumably lie in the maintenance and defence of capitalism' (Miliband, 1977, p. 31). In short, the basic interest of the dominant class can be defined as the securing of its dominant position in society and, therefore, the relations of production in which this dominance is rooted. 'Class success means the ability of a dominant class to maintain its position in society, and to contain and subdue any challenges to its power and privileges' (Miliband, 1984, p. 5). Conversely the basic interest of members of the working class or proletariat is to improve the terms on which they contract with capitalists, reduce the amount of surplus labour they perform, and, according to classical Marxism, ultimately end their subordination altogether through transformation of the relations of production in which that subordination is rooted (Miliband, 1977, p. 33).

It is clear from these brief definitions of the concepts of the 'needs of capital' and 'class interests' that the interests of capitalists and the needs of capital are closely related: if the 'true interests' of capitalists consist in the maintenance of capitalism then they consist in the securing of those essential requirements which have to be met in order for capitalism to continue. This congruence is not surprising given that the capitalist class is defined in terms of the relations of 'ownership' that constitute the economic structure. Although the basic interests of the proletariat are defined as being antagonistic to those of the capitalist class, as being anti-capitalist, lying in revolutionary form in the overthrow of capitalist relations of production, there is in fact a degree of congruence between these interests and the interests of capitalists/ needs of capital. This congruence arises from the fact that labour power, the source of surplus value, is dependent for its reproduction on that of the proletarian who is its owner, and hence on the 'well-being' of the latter. Hence proletarians who demand a reduction of exploitation to ensure their own health may also, thereby, contribute to the 'health' of the system. (This congruence is exemplified by examples of welfare reform: Cohen, 1978, pp. 294–6; Gough, 1979, pp. 55–6). Nevertheless to the extent that the interests of the working class figure in the explanation of the state they may provide a form of economic determination that runs counter to alignment of the state with the interests of the capitalist class/needs of capital (Wetherly, 1988).[17]

For the moment we will narrow our focus to the relation between the interests of capitalists and the needs of capital which are the primary concern of the theory of history. The famous statement by Marx and Engels in the *Communist Manifesto* that the bourgeoisie has conquered 'exclusive political sway' refers to the state 'managing the common affairs of the whole bourgeoisie' (Marx & Engels, 1976, p. 486). As has been noted, this reference to common affairs or common interests of the whole class implies that there are also particular interests of units (i.e. individual firms) or 'fractions' of capital. Common or class-wide interests may be defined as the basic interests of the class in the maintenance of capitalism and therefore include the needs of capital. But it does not follow that all common interests are requirements of the system. The notion of need as precondition or prerequisite suggests that the maintenance or viability of the economic structure is at issue: if identified needs are not satisfied the stability or reproduction of capitalist relations of production, of the circuit of capital and the accumulation process, will be called in question. But there may conceivably be interests which are common to the bourgeoisie but which do not have this critical status: if these interests are not met the economic structure may be subject to some disruption of its normal functioning but its viability will not be threatened. The distinction being suggested here may be formulated in terms of needs and benefits. We will seek to clarify this conceptual distinction shortly through elucidation of the needs of capital.

Thus we have drawn two sets of distinctions within the category of 'interests of the capitalist class'. Taken together these provide a four-way classification which shows that 'needs of capital' constitute a subset of dominant class interests. The logic of this classification is that common interests involve the system as a whole whereas particular interests concern the operation of specific fractions of the dominant class or individual units of capital (firms).

Classification of the interests of the capitalist class

		With Reference to Constituents of the Class	
		Common	Particular
With Reference to the Maintenance of the System	Needs	Needs of Capital in General	Needs of Fractions of Capital
	Benefits	System Benefits	Benefits of Fractions of Capital

The *Communist Manifesto* says that the state manages the common affairs of the bourgeoisie; that is, needs of capital and system benefits. However this claim need not be taken as implying that the state manages *all* the common affairs of the bourgeoisie, or even *only* these affairs. The state could be conceived as not taking full charge of these affairs and as managing some other affairs – interests of particular units of capital, the subordinate class, or non-class interests. Indeed it seems highly unlikely that the state *fully* and *exclusively* manages the common affairs of the bourgeoisie. Within the category of common interests we have distinguished between system needs or 'needs of capital' – understood as essential conditions of existence – and system benefits – understood as conditions favourable to capital. In order to approach the question of which affairs the state does manage it is necessary to make a distinction between those conditions – needs and benefits – which are secured and reproduced within the economic structure itself by the actions of the bourgeoisie and/or the impersonal rationality of the system and those which are extra-economic. We have seen that the circuit of capital recreates the basic conditions for its own renewal – specifically, the basic 'ownership positions' of capitalists and proletarians – up to a point. However the circuit is not characterised by complete self-closure or autonomy for there are certain conditions which can only be secured extra-economically by means of political action. In these cases we can say that state action is *required*. It is possible to conceive that in other cases these conditions may not require state action but may be more effectively secured thereby so that state action is *desired*. The range of state actions may encompass, *inter alia*, system needs and system benefits, but a crucial question is whether it is possible to identify system needs which require state action; that is, conditions which are requirements for the existence of capital and for which to be secured state action is required. It is to the identification of such conditions that we turn in the next chapter.

6
A Theory of the 'Needs of Capital'

Introduction

The nature of the economic structure that explains the character of superstructural phenomena is its need to be 'stabilised'.[1] The needs of the economic structure – or, more generally, needs of capital – are functional requirements, that is, conditions that must be met for capitalism to continue.[2] There are needs of capital because a capitalist economy, left to its own devices, is unstable in the sense that it is not self-sufficient and not capable of ensuring its own maintenance or reproduction. Thus the needs of capital consist in the forms or sources of this instability and are, by extension, needs for external conditions that will eliminate or effectively manage it. Superstructural phenomena are as they are because, being so, they secure these functional requirements or conditions.

In order to develop a theory of the needs of capital we need to start with need as a concept, and this has been most extensively analysed in theoretical work in relation to human needs (Plant et al., 1980; Doyal & Gough, 1991; Gough, 1992). This theoretical work is relevant to the analysis of 'system needs' because, we argue, the same concept of need is in play in each domain. However, before applying this concept in a theory of the needs of capital, we will confront the argument that social systems do not have needs.

The concept of need

Need statements take the form 'A needs B for C' (Plant et al., 1980, p. 26; also Doyal & Gough, 1991, p. 39). 'A' here might be an individual person or, as we will argue later, a social system. 'A' is said to need 'B' as a means to some end or purpose, 'C'. 'C' constitutes the 'end goal, purpose or function which the object is ... needed for' (Plant et al., 1980, p. 26). Strictly then the referent of need is this 'end goal'. The difficulty in elaborating a theory of need – whether human need or system need – is whether it is possible to identify certain end goals which constitute needs that all entities of that sort have (in virtue of being entities of that sort) and which are distinct from 'wants' or 'benefits'. In the theory of human need the key criterion is harm.

> If a person is held to have a need for something, then it is assumed that he will be *harmed* by his not having it, and his getting what he needs will overcome this harm or will be a remedy for his condition ... The assumption ... is that there is a certain state of human flourishing or welfare, and if a person fails to achieve this state he will ail or will be harmed. *Needs are what are necessary to achieve this condition of flourishing* (Plant et al., 1980, pp. 33–4).

In similar terms Doyal and Gough claim that 'If needs are not satisfied by an appropriate "satisfier" then *serious harm* of some specified and objective kind will result, (1991, p. 39). Thus the end goal 'C' is defined as a condition of flourishing, and needs and their satisfaction are defined in terms of whatever 'B' items are necessary for some entity 'A' to achieve this condition or, what amounts to the same thing, to avoid serious harm. According to Doyal and Gough all humans share the same basic needs – which are, therefore, universal – in virtue of being human.

A theory of the 'needs of capital' must then identify conditions which must be met if the system is to avoid 'serious harm' (or analogous term), and which are necessary conditions in virtue of the *nature* of the system and so shared by all systems of that type. Such are 'basic (system) needs'. It is evident that there may be different ways of satisfying basic needs – different 'specific satisfiers' (Doyal & Gough, 1991, p. 170) may be 'functionally equivalent'. In Doyal and Gough's conceptual framework this equivalence is expressed by saying that what all specific satisfiers have in common, what identifies them as such, is that they possess 'universal satisfier characteristics'. These universal satisfier characteristics are otherwise referred to as 'intermediate needs'. These distinctions generate the following hierarchy (based on Doyal & Gough, 1991, p. 170, fig. 8.2).

UNIVERSAL GOAL
(Avoidance of Serious Harm/
Condition of Flourishing)

BASIC NEEDS

INTERMEDIATE NEEDS
(Universal Satisfier Characteristics)

SPECIFIC SATISFIERS

Intermediate needs constitute all derived or second-order goals which must be achieved if the first-order goals or basic needs are to be attained (Doyal & Gough, 1991, p. 157).

Intermediate needs are such because their achievement is necessary for the attainment of first-order goals, such attainment being a precondition of 'avoidance of serious harm'. In turn 'universal satisfier characteristics can be regarded as goals for which specific satisfiers can act as the means'. (Doyal & Gough, 1991, p. 157). For example, Doyal and Gough argue that physical health and autonomy constitute basic needs which must be satisfied (at 'optimum' levels) for individuals to flourish. Relevant intermediate needs include such things as 'adequate nutritional food and water', 'adequate protective housing', 'appropriate health care' and so on, and these can be met through a range of specific satisfiers, such as different policies.

In the domain of human need, needs are defined as objective (i.e. as distinct from wants or preferences) and are identified as universal preconditions of human flourishing (i.e. applicable to all humans).[3] In line with this conception, system needs ought to be defined objectively, in terms of the intrinsic nature of the system in question and the preconditions or functional prerequisites for the system to reproduce itself or survive. Statements concerning the needs of capital should then comply with the generic form of need statements (A needs B for C): they involve claims that certain conditions (B) must be secured if the capitalist economic structure (A) is to have the capacity for continued reproduction (C).

Needs of social systems

Gough is sceptical about the propriety of applying the concept of need to social systems. This is because 'Capital is not an entity in the same way as people, and there is a danger of reifying the category – of imbuing it with lifelike qualities. Moreover, to speak of the 'needs' of capital is to resort to functional explanations of state policies, whereby the consequences of a policy explain its origins' (2000, p. 14). In respect of functional explanation, Gough states that though capitalist economies do have functional requirements it does not follow that state polices can be functionally explained by these requirements. On this last point Gough is correct: functional explanations do not follow from function statements. Causal mechanisms and/or empirical evidence are needed. However, Gough does not rule out the possibility of valid functional explanation, agreeing with Cohen's response to Elster on mechanisms.[4] For the moment, though, we are concerned merely with the existence and, if they exist, character of the functional requirements of a capitalist economy. Gough appears to be ambivalent on this question: cautioning against the idea of 'needs' of capital because it is not lifelike in the way that people, who do have needs, are, yet accepting that there are functional requirements of capitalist economies. The only way to square this is to say that things, like capital, that aren't lifelike can have needs. It is possible to analyse the needs of capital while avoiding the danger of reification. A similar objection is made by Giddens who argues that

> social systems ... do not have any need or interest in their own survival, and the notion of 'need' is falsely applied if it is not acknowledged that system needs presuppose actors' wants (1976, p. 343).

The first part of this statement is certainly true, for Gough's reason that social systems are not 'lifelike': they are not subjects with wants, interests or 'end goals'. These are things that only actors can have. The claim that 'system needs presuppose actors' wants' can, however, be taken in two ways. One of these is that the idea of 'system needs' is merely a form of expression for what are really, at root, the wants of actors. System needs are, in other words, reducible to actors' wants. According to this reasoning we should do away with 'system needs' and refer only to actors' wants. For example, if we want to specify the conditions that must be met for capitalism to survive we should recognise that capitalism has no interest in or need for its own survival, and only certain actors within the capitalist system can choose and act on this end goal. However this does not show that we can replace statements about system needs with statements about actors' wants, for need statements specify objective conditions that must be met if capitalism is to continue. If actors want capitalism to continue then they must act in accordance with these objective conditions. The needs and the wants are clearly distinct: the needs exist regardless of what actors want. A second sense of 'presuppose' is that system needs, defined in this objective way, can only explain anything if they are expressed as actors' wants. For example the needs of capital can only have explanatory power if actors choose the survival of capitalism as their end goal. But then the explanatory burden seems to fall on the wants of actors since they could conceivably have made different choices. The needs count for nothing, it seems, if they do not coincide with what actors happen to choose as their purposes.

If actors just 'happen to choose' purposes that coincide with needs then need-satisfaction will be purely fortuitous. Actors could choose differently and then needs wouldn't be satisfied. But wants and needs may be more connected than this, and they must be connected if we are to make the step from function statements to functional explanations. The connection is that system needs may shape actors' wants as end goals, or shape their second-order wants as means to their end goals. For example, actors do not just 'happen' to choose the survival of capitalism as their end goal. This end goal constitutes the basic class interest of the capitalist class and is thus strongly influenced by the positions of capitalists within the relations of production. Thus we could say that needs determine wants in the same sense as that which Cohen makes of the claim that being determines consciousness (1988, chapter 3). State dependence on revenue generated in the capitalist sector is an example of system needs shaping second-order goals, for state managers are constrained to meet the needs of capital so as to ensure a healthy economy as a means of realising their own end goals.[5] In response to Giddens, we can say that the notion that system needs presuppose actors' wants is falsely applied if it is not acknowledged that wants may be powerfully shaped by system needs as a consequence of the structural locations of these actors.

However, there is a fundamental sense, in the theory of history, in which the needs of capital do presuppose actors' wants in the first meaning that system needs are reducible to actors' wants. According to the theory of history capitalism is selected and persists because, and so long as, capitalist production relations are forms of development of the productive forces. Therefore the needs of capital are conditions that must be met for productive progress. But the underlying cause of productive development through history is the basic human interest in reducing scarcity. Thus the needs of capital presuppose, in the sense of being reducible to, actors' wants as defined by this basic human interest.

Capitalism, the market and competition

The theory of human need developed by Doyal and Gough identifies a 'universal goal' defined in terms of the avoidance of serious harm. Although the same basic concept of need is in play in a theory of the needs of capital as in a theory of human need, these terms have to be recast. For the capitalist system does not have goals, and ideas of 'harm' and 'flourishing' will be very difficult to operationalise. These terms can be replaced by an 'ultimate system need' defined in terms of maintenance or reproduction of a capitalist economy. Needs refer, in other words, to extra-economic conditions of existence of a capitalist economic order. This is understood in terms of a set of conditions that is 'good enough' to secure the reproduction of capitalism rather than a notion of the 'health' of the system. Doyal and Gough do, as noted, incorporate a notion of the level of need satisfaction into their theory in terms of an 'optimum'. But this idea is problematic in the domain of human need and, perhaps, more so in that of system needs. Clearly, notions of 'health', and of 'progress' and 'decline', are often applied to social systems. The 'health' of a society or economy may usually be conceived in terms of its contribution to the satisfaction of human needs, but it may be possible to define the health of the system in its own terms, such as the rate of profit in capitalism. However it does not seem possible to identify system needs in terms of some threshold level of functioning, so the concept of need is confined to the requirements for reproduction of the system.

In order to identify the continuity of a social system, and thereby be able to think about the conditions which are essential for such continuity (system needs), it is necessary to define the system itself. We have defined the nature of a capitalist economic order not just in terms of the economic structure but to include the abstract analysis of the circuit of capital and process of accumulation. By identifying essential characteristics which all capitalist economies at all stages of development exhibit this enables us to identify structural continuity when faced with ongoing social change and different 'models' of capitalism.[6]

Capitalism refers to a particular type of economic structure and production process. As such it can be analysed, widening the focus, on three levels. First, capitalism may be understood as an economic structure *in general*. In other words, capitalism belongs to the general category 'economic structures' and is to be understood not only in terms of what is peculiar to it but also what it shares with other members of this category. There may be generic conditions of existence or needs which all economic structures have, regardless of their particular character. For example, all societies must ensure biological reproduction through procreation and childcare (Doyal & Gough, 1991, pp. 76–90). In addition the capacity to work must be reproduced on a daily basis. Thus in characterising the welfare state as 'the use of state power to modify the reproduction of labour power and to maintain the non-working population in capitalist societies' (1979, pp. 44–5), Gough adds that 'the continual reproduction of [labour power] ... is ... a necessary condition of all human societies' (1979, p. 45).

Second, capitalism belongs to that type of economic structure that may be labelled 'class-divided' or, as by Marx in the Preface, 'antagonistic'. As such it shares certain conditions of existence with other antagonistic forms. Specifically, the productiveness of labour must be sufficiently high to produce a surplus and there must be mechanisms through which this surplus is appropriated by the dominant class. These are the basic conditions for exploitation to occur. Third, capitalism is a particular type of class-divided economic structure and, as such, may have conditions of existence that are peculiar to it or, at least, peculiar forms of the conditions of existence of the class-divided type of economic structure. Thus capitalism is to be understood as a particular type within class-divided forms of the generic category of economic structures. All societies have economic structures, some societies have class-divided forms, capitalism is a particular class-divided form.

Now let us sharpen our focus on capitalism. Here we need to begin by observing that capitalism is a particular form of (monetised) market system. It has, that is, two aspects: it is a market system and it is capitalist. First, as a *market* system, production is for exchange (mediated by money), and resources are allocated via the 'price mechanism'.

Other kinds of market economy are, of course, conceivable, such as simple commodity production and forms of 'market socialism'. What most distinguishes a *capitalist* market is that labour power is a commodity and production is for profit (M – C – M rather than C – M – C). Capitalism is a form of market system in which, not only is production for sale, but the ownership position of the direct producers, owning none of the means of production they use, means that their livelihoods (barring 'escape routes') depend on selling the labour power that they do own. Thus 'what most distinguishes capitalism from other forms of producing goods and services is the generalization of the commodity form to labour-power' (Jessop, 2002, p. 12). The recognition that capitalism is a particular type of market system is important because there may be conditions of existence of markets in general – such as a universal medium of exchange, and legal rules to enforce contracts. As a particular form of market system there may be conditions of existence which are peculiar to capitalism, or the conditions of existence of markets may appear in peculiar form. For example, particular legal rules will be required to create rights which match the particular configuration of powers structured by the 'ownership' positions of capitalist relations of production (Cohen, 1978, pp. 231–6). In particular, the generalisation of the commodity form to include labour power, but as a fictitious commodity, entails specific conditions of existence related to the reproduction of this commodity (Jessop, 2002, p. 13). Understood in this way, the defining features of capitalism may be set out as follows:

i)   as a market system production is for *exchange* and producers operate in conditions of rivalry or *competition*;
ii) as a capitalist system there is *private ownership* (in the form of the ownership positions of capitalists and proletarians) which means that: capitalists and proletarians contract as buyers and sellers of labour power in a labour market, the producers are units of capital, and the motive of production is *profit*.

The needs of capital are those conditions necessary for capitalism to continue; that is, conditions necessary for the maintenance of capitalist relations of production. This entails not simply the 'ownership' positions of capitalists and proletarians described by Cohen but the continual renewal of the circuit of capital involving the self-expansion of value via exploitation. Capitalist relations of production involve not one but two key types of relationship: the 'vertical' relationship of exploitation of labour by capital, and the 'horizontal' relationship of competition between individual units of capital.

It can be argued that the 'vertical' relationship is more fundamental in the sense that competition is not peculiar to the capitalist type of market system, whereas the particular form of the relationship of exploitation is definitive of capitalist relations of production. Further, competition is a variable factor within capitalist economies, subject to the general tendency of increasing concentration and centralisation of capital and to varying degrees of concentration in different markets. However competition is characteristic of capitalist economies and can be seen as a defining feature. The importance of competition for an understanding of the needs of capital is twofold: as a stimulus and as a barrier. First, competition provides the impetus to accumulation (enlargement of the circuit) and, thereby, development of the productive forces. Although the profit motive provides some stimulus to productive development, as capitalists have an incentive to improve efficiency (productivity) in order to increase profits, it is competition rather than greed that is the key driver. Competition forces firms to strive for efficiency gains in order to survive, and the prime mechanism is accumulation. This suggests that competition is a key ingredient of the success of capitalist production relations as forms of development of the forces of production. And, although competition is an intrinsic feature of these relations, it has to be regulated as an external condition of the reproduction of a capitalist economy, that is, as a need of capital. This is because the tendency to increased market concentration is an outcome of the competitive process (oligopoly and monopoly).[7] As a barrier, the importance of competition is that it militates against the securing of certain needs of capital within the circuit, so that these needs must be secured externally. Because capitals are fragmented and competitive they either cannot, individually or collectively, secure certain conditions of existence, or may actually threaten or undermine some such conditions. This problem is conventionally defined in terms of 'market failure', including the inability of competitive markets to supply 'public goods' and the generation of 'social costs'.

Accumulation and legitimisation

O'Connor's influential analysis of *The Fiscal Crisis of the State* (1973) involves a conceptualisation of the 'functions of the state' which provides a useful starting point for thinking about the needs of capital. According to O'Connor the capitalist state must try to fulfil two basic and often mutually contradictory functions – accumulation and legitimization. This means that the state must try to create or maintain the conditions in which profitable accumulation is possible. However, the state also must try to create or maintain the conditions for social harmony.... State expenditures have a twofold character corresponding to the ... two basic functions: social capital and social expenses. Social capital is expenditure required for profitable capital accumulation; it is indirectly productive.... The second category, social expenses, consists of projects and services which are required to maintain social harmony (1973, pp. 6–7).

Social capital is broken down into social investment and social consumption.

Social investment consists of projects and services that increase the productivity of ... labour power and, other factors being equal, increase the rate of profit ... Social consumption consists of projects and services that lower the reproduction costs of labour and, other factors being equal, increase the rate of profit (1973, p. 7).

For O'Connor, the creation of conditions for profitable accumulation seems to be seen as a function of the state in virtue of the in-built impulse to accumulate characteristic of capitalist relations of production. For the theory of history accumulation is important for the larger reason of its connection with the development of the productive forces. In this connection, accumulation is also basic to legitimisation, in the sense of an adequate level of consent for the maintenance of a capitalist economy. For, according to the theory of history, capitalist relations of production are selected because, and so long as, they constitute forms of development of the forces of production. Accumulation is driven by competition and profit. Competition is the key driver since in competitive conditions firms must accumulate in order to survive. However profit is a precondition since firms will only accumulate in the expectation of profit (even though profit by itself imparts a relatively weak impulse to accumulation). What capital requires is *profit* (surplus value) – profit is the *raison d'etre* of the circuit.

There is some ambiguity in O'Connor's formulations, which refer both to creating 'conditions in which profitable capital accumulation is possible' and to the function of 'social capital' expenditures to 'increase the rate of profit'. It is true that capitalism needs profit in order to continue but not an *increase* in the rate of profit. There must be profit for the circuit of capital to be renewed and there may be a minimum rate of profit which is necessary for capitalism (or individual units of capital) to continue. However it is not justified to go beyond that to say that an upward *trend* in the rate of profit is needed. It is, in other words, in the interests of capitalists but not a need of the capitalist system, of capital, to increase the rate of profit.

Profit depends on the balance between the wage, the level of productivity and the length of the working day (Sweezy, 1942, pp. 64–5). The reproduction costs of labour power, to the extent that they are incurred by capital, can be incorporated into this equation by adding them to wage costs.[8] Given that the wage and the productiveness of labour are both focal points of class conflict, it is conceivable that surplus value may be reduced to zero, or become negative, as a result of an unfavourable balance of these factors. Thus the need for 'social capital' expenditure by the state to lower reproduction costs and/or raise productivity may be argued on the grounds that exploitation does not, in fact, occur 'automatically' within the circuit of capital. Nevertheless, the need for social capital expenditures should be set against the autonomous capacity of the circuit to generate profit through the chronic imbalance of power between capital and labour and the recuperative function of economic crises. Briefly, failure to produce surplus value will trigger a crisis which tends, through expansion of the 'reserve army of labour' and downward pressure on wages, to restore the conditions of profitability. To the extent that economic crisis is an effective recuperative mechanism, 'social capital' expenditure to increase the rate of profit does not seem to constitute a chronic, as opposed to acute, need of capital.

The claim that 'social capital' expenditures may contribute to profitability through lowering the reproduction costs of labour power may be based on two grounds: simply transferring these costs from capital to the state, or lowering such costs. However there are some difficulties in the way of both of these arguments. Against the idea of a transfer of costs from capital to the state it can be argued that state expenditure is a drain on surplus value (Fine and Harris, 1976). It is arguable that state expenditure may be financed through taxation of wages rather than profits, but this may have the effect of stimulating demands for compensating wage increases. In this way social capital expenditure may displace rather than solve the problem of an unfavourable balance of factors in the production process. Second, if it can be shown that reproduction activities and investment projects can be undertaken at lower cost when organised by the state rather than capital then social capital expenditure may still boost profitability even if it is financed out of surplus value. It is possible that the centralisation of investment and reproduction functions within the state sector may yield some economies of scale, but it is difficult to argue that there is likely to be a general productivity differential in favour of the state sector. Indeed there is reason to think that productivity differences are more likely to favour the capitalist sector in virtue of the coercive force of competition. These considerations suggest that the argument for social capital expenditure as a need of capital is weak if expressed in terms of securing profitability by transferring certain costs of production from the capitalist to the state sector.

O'Connor also argues that the function of 'social capital' expenditures may be to increase the productivity of labour and this is a stronger argument. This is because competition is both a stimulus and barrier to productive improvement. The analysis of the circuit of capital suggests that competition between individual units of capital provides a powerful impulse to productivity growth via accumulation and labour-saving technical change. On the other hand, however, the competitive relationship between capitals may inhibit productivity growth in a number of ways. O'Connor argues that social capital expenditure can be explained in terms of the increase in the social character of production associated with the monopoly stage of capitalist development. In this context 'projects are socialised because costs often exceed the resources of or are regarded as unacceptable financial risks by the companies immediately concerned' (1973, p. 101). Thus capitalist relations of production develop the productive forces to a point where the scale of physical capital projects exceeds the capacity of individual competitive units of capital for investment. Competition may inhibit productivity-enhancing investments in other ways. Competition may squeeze the rate of profit and so, while compelling capitals to accumulate, simultaneously restrict internal funds available for investment. Innovation may be inhibited by 'public good' characteristics which make it difficult for firms to internalise the benefits. Finally innovation may be hindered by the prevalence of a strategy of imitation rather than initiation in order to limit cost and risk. These considerations at least suggest the possibility that capitalist relations of production may not exhibit a straightforward in-built tendency to productivity growth. It follows that there may be a need for state action, such as social investment, to overcome these systemic inhibitions to innovation. Notice that the requisite state action may take the form not only of capital projects as emphasised by O'Connor but also regulation. For example the patent system provides an incentive to innovate by ensuring that benefits are internalised and encourages a strategy of initiation.

The claim that social capital expenditures are needed to increase the productiveness of labour seems to contradict the theory of history, since capitalism is supposed to be selected precisely in virtue of its powerful tendency to increase productivity. The argument must be that the *tendency* to productive growth is imparted by the relations of production but requires state action for that tendency to manifest itself fully in *actual* productivity growth. The *impetus* for technological development is coming from the economic structure but it is beyond the autonomous capacity of the structure to *organise* such development fully. That conception seems to preserve the proper historical materialist relationship between base and superstructure.

This understanding of the incapacity of capital to *organise* investment projects provides a second and more fruitful way of thinking about the contribution of social capital expenditure to the needs of capital than a focus on costs. The abstract analysis of the circuit of capital assumes away the problem of organising the inputs to production, both constant and variable capital. The capitalist simply finds these inputs available in the market place. Thus the circuit of capital begins with a simple act of exchange (M–C). O'Connor's argument shows that the circuit may break down at this point because physical capital projects become too large/risky for individual units of capital to undertake. Yet constant capital inputs are produced within the circuit. Labour power, on the other hand, is largely reproduced outside the circuit so the incapacity of capital is greater with respect to the organisation of this input.[9] Social consumption expenditures may then be needed not so much, as O'Connor suggests, because they *lower* the reproduction *costs* of labour power but because the reproduction of labour power cannot be organised by capital. This problem has a number of component elements.

In our characterisation of the economic structure it was suggested that the relationship of exchange between capital and labour, the wage-labour relationship, is engendered by the respective 'ownership' positions of capitalists and proletarians. However this is a simplification which in fact conceals a fundamental condition of existence of capitalist relations of production. The problem which must be overcome for such relations to exist is, as Offe puts it, that 'individuals do not automatically enter the supply side of the labour market' (1984,

p. 92). The ownership positions of capitalists and proletarians may be said to favour the formation and maintenance of the wage-labour relation but do not in themselves necessitate or entail it. For

> there is no reason why those individuals who find themselves dispossessed of their means of labour or subsistence [(passive proletarianisation)] should spontaneously proceed to 'active' proletarianisation by offering their labour power for sale on the labour market (Offe, 1984, pp. 92–3).

This problem seems to bear most heavily on the origins of capitalism but in fact has to do also with its persistence. The wage-labour relationship seems to depend on such individuals: a) lacking, or perceiving themselves to lack, any alternative to, or 'escape route' (Offe, 1984, p. 93) from, wage labour; b) being coerced; or c) perceiving wage labour to be the best alternative. A variety of escape routes is conceivable including subsistence outside of capitalist relations of production, social mobility, and 'the liquidation of the commodity form of labour power itself' (Offe, 1984, p. 93). Short of the latter, the first two are inherently limited. Welfare states are not intended to, and do not, offer realistic opportunities to subsist outside of capitalist production relations, especially for those of working age who are fit to work. Social mobility offers an avenue for escape for individuals but is limited in scope and cannot, by its nature, be an escape route for the whole class. Coercion may be used to compel active proletarianisation or block various escape routes, but reason and the record of history both suggest that capitalist relations of production could not persist in a relatively stable fashion on the basis of reliance on the routine, as opposed to exceptional, use of force. These considerations suggest that capitalist relations of production depend on 'dispossessed potential workers' (Offe, 1984, p. 94) perceiving wage labour to be the best alternative; that is, on a significant level of consent. 'They must consider the risks and burdens associated with this form of existence as *relatively* acceptable; they must muster the *cultural motivation* to become wage-labourers' (Offe, 1984, p. 94).

If such cultural motivation was spontaneous, if wage labour really was the only or best alternative, then the transformation of labour power into a commodity, 'active' proletarianisation, would not be a problem for capital. However the burden of Offe's, as of any Marxist, argument is that the consent of 'dispossessed potential workers' to becoming actual wage labourers is not spontaneous in virtue of the conflictual nature of the capital-labour relation. For,

> according to the Marxist anthropology of labour and theory of alienation, the special character of wage labour implies that the willingness of workers to actually sell their labour power cannot be regarded as self-evident (Offe, 1984, p. 96).

This means that the 'transformation of dispossessed labour power into wage labour ... cannot be explained *solely* by the "silent compulsion of economic relations" (Offe, 1984, p. 96). It cannot be explained, that is, solely by the ownership positions of capitalists and proletarians, but must be organised by extra-economic means. Thus the organisation of this transformation constitutes a basic condition of existence of capitalist relations of production. The transformation is effected in part through coercive means such as 'the criminalisation and prosecution of modes of subsistence that are potential alternatives to the wage-labour relation' (Offe, 1984, p. 96), but more importantly through the organisation of consent through, for example, 'the state-organised procurement of norms and values, adherence to which results in the transition to the wage-labour relation' (Offe, 1984, p. 96).

According to Offe the entry of individuals into the supply side of the labour market is only one aspect of the problem, and there are two further component parts: the reproduction of labour power or maintenance of labour capacity; and, the quantitative control of the proletarianisation process. The problem of reproduction of labour power is that 'not all members of society could function as wage-labourers unless certain basic reproduction functions (especially in the domain of socialisation, health, education, care for the aged) are fulfilled' (Offe, 1984, p. 94). In other words, capitalist relations of production depend not only on the willingness or cultural motivation of individuals to enter the supply side of the labour market but on their capacities to function as wage labourers. The point is that the capacity to work is used up in the process of doing work and thus needs to be continually renewed, but this renewal is not secured within the circuit of capital. Here a distinction can be made between daily and generational reproduction: daily reproduction refers to the day-to-day capacity to labour, and generational reproduction to the care and upbringing of children. This distinction cuts across another, between the working and non-working parts of the population, children being part of the current non-working but the future working population (Gough, 1979, p. 47).

Thus generational reproduction involves maintenance of one part of the non-working population.

In addition the boundary between the working and non-working parts of the population is not fixed: among the (socially defined) 'population of working age' are those who are not members of the working population but who might be classed as potential workers. For example during the postwar years in the UK the working population has expanded in part due to the increased participation rate among married women, and there has been a corresponding fall in the proportion of 'housewives' in the population of working age. Thus it is possible to distinguish five groups within the population:

- the labour force, defined as those in work
- the reserve army of labour, defined as those currently without employment but who are available for work
- potential workers, e.g. housewives
- the future working population, i.e. children
- the non-working population, defined as those unable to work: the elderly, sick and disabled.

The reproduction of labour power involves the maintenance of the first four categories – the current, reserve, potential and future labour force[10] – and entails reproduction or maintenance of 'the capacity to do useful work' (Foley, 1991, p. 296). We can distinguish two aspects of productive capacity corresponding to Marx's distinction between abstract and concrete labour. The reproduction of labour power involves the maintenance of the capacity to work in general (given by health, cognitive ability, etc.), but also to do specific forms of useful work (requiring specific skills and forms of knowledge) corresponding to positions within the division of labour at a particular stage of development. Further, the reproduction of labour power involves 'specific patterns of socialisation, behaviour ... and personality structures' (Gough, 1979, p. 46), what Offe refers to as the 'cultural motivation' necessary for active proletarianisation.

Reproduction of labour power involving these three aspects – general capacity, particular skills, cultural motivation – and the four segments of the workforce – current, reserve, potential and future – is a need of capital not, to repeat, because this function of the state lowers the reproduction *costs* incurred by capital. Rather, it is fundamentally because it is beyond the capacity of capital – individually and/or collectively – to *organise* this function that it constitutes a need of capital. The circuit of capital cannot be autonomous in this respect since it relies on a supply of labour power whose reproduction, as a 'fictitious commodity', essentially takes place away from the circuit. That is not to say that capital has no involvement in the reproduction of labour power or that such reproduction is not at all effected within or via the circuit. The most basic mechanism whereby labour power is reproduced is via the wage and the purchase of consumption goods (although the wage may not always be adequate for reproduction). Individual units of capital may undertake reproduction tasks in relation to their own workforces in the forms of: training, attempts to shape organisation 'culture', and occupational welfare. However these mechanisms cannot provide an adequate response to the need for reproduction of labour power. Competition between capitals undermines reproduction because of the pressure to reduce unit costs and maximise effort and because there is a disincentive to undertake reproduction tasks where the benefits may not be retained within the firm. Even where the wage is sufficient to allow reproduction of the general capacity to work capital has no control over the pattern of consumption on which the wage is spent. Finally, capital cannot directly organise the reproduction of labour power in respect of the reserve, potential and future segments of the workforce. It is clear, then, that the reproduction of labour power is largely external to the circuit of capital.

The question of the capacity to work links up with the requirement that, for exploitation to be possible, the productivity of labour has to be high enough to produce a surplus. Exploitation however presupposes not merely the productive capacity or potential of the workers but the actualisation of that potential. The workers have actually to produce a surplus. Further, exploitation presupposes that this surplus is not merely produced but appropriated by capital. Hence regulation of the capital-labour relation, the securing of conditions for exploitation, involves four elements:

1. workers have to *enter* the supply side of the labour market with
2. the *capacity* to produce a surplus, but
3. a surplus has actually to be *produced* and
4. *appropriated*.

The point is that, from the standpoint of capital, exploitation is far from automatic. Apart from the requirements of entry of individuals into the supply side of the labour market and their capacity to work – conditions which cannot be secured within the circuit – exploitation requires production and appropriation of surplus product. These last two requirements depend essentially on conditions internal to the circuit. Normally the production and appropriation of surplus value will be secured within the circuit by capitalists acting individually or in concert (e.g. through employers organisations). In other words in respect of production and appropriation of surplus value the capital-labour relation will normally be self-regulating. However this capacity for self-regulation cannot be guaranteed so that extra-economic intervention may be required, such as wage control.

The third component problem of the transformation of non-wage labourers into wage labourers identified by Offe is the quantitative control of the proletarianisation process. In other words, 'there must be, in the long run, an approximate quantitative balance between those who are "passively" proletarianised ... and those who are able to find employment as wage labourers given the volume of demand on the labour market' (Offe, 1984, p. 95). There is likely to arise within capitalist economies 'a structural problem of a long-term discrepancy between demand and supply' in respect of labour power 'and in particular the potential excess of supply' (Offe, 1984, p. 99), that is, the reserve army of labour. In periods of rapid accumulation, of course, the potential excess of demand, or labour shortage, may be a problem. This discrepancy between supply and demand arises, again, because the reproduction of labour power, as a fictitious commodity, takes place outside the circuit of capital. It is 'treated *as a commodity* but, unlike other commodities, its coming into being is not *based* on expectations of saleability' (Offe, 1984, p. 99; see also Jessop, 2002, p. 13). Thus regulation of the capital-labour relation is needed in the form of quantitative control to ensure a balance between 'passive' and 'active' proletarianisation. This involves

> the institutional 'storage' of that portion of the social volume of labour power which (because of conjunctural and structural changes) cannot be absorbed by the demand generated by the labour market (Offe, 1984, p. 99)

or, in periods of labour shortage, the institutional 'release' of new sources of labour power.

'Accumulation', it will be recalled, is one of two functions that the state, according to O'Connor, must fulfil. The second, 'legitimisation', is defined in terms of maintaining or creating 'the conditions for social harmony' (1973, p. 6) or, in other words, an adequate level of consent.

Although it appears that 'legitimation' is very similar to what Offe calls 'cultural motivation' as an aspect of the reproduction of labour power, it may be argued that a wider conception of social harmony or consent is involved. For if certain conditions of existence are necessary for capitalism to continue, and if securing these conditions requires state action, then there must be 'sufficient consent' to the political order to allow these functions to be fulfilled. It follows that 'cultural motivation' is both an aspect of the reproduction of labour power and of a wider sense of legitimation. For this reason it may be tidier to present legitimation and reproduction as distinct needs of capital, with cultural motivation as an aspect of the former.

Legitimation is a need of capital insofar as consent does not arise spontaneously or autonomously within the circuit of capital and is necessary for capitalism to continue. It follows from the Marxist conception of the relations of production that consent is not spontaneous since these relations are inherently antagonistic. There are mechanisms to secure consent that operate within the circuit, that is autonomously; notably attempts within capitalist firms to influence worker attitudes and organisation culture, but it seems clear that such mechanisms will not be sufficient by themselves. That the organisation of consent has come to be seen as the 'normal' form of rule in capitalist societies is not the same thing as saying that it is necessary. In contrast to this emphasis on legitimisation, Holloway and Picciotto (1977, p. 79) argue that it is the antagonistic or conflictual nature of the relations of production together with the fact that coercion is absent from them which permits and requires an extra-economic apparatus of coercion, the state. Thus both coercion and consent may be seen as needs of capital arising from the antagonistic nature of the relations of production. It might be better to say that capital needs *compliance*, that is action in accordance with the relations of production, and that such compliance can be secured, roughly speaking, through a combination of coercion and consent. Held distinguishes in a more sophisticated way 'between different grounds for obeying a command, complying with a rule, agreeing or consenting to something' (1984a, p. 301). At one end of a continuum is 'ideal normative commitment' and at the other 'coercion, or following orders'. This shows that the grounds for compliance can range between that to which compliance is given being 'what in ideal circumstances ... we would have agreed to do' (1984a, p. 302) and 'there [being] no choice in the matter' (1984, p. 301). Offe's concept of cultural motivation is consistent with active proletarianisation occurring on the basis that 'escape routes' are blocked by coercive power. Thus consent and coercion are not alternatives but are likely to exist in combination. It is unlikely, on the one hand, given the conflictual nature of the relations of production, that anything approaching 'ideal normative commitment' can be secured. Consent is, rather, likely to be unstable and to require backing by coercive power. Coercion, on the other hand, is unlikely to be sufficient to ensure compliance without some measure of consent.

O'Connor's framework, with its emphasis on state expenditure and the fiscal crisis, omits the provision of a legal order. Yet law or regulation may be used as an alternative to direct provision by the state in order to secure external conditions of accumulation. For example regulation may be set alongside state provision of services as two sets of activities that comprise the welfare state (e.g. Gough, 1979, pp. 3–4). From within the state-derivation tradition Altvater puts greater emphasis on the provision of a legal order (see Jessop, 1984, p. 91). One of four functions of the state is identified as 'establishing and guaranteeing general legal relations, through which the relationships of legal subjects in capitalist society are performed' (1978, p. 42). We have seen that Cohen also emphasises legal relations as an aspect of the superstructure, making effective the distinction between these legal relations and economic relations of production by deploying a distinction between (structural) powers and (superstructural) rights (1978, p. 219).

It might be argued that law is not so much a need of capital in itself but rather the means through which certain needs may be secured (i.e. an 'intermediate need' in the vocabulary of Doyal and Gough). Certain welfare 'functions' of the state which contribute to the reproduction of labour power might be undertaken through direct provision or by regulation. For example the state might attempt to secure a minimum income through income support policy or through regulation of the wages system such as minimum wage legislation. In this case it would be clear that law is a possible mechanism for securing a need of capital but is not in itself a need.

However, for Altvater (1978), and for Cohen (1978), law in itself is, in some respect, a need of capital. Altvater says that the subjects in capitalist society are constituted as legal subjects and the relationships of these subjects are performed through legal relations (1978, p. 42). Presumably this is intended to cover both the relations of production in the strict sense that Cohen uses that term (i.e. the 'ownership' positions of capitalists and proletarians) as well as relationships of exchange between commodity owners including the sale of labour power, exchange between units of capital and purchase of consumption goods. However this does not explain why it is necessary for these relationships to assume legal forms, why they cannot be carried on in non-legal forms. For Cohen the necessity of law is an exemplar of the more general claim that 'bases need superstructures' (1978, p. 231), and the requirement for (legal) property relations to match relations of production is explained in terms of the securing or stabilising of the latter by the former:

> In human society might frequently requires right in order to operate or even to be constituted ... Powers over productive forces are a case in point. Their exercise is less secure when it is not legal. So, for efficiency and good order, production relations require the sanction of property relations ... production relations require legal expression for stability ... (1978, p. 231).

Powers can, conceivably, exist without rights and rights without powers. It might be possible to conceive different powers whose requirements for rights vary along a spectrum between those which cannot be constituted except in legal form and those which are secure in their operation without matching rights. Cohen indicates that the case of powers over productive forces falls somewhere in between these extremes: they do not absolutely require matching rights and can conceivably be exercised in their absence, but would be more secure in legal form. Property relations can, nevertheless, still count as a need of capital on the basis that the economic structure would not be stable in their absence. According to Cohen, when powers are matched by rights they are 'legitimate' and the rights, correspondingly, are 'effective' (1978, p. 219). Relations of effective power over productive forces (e.g. the ability to use them and to prevent their use by others) which relations of production comprise have to be obtained and sustained. Where there is a matching set of rights we can say that the economic powers exist because of the existence of the rights. It is through the law that the economic powers are obtained and sustained. Thus 'in law-abiding society men have the powers they do because they have the rights they do' (Cohen, 1978, p. 232).

To say that a society is law-abiding is, arguably, to say two things about it: that the legal form is characteristic or dominant, as opposed to, say, traditional or charismatic forms of authority; and, that individuals normally act in compliance with laws. When society is law-abiding in both these senses we can say that people have the powers they do because they have the rights they do – for powers are typically expressed in legal form and laws sustain powers because there is compliance with them. However there are problems with this argument. It relies on the claim that powers are, by themselves, unstable and need to be stabilised, but only shows that law is among the possible ways of securing this stability. Powers might conceivably be sustained by the use of non-legal means such as tradition or force (Cohen, 1978, pp. 223–4). Given that possibility it seems difficult to maintain that law is a need of capital. We seem to be back with law as a means, in this case as one among other possible means of sustaining economic powers. This still leaves the second aspect of a law-abiding society: that there is general compliance with laws. To indicate, as Cohen does, that rights sustain powers by making them legitimate simply begs Held's question of what is meant by legitimation or, in other words, what is the basis of compliance with rules. Thus underlying the alleged need for law is the more fundamental need for compliance which is secured by some combination of coercion and consent.

Cohen's argument for the necessity of law is weakened by the possibility of other means of sustaining powers and by failure to recognise the need to secure compliance with laws. However it might be argued that the codification of the relations of production as general legal relations between legal subjects is the only effective way of ensuring the continuity and stability of those relations. Compliance requires knowledge of what is to be complied with and this can be achieved through the codification of complex relations as rules or laws. Laws, in this sense, provide understandings of social relations and roles, and the focus for the organisation of consent. Crucially, also, laws define boundaries for the use of coercive power. The argument here is that though law is not sufficient in itself since compliance has to be secured, it is in fact necessary because it would not otherwise be possible to organise the stable and continuous performance of roles which comprise the relations of production.

Summary

We will now attempt to summarise this analysis of the needs of capital and relate it to the conceptual vocabulary and framework developed by Doyal and Gough. A diagrammatic presentation is given below.

ULTIMATE SYSTEM NEED
Maintenance of Capitalist Relations Of Production
(as forms of development of the productive forces)

BASIC NEEDS
Profit
Production and Appropriation of Surplus Value

INTERMEDIATE NEEDS
1. Bourgeois Legal Order and Money
Private Property, Exchange

2. Compliance
Legitimation/Consent, Coercion

3. Regulation of the Capital-Labour Relation
Entry into the Labour Market
Productive Capacity
Productive Performance

4. Regulation of Competition

5. General Material Conditions
Infrastructure

SPECIFIC SATISFIERS
State Policies

The ultimate goal or system need (analogous to 'universal goal' in Doyal and Gough) is defined in terms of the maintenance of capitalism, in other words the maintenance or stabilisation of the relations of production which comprise the economic structure. This is to be understood not narrowly in terms of the ownership positions of capitalists and proletarians but in the wider sense of the renewal of the circuit of capital. This understanding follows Doyal and Gough in defining the 'universal goal' in terms of the intrinsic nature of the entity whose needs are in question. Hence the needs of capital are those conditions which must be met if capitalism is to continue. However, according to the theory of history, the maintenance of capitalist relations of production is seen in the context of the higher order goal of developing the productive forces and enlarging the surplus product. Thus the maintenance of capitalism is linked to the basic human interest in material progress.

Following Doyal and Gough we can distinguish between basic and intermediate needs. Basic needs are first-order goals (or conditions) which are preconditions of the renewal of the circuit of capital. Recall that these needs are distinguished from system benefits in virtue of their indispensability to the continuance or maintenance of the system. Intermediate needs constitute derived or second-order goals (or conditions) which must be achieved if basic needs are to be met. A further stage in the analysis would be to identify 'specific satisfiers' which are means for the attainment of intermediate needs. It is at this point that a concept of functional alternatives would be relevant: intermediate/basic needs are necessary conditions for capitalism to continue but there might be alternative (functionally equivalent) means of securing these conditions. Recall, in this connection, that it is possible to conceive some functional requirements of capital being secured, autonomously, within the circuit: here we are concerned with those needs which are not secured in this way and where, consequently, extra-economic conditions of existence are required. 'Specific satisfiers' would thus comprise specific state policies.

The basic need of capitalism is profit. Profit is the rationale of the circuit as a process of 'self-expanding value'. More specifically profit presupposes both that a surplus is generated within the production process and that this surplus is appropriated, in other words the exploitation of labour by capital occurs. Thus the *production* and *appropriation* of surplus constitute the basic needs of capital. Exploitation takes place within the circuit of capital through the exchange of equivalents and the peculiar character of labour power which permits, through the performance of actual labour, the production of a quantity of output with a value greater than its own (surplus value). However the circuit is not autonomous: exploitation depends on conditions which cannot be secured within the circuit and which, therefore, constitute extra-economic conditions of existence. These conditions comprise the five intermediate needs. Two of these – the provision of a legal order and the securing of compliance – may be termed external conditions, and the other three – provision of the general material conditions of production, regulation of the capital-labour relation and regulation of competition – general conditions within production. Since each of these has already been discussed at some length only brief comments on each are necessary here. In considering each in turn it should be recognised that they are in fact interrelated.

A **legal order** is necessary because it defines the roles which constitute the relations of production and whose performance entails structural continuity. Through the provision of a legal order basic powers are matched by, and become codified as, rights. The legal form is necessary because it confers upon social relations stability and continuity. Of particular importance is the securing of private property rights (the ownership positions of capitalists and proletarians) and the system of exchange. Exchange also requires provision of a generally accepted means of payment or universal exchange equivalent, i.e. **money**. However for a legal order to have this effect society must be law-abiding; that is there must be a sufficient degree of acceptance of and **compliance** with production relations and the legal form in which they are expressed. Such compliance is problematic because of the antagonistic character of capitalist production relations. The notion of compliance is used here in preference to legitimation because it permits the securing of consent through ideological means to be seen in conjunction with the requirement for extra-economic relations of force to guarantee class domination.

The provision of a legal order and compliance provide the conditions for active proletarianisation, i.e. entry of potential workers into the supply side of the labour market. The ownership positions of capitalists and proletarians (which are legally constituted) do not in themselves entail active proletarianisation – there has to be what Offe terms 'cultural motivation'. Entry into the supply side of the labour market is only one aspect of cultural motivation and 'entry' is only one aspect of the need for **regulation of the capital-labour relation**. Capital requires not merely entry of workers into the labour market but also quantitative regulation (matching of supply to demand) and favourable terms of exchange (recall that profitability is determined by, within a given working day, the productiveness of labour and the wage).

The productiveness of labour depends on both productive capacity and the actual performance of labour (i.e. both labour power and labour), these being the other aspects of the regulation of the capital-labour relation. Maintenance of the capacity to work (which includes that of reserve, potential and future workers) is what is often referred to as the reproduction of labour power and largely takes place away from the circuit of capital. Analytically we may distinguish between the general capacity to work (abstract labour) and the capacity to undertake specific forms of useful work corresponding to a specific form of the division of labour (concrete labour). In the first aspect the need of capital for labour power clearly corresponds with basic human needs. The capacity to work, we have argued, also involves appropriate beliefs and attitudes and these are also crucial to the actual performance of labour. Hence cultural motivation is intrinsic to all three elements of the regulation of the capital-labour relation. All three elements are, to repeat, essential to the production and appropriation of surplus value.

Regulation of competition is necessary because of its role as key driver of the accumulation process. Finally, provision of the general material conditions of production (infrastructure) is needed because of, as argued earlier, the incapacity of capital to organise certain of these inputs.

The importance of this presentation of the needs of capital, as a sub-category of the interests of the capitalist class, is the claim that such needs make an important contribution to explanation of the state. Expressed simply, the needs or functional requirements of capital constitute the point of reference for functional explanation of the state: in this view some actions of the state are as they are because of the way such actions satisfy these functional requirements. In other words the needs of capital constitute key conceptual foundations of a Marxist theory of the state. But only foundations. If there are needs of capital their identification is really an aspect of the theory of the economic structure and does not in itself allow us to infer very much, if anything, about the state. If we are to believe that the state does indeed act to meet those needs a plausible theory of the state is needed.

7
State Autonomy – A Conceptual Framework

Introduction – the relative autonomy of the state

The principle of economic determination entails that economic phenomena explain (or determine) non-economic phenomena. The reach of economic determination within Marxist theory may be clarified by distinguishing between the claims of Marxist sociology and the theory of history.[1] The sociology does not claim that all non-economic phenomena are explained in economic terms, but it does claim that they are (or may be) so explained in their 'broad lines' (Cohen, 1988, p. 177). The theory of history, understood as a 'restricted' doctrine, is more limited in scope. This is because a restricted range of non-economic phenomena is *functionally* explained by the nature of the economic structure. In other words the theory of history restricts itself to explanation of only those non-economic phenomena that are 'economically relevant' in the sense of meeting some functional requirement or 'system need' of the economic structure. It is only these non-economic phenomena that are included in the 'legal and political superstructure'. In general terms the function of the superstructure is to 'stabilise' the economic structure.[2]

Thus the theory of history restricts both the economic and non-economic elements of economic determination. 'The nature of the economic structure functionally explains the character of the legal and political superstructure' essentially means 'the functional requirements of the economic structure explain the occurrence of non-economic phenomena that meet those requirements'.[3] In other words the theory of history does not exhaust economic determination – there may be other economic causes of other non-economic effects. These fall outside the scope of the theory of history, but may come within the ambit of Marxist sociology.

Although the terms 'state' and 'superstructure' are not synonymous the designation 'legal and political' does suggest that the superstructure has to do largely with the state. Since functional explanation is intended to capture the effects (functions) of the superstructure on the economic structure, it will largely be concerned with the uses of state power, that is, a range of state actions or forms of intervention directed at the economy. As well as functions, the form of the state may also be functionally explained where reorganisation occurs so as to alter the 'strate.g.ic selectivity' of the state in line with the interests of the capitalist class and/or needs of capital.

The issue of the (relative) autonomy of the state now arises, that is, whether the functionally explained form and functions of the state are reducible to the functional requirements of the economic structure. One way of thinking about the explanatory autonomy of the state is that it entails its non-reducibility to the nature of the economic structure. In this vein, though conceived more narrowly, Elster argues that

> the state has explanatory autonomy when (and to the extent that) its structure and policies cannot be explained by the interest of an economically dominant class ... autonomy is defined ne.g.atively, as the absence of class interest explanation (1985, p. 405).[4]

In this sense autonomy points to a gap in the explanation – the part that the explanation cannot reach. It points to the need to identify other types of explanation or causal influences that bear on the state's structure and policies. In other words the state has explanatory autonomy in relation to a specific explanation (here, class interest), but this does not preclude, in principle, the possibility of a fully determinate account of the structure and policies of the state.[5]

The gap might be filled by explanation in terms of other types of interests and social forces and/or by structural constraints so that, in the end, a fully determinate society-centred account of the state is possible, at least in principle. On the other hand, autonomy might be understood, in part, in terms of the independent capacity of the state to pursue its own interests, that is, by invoking a state-centred explanation. It is this meaning, the power of the state to act and not simply be determined by external forces and pressures, that is often found in Marxist conceptions of relative autonomy (Miliband, 1977; Block, 1987).

Although Elster refers to the *absence* of class interest explanation, the suggested dichotomy between autonomy and reductionism is misleading. It is better to say that the state has explanatory autonomy *to the extent that* class interest (or economic) explanation is absent. This means that autonomy is greater (or less) according to whether the power of economic explanation is less (or greater). In Marxist theory the concept of relative autonomy is intended to capture this 'in-between' position, avoiding both reductionism and simple autonomy. But there is a range of 'in-between' positions with greater or lesser degrees of autonomy. More specifically, then, relative autonomy is intended to convey the explanatory *primacy* of the nature of the economic structure and, correspondingly, the severely *restricted* scope of state autonomy. Though the state has potential for autonomy, its actual autonomy is confined or constrained by the causal power that the economy exercises over it. The aspects of the structure and policies of the state that are functionally explained by the economy are *largely* or primarily explained in this way. To make good this claim we will defend two arguments against criticisms from Jessop: that the state should be conceived as a subject capable of exercising power, and that a multiplicity of causal chains is compatible with the existence of strong tendencies in social theory.

The potential for state autonomy

The potential autonomy of the state may be related to three considerations: the institutional separation of the state from civil society; the nature of the state as a 'power container'; and, the force of society-centred pressures and influences. Institutional separation is a key characteristic of the form of the capitalist state which means that its operation is autonomous from the operation of the economy and the circuit of capital. The state has its own 'institutional logics and modes of calculation' distinct from those of the economy (Jessop, 2002, p. 41). Further, the state has its own personnel, in principle separate from actors in the capitalist market. These factors create the *potential* for state autonomy, but this involves something else: the capacity of the state to act and to exercise power in its own interests. Without this state-centred conception the state, despite its distinct institutional materiality and logic, is simply a reflection of society-centred pressures and forces. Finally, the actual autonomy of the state depends on the balance between its capacity to project its own interests and power out to the economy and civil society and the society-centred pressures and forces to which it is subject.

The idea of state autonomy relies on the concept of the state as a subject or agent capable of deciding how to act. The autonomy of the state is, then, analogous to the autonomy of other agents, an idea closely bound up with freedom. In Lukes' conception freedom consists in 'the non-constraining of the realisation of agents' purposes' and, consequently, 'freedom is diminished when agents' purposes are prevented from being realised' (1985, p. 71). This approach, then, focuses attention on the nature of the constraints that may diminish freedom. In Lukes' view autonomy has to do with whether the purposes whose non-constraint is essential for freedom are 'genuinely ... [the agent's own], autonomous rather than heteronomous, self-directed rather than imposed or induced' (1985, p. 74). Thus freedom and autonomy are distinguished: freedom has to do with the absence or presence of constraints on the realisation of agents' purposes, whereas autonomy has to do with whether those purposes are self-determined. If we can think of the state as potentially having its own purposes economic explanation may work by influencing these purposes and/or by constraining their realisation.

Rejecting this approach, Jessop (1984) warns against treating the state as an 'originating subject endowed with an essential unity' (p. 222) and argues that 'the state should not be seen as a subject capable of exercising power' (pp. 223–4). In this view 'state power is an explicandum, not a principle of explanation' (1984, p. 225). The concept of the state as a 'subject' does not in fact presuppose its 'essential unity' in the sense of constituting a singular unified actor with a unified set of interests. For 'the state' is really 'the state system', which comprises a complex set of institutions. The unity of this system, to the extent that it occurs, has to be achieved politically, but this allows that such unity is, to some extent, achievable.[6] In any case, the idea of the state as a 'subject' is really a claim that *state managers* are capable of exercising power. Against this Jessop argues that to make such a claim

> is at best to perpetrate a convenient fiction that masks a far more complex set of social relations that extend far beyond the state apparatus and its distinctive capacities. ... While the constitutionalization and centralization of state power enable responsibility to be formally attributed to named officials and bodies, this should not lead us to fetishize the fixing of formal political responsibility at specific points and/or in specific personages. We should always seek to trace the circulation of power through wider and more complex sets of social relations both within and beyond the state (2002, pp. 40–1).

It is true that the exercise of state power is not *simply* a question of the decisions and actions of state managers, since it does involve 'more complex sets of social relations'. Jessop also expresses this complexity in terms of the range of social forces involved so that 'state power is a complex social relation that reflects the changing balance of social forces in a determinate conjuncture' (Jessop, 1984, p. 221). More fully, state power is not a simple reflection of these social forces but 'a form-determined, institutionally mediated effect of the balance among all forces in a given situation... a form-determined condensation of social forces in struggle' (1984, p. 225).

Thus state power cannot simply be a question of what state managers do because there is a range of other social forces involved, and because the balance among all these forces 'is institutionally mediated through the state apparatus with its structurally inscribed strategic selectivity' (Jessop, 2002, p. 40). State power is an effect of both the balance and the mediation. However Jessop seems to jump from the true assertion that state managers do not exercise state power *exclusively* to the false one that they do not exercise it *at all* (except in fiction).

Yet Jessop's approach must allow that state managers are among the social forces that state power reflects (Jessop, 1990, pp. 269–70). This point can be expressed more generally to include other actors within the state system. Thus Jessop argues that to reject the concept of the state as a power subject is not 'to deny the influence of political categories such as the military, bureaucrats, or parliamentary deputies' (1984, p. 225). This means that state managers and other actors are involved in, or contribute to, the exercise of state power. In other words, state managers do exercise power, neither 'exclusively' nor 'not at all', but 'to some extent'. The question is to what extent, and this has to do largely with the interests and strategies of these actors relative to other social forces and the strategic selectivity of the state apparatus. This is, in other words, a question of the relative autonomy of state managers.

Jessop insists that the state is 'merely an institutional ensemble' (1990, p. 270), and the point of the term 'merely' seems to be to distinguish between the state as institution(s) or apparatus(es) and the social forces which condition and are conditioned by it. This fits with the idea of the state as a strategic 'terrain' on which social forces act. But this is, at best, a one-sided characterisation of institutions. For the state, like other institutions, comprises a set of roles, and these roles are occupied and performed by real individuals. The idea that state managers are just among the category of social forces whose interests are mediated by state institutions suggests that they have the same relationship to these institutions as other forces and interests. However this fails to recognise a crucial distinction: namely, that state managers and other 'political categories' are defined by their location and performance of roles *within* state institutions whereas other social forces are essentially external to those institutions. The roles of the former are directly, though to varying degrees, involved in the exercise state power, whereas the latter are formally excluded from the decision making processes involved in this exercise of power. The state, then, is not simply a prism through which state power is mediated as a condensation of social forces; it is in fact the originating source of state power.

Further, the roles of state managers within the state system carry with them distinctive interests, as Jessop himself acknowledges:

in addition to other forces and interests constituted wholly or predominantly outside the state system, the state system itself engenders *sui generis* political interests ... [including] the interests of state managers ... [or] officialdom (1990, p. 269).

But this strengthens the concept of the state as a subject capable of exercising power, for state power is not simply a reflection of external forces and interests. It is both internally generated through the deployment of resources organised by the state as a 'power container', and reflects distinctive interests of officialdom generated within the state system in virtue of the roles they perform.

Seen in this way, as a power container, the state is like other institutions. For example, a capitalist firm is an institution comprising a set of relations of effective control or power. In Jessop's terms it might be described as the institutional mediation of economic power. As a private institution within civil society the firm is not as accessible to external forces as state institutions in the public realm, particularly in democratic polities. However a range of social forces external to the firm, such as consumer groups, do weigh in the balance which is reflected in economic power. We can say that economic power largely reflects the balance among class forces as they are constituted at the level of the firm. Jessop might argue that the firm, as institution, should not be seen as a power subject although this is not to deny the influence of economic categories such as capitalists and managers. Yet the firm is conventionally treated as a power subject or collective actor which exercises power and this is in recognition of the fact that capitalists and managers, categories which are defined by their roles within the institution, do exercise power. If that is a legitimate theoretical move then so, arguably, is the treatment of state institutions as power subjects. Alternatively if we extend Jessop's argument no institution can be treated as a power subject: everything simply reflects social forces. In treating the state as a subject capable of wielding power our approach is in line with that of Miliband. For

> it is these institutions [of the state] in which state power lies, and ...
> is wielded ... by the people who occupy the leading positions in
> each of these institutions ... the state elite. ... [T]he state elite ...
> does wield state power (Miliband, 1969, p. 54).

This orientation explicitly brings the state into the equation as a 'subject' potentially capable of exercising power in its own right. 'Potentially' because it is the task of state theory to show how far the state is actually autonomous and how far it is controlled by economic (and/or non-economic?) explanation. Rather than deny, with Jessop, this potential autonomy the question is how far it is realised. This focuses a central tension or dilemma within Marxist theory: between conceiving the state as effect of a determining economic structure and as autonomous institution. This tension may be seen as one of the central problems of Marxist theory and can be seen equally in Marx's own writing on the state, as exemplified by Miliband's 'primary' and 'secondary' views, and in debates within contemporary Marxism and between Marxism and 'ex-Marxism' (Geras, 1988).

The difficulty is to develop a convincing understanding of economic determination which does not amount to economic reductionism or determinism, that is which does not deny the possibility of non-economic determinations and/or the state possessing some degree of autonomy or specific effectivity. A rejection of determinism entails that the explanatory reach of Marxism is limited, that the explanations it provides are likely to be incomplete. Yet this concession is to be made while maintaining that economic determination has primacy, that it is not simply one among many forms of determination. This problem can be approached through a consideration of the functional construal of the base-superstructure relation.

Functionalism and determinism

The functional construal of the theory of history solves a problem that might otherwise fatally weaken economic determination. For the dependence of the capitalist economy on certain extra-economic conditions of existence and the central role of the state in securing these conditions suggests that the state constitutes a principle of explanation. Thus some obvious truths about the relationship between the state and the market seem to turn economic determination on its head. However functional explanation puts it back on its feet since, in this view, 'superstructures are as they are because, being so, they consolidate economic structures', that is, they 'have the character they do because production relations require that they have it' (Cohen, 1978, p. xi and p. 231). Thus functional explanation of the state by the economic structure achieves consistency between the stabilising influence exerted over the economic structure by the state and the explanatory primacy which the theory of history assigns to the economic structure.

However Cohen's defence of an 'old fashioned' historical materialism has, arguably, a strongly determinist character, and determinism is highly controversial. The functional construal of the theory of history might be described as a form of technological determinism insofar as explanatory primacy is assigned to what is technological – the productive forces. It might be described (in its second stage) as a form of economic determinism insofar as explanatory primacy is assigned to the economic structure *vis-à-vis* the legal and political superstructure. Although Cohen does not pay attention to the question of determinism, some discussion of this troublesome term is clearly warranted.[7] It might be argued that, far from being controversial, determinism is generally regarded as a 'bad thing'. Thus 'for some time there has been a strong reaction among marxist theorists against economic reductionism' (Jessop, 1990, p. 79). Marsh claims that the 'coherent core' of Marxism is characterised by rejection of determinism, alongside the other related 'errors' of classical Marxism, economism and structuralism (1999a; see also Hay, 1999). All social theory must operate with some notion of determinate causal relations between social phenomena or events so that, understood in this way, reductionism may be seen as intrinsic to the very idea of explanation. As McLennan argues, 'some regulative notion of explaining the events of one domain [e.g. the political] in terms of those of another [e.g. the economic] remains close to the heart of what we mean by "explanation" itself' (McLennan, 1996, p. 58). However reductionism is often understood, and criticised, as the stronger claim that there is an 'invariant conjunction of events' between the two domains (Bhaskar, 1991, p. 139). Thus Jessop defines reductionism as the claim

> that the forms and functions of non-economic systems *necessarily correspond* to the forms and functional needs of the economy. It also treats economic factors as the mechanism which generates this correspondence. In this sense it denies that non-economic systems have any significant autonomous institutional logic and also denies they can have significant independent effects on the economy (1990, p. 79, emphasis added).

This closely follows Bhaskar's definition of determinism, 'normally understood as the thesis that for everything that happens there are conditions such that, given them, nothing else could have happened' (1991, p. 139). A determinist reading of the base-superstructure metaphor would then seem to entail that

1. for every action of the state (that is economically explained or superstructural)
   (for everything that happens ...)
2. the character of the economic structure is such that, given a structure of that character ...
   (there are conditions such that, given them ...)
3. these actions are uniquely determined.
   (nothing else could have happened.)

The crucial clause in this phrase is, of course, that 'nothing else could have happened', that what happens at the superstructural level is uniquely determined at the economic. In Jessop's words, that it 'necessarily corresponds'. This can be extended from analysis of a particular case to a generalisation, or law, about the causal relationship between the event mentioned in 1. and the conditions specified in 2. Indeed, it can be argued that the particular case in which a thing happens following certain conditions occurring (i.e. B follows A) may be accepted as an explanation of B when it is supported by a generalisation to the effect 'whenever A then B'.

Similarly functional explanations may be related to such generalisations or laws. Cohen analyses functional explanation as a type of 'consequence' explanation in which the cited consequence performs a function (i.e., roughly, is beneficial for some other item). A consequence law is simply a generalisation that whenever an item would have a particular consequence that item occurs. A consequence statement is deemed explanatory if there is a valid consequence law which it instantiates. Thus the (descriptive) function statement

'state action X performs the function of stabilising economic structure Y'

would be rendered functionally explanatory of X by the generalisation or law that

'whenever a particular state action would stabilise the economic structure (favoured by the productive forces) that state action occurs'.

The debate about determinism concerns, in effect, the strength of the term 'whenever' with which the statement of the law commences. That 'whenever' can mean just that is contested by the claim that 'laws set limits rather than prescribe uniquely fixed results; and that, in general, laws must be analysed as the tendencies of mechanisms' (Bhaskar, 1991, p. 139), rather than as involving 'necessary correspondence'. 'Whenever A, then (invariantly) B' is rejected in favour of 'Whenever A, then (there is a tendency to) B'. In functional explanation this involves a double weakening: instead of 'Whenever A would perform function B, A occurs' we have 'Whenever A would tend to perform function B, A tends to occur'.

The analysis of laws as tendencies is based upon the existence, in general, of a multiplicity of causes or determinations. Thus, returning to Jessop's definition of reductionism, necessary correspondence is rejected precisely because it is not merely economic factors that generate this (spurious) correspondence. In other words, economic explanation is disrupted by non-economic factors. The operation of multiple determinants (or causal influences) undermines economic explanation in two, related, ways. First, it may lead us to downgrade the weight of economic factors in explanation simply because there are other factors to take into account and these might turn out to be weighty. However they might not be weighty, so the primacy of economic explanation can be defended by showing that economic factors exert greater causal influence than other, non-economic factors. Thus simply invoking multiple determinants cannot succeed as an argument for rejecting economic determination because it is possible that economic factors are the most important (Wetherly, 2001). The second argument, however, is that the existence of a multiplicity of determinants underlines 'the contingency and indeterminacy of social and political change'. Although economic factors may prove weighty in a *specific* case, and we may characterise this as a case of economic explanation, we may not infer a generalisation from this case because the various causal influences or chains may interact differently to produce a different outcome in a different case. Thus Jessop's 'contingent necessity' recommends the analysis of specific cases and argues against the possibility of a general theory. In some cases the nature of the economic structure may be decisive in explaining the structure and/or policies of the state, but in other cases it may not be. It follows that any claim that the superstructural level necessarily corresponds to the economic structure must be rejected.[8]

The theory of history does appear to be committed to a general theory of the state, and one that is of an extraordinarily ambitious kind. It is not just the state in capitalist society that is functionally explained by the needs of the economy but all historically existing forms of state, for all societies have a 'base' and a 'superstructure' and these are always functionally related. Shorn of a general theory of the state this historical reach appears to be called in question. What is more, the much larger claims which the theory makes about the progressive, directed nature of history are also called in question. For the first of the two stages of functional explanation – of the relations by the forces – depends upon the second – of the superstructure by the economic structure. The relations of production 'selected' by the forces require for their own stability a particular legal and political superstructure. If they don't get it they will not serve as effective 'forms of development' of the productive forces. Thus the progress which the theory says is the content of history might founder.

It is only a restricted catalogue of non-economic phenomena that, according to restricted historical materialism, are functionally explained by the nature of the economic structure – only those that are economically relevant in the sense of being necessary in order to stabilise an otherwise unstable structure. Beyond this catalogue the theory makes no explanatory claims – either about the relative weighting of economic and non-economic factors, or about the contingency of their interaction. The theory only, but crucially, requires that these other phenomena do not interfere with the functional relationship between base and superstructure. Historical materialism therefore cannot allow non-superstructural non-economic phenomena to be generated without constraint. The requisite constraint is just that such phenomena neither help to stabilise the economic structure (since such stability would then be merely fortuitous) nor generate negative or destabilising effects at the economic level.

Neither the positive nor the negative form of economic determination excludes the specific effectivity, or autonomy, of the political level altogether. First, that certain extra-economic conditions are required does not stipulate how they are secured. There might be a range of functional alternatives at the political level (i.e. 'specific satisfiers') rather than a unique solution to the functional needs of the economy, and which of these prevails might be determined by specifically political factors. For example, the needs of the economy might be secured through alternative accumulation strategies. Similarly the forms of non-superstructural phenomena may be variable and determined by political factors, only within the constraint that the consolidation of the economic structure is not threatened. Second, functional requirements do not have to be satisfied optimally but only to a standard that is 'good enough'. For example, accumulation strategy A may be functionally superior to B but either may be good enough in securing adequate conditions for accumulation to be sustained. Or, strategy A may be implemented more or less successfully or effectively, so long as its implementation is adequate to the needs of the economy. Third, the effectivity of the political might be conceived in terms of the timing of superstructural adjustments to basic requirements. There might, in other words, be a lag between economic structural change and the appearance of the appropriate state structure or policy. Similarly, there might be intervals of limited duration in which non-superstructural phenomena generate dysfunctional effects for the economy. However if we go further than these limited forms of effectivity of the political and say that political factors can override economic determination to the extent of determining not only the precise form, effective implementation and timing of superstructural solutions but whether or not they appear then we will be leaving the theory of history behind.

At least, if the central explanatory claims of the theory of history are analysed as the 'tendencies of mechanisms' then these must be construed as *strong* tendencies. If the system need of the economic structure is one among many determinations the theory requires that it *usually* overrides these others and, conversely, that it is *rarely* overridden by them. Economic determination must be the dominant explanatory vector. The strong tendency that the theory of history demands entails that economic determination leaves little room for state autonomy (or non-economic determination). Such a strong tendency may be defended on theoretical and empirical grounds. The theoretical grounds are in two forms: first, the admissibility of strong tendencies in social theory in general; second, the plausibility of strong tendencies in the specific case of the theory of history.

On this second count the theoretical grounds are provided by the arguments for the 'structural' and 'instrumental' mechanisms already set out. These may be labelled 'capital-theoretical' and 'class-theoretical' approaches (Jessop, 1990). The former emphasises the structural dependence of the state on the process of capital accumulation such that the interests of the economically dominant class/needs of capital are imposed on the state by the impersonal logic of capitalist relations of production. The class-theoretical approach emphasises class agency; the resources that the economically dominant class is able to bring to bear in political class struggle and the political power wielded by the class either directly in virtue of its command over the leading positions within the state or indirectly through the pressure it is able to bring to bear against the state. The distinction between the two approaches may be neatly summarised in terms used by Elster in a discussion of the relation between the government (B) and the dominant class (A) as a 'strategic game'. (Note that this game-theoretic approach assumes that the state can be treated as a subject, capable of exercising power, etc.). B avoids policies unacceptable to A because: 'A has the power ... to dethrone him' (class-theoretical approach); and/or, because 'what is bad for A is also bad for B', that is, 'the need to avoid killing the goose that lays the golden eggs' (capital-theoretical approach).

The admissibility of strong tendencies in social theory is opposed by Jessop's arguments for 'contingent necessity'. This rests on the link between the existence of multiple determinants and contingent outcomes. Because there are many possible causal influences, and these may interact in different ways, outcomes must be indeterminate. Or, rather, it is only permissible to speak of necessity in terms of the contingent way these causal chains interact in each specific conjuncture – thus, contingent necessity. But it is inadmissible to make general statements about outcomes (i.e. about the outcome that will generally or normally be produced) just because of the inherent contingency of the interaction of causal chains. Each specific conjuncture (or each production of an outcome) is essentially unique. However there is no automatic link, as Jessop seems to believe, between complexity and contingency. The claim that within a set of causal influences any, some or all might, or might not, exercise causal influence requires argument just as much as the claim of explanatory primacy for one of the set. Why should we believe, *a priori*, that each determinant is, in general, no more (or less) likely than any other to exercise influence? On the face of it this is in fact a most implausible assumption and therefore it is a proper objective of theory to elucidate the relative strengths of a set of causal factors. There seems to be no good reason to rule out the possibility that some causal factors will, in general, be more potent than others.

In effect Jessop's contingency approach seems to amount to characterising the causal impact of the various social forces as weak tendencies. A weak tendency can be thought of as one that may often be frustrated or blocked and/or, when it operates, usually only imparts a weak causal influence. Jessop's multiple determinants are weak tendencies in the sense that class and non-class social forces are latent or potential causal influences that can and may play some part in explaining the state, but need not. The causal influence of capitalist relations of production is seen by Jessop as one weak tendency among others. This shows that tendencies are requisite elements of social theory. If this is correct there *must* be, at least, weak tendencies, and it seems to follow that there *might* be strong tendencies. Economic determination might be such a strong tendency. Jessop's argument does not succeed in showing that it cannot be such.[9]

State autonomy – a conceptual framework

The state, in our conception, can be treated as a subject capable of exercising power and, therefore, as potentially autonomous. The question is to what degree this potential is realised. The idea of the 'relative autonomy' of the state expresses the claim that economic determination of the state (to the extent that it is, in part, superstructural) is a strong tendency. The principle of economic determination claims that the autonomy of the state is severely constrained by the nature of the economic structure.

More precisely we can understand the relationship between base and superstructure in terms of Lukes' distinction between the related concepts of freedom and autonomy. This distinction can be rephrased in terms of means and ends. Autonomy concerns the determination of ends (are they the agent's own?) and freedom is a question of the extent to which the realisation of these ends (however determined) is constrained. This largely boils down to the extent to which the agent is constrained in determining the requisite action in pursuit of these ends or, in other words, in deploying the requisite means. Thus autonomy and freedom concern the determination/constraint of, respectively, ends and means: to be autonomous (free) is to determine one's own ends (means).[10]

The concept of autonomy presupposes that the agent has (or might have) purposes that are genuinely its own. It seems implausible that any agent (however conceived) could ever be fully autonomous, in the sense of having purposes that are all and only genuinely its own, uninfluenced by, say, the situation of the agent. But, equally, a total lack of autonomy is also generally implausible. Some purposes might be purely self-directed, some might be wholly induced, and some might be mixed. Autonomy seems to require that (at least some) purposes are (at least in part) chosen by the agent and therefore express free will. In this sense autonomy seems to entail unpredictability. But some purposes might be seen as inherent in the type of agent in question, rather than freely chosen. For example, the modern state might be said to have a particular nature from which certain purposes follow regardless of the particular historical situation. In this vein Poggi asserts that the operation of political power has as its object 'the ability to control and direct the use and development of a society's ultimate resource – the activities of the individuals making up its population' (1990, p. 8). In pursuit of this object the peculiar uses of political power

> normally consist in safeguarding a given society's territorial boundaries against aggression and encroachment from outsiders; and in imposing restraints upon those individuals or groups within a given society which use or threaten to use violence or fraud in pursuing their special interests (1990, pp. 8–9).

Here we have an understanding of the distinctive purposes of the state as agent which derive from its very character as a state. All definitions of the state which assert that the state 'monopolises rule making within its territory' (Hall & Ikenberry, 1989, p. 2) or claims a monopoly over the use of coercion implicitly make the same point. Hall and Ikenberry claim that 'fully-fledged "stateness" has been an aspiration for every state in history' (1989, p. 2). In other words every state has aspired, as its own purpose, to exercise a monopoly of rule making.

Whatever the genuine self-directed purposes of the state may be, the theory of history is primarily interested in the influences and constraints upon the state emanating from the economic structure. The point of a Marxist argument is to show that the state is a capitalist state in the sense that it meets the functional requirements or preconditions of the economic structure. Further, that this is so because of the way it is situated within a capitalist society and is, therefore, influenced and constrained by the nature of the economic structure. In other words, the state is the effect of economic determination. What its genuine own interests or purposes are (or would be) is a secondary question, and to that extent it may be said that the state as such is under-theorised within this approach.

We can turn, again, to Lukes for a characterisation of freedom-diminishing constraints in terms of three kinds.

> First, such constraints may be external (like handcuffs) or internal (like inhibitions) ... Second, constraints may be positive (like prohibitions and taboos) or negative (like a lack of money or knowledge) ... Third, constraints may be personal or impersonal in origin: they may result directly from specified intentional acts by specific persons (as when a dictator imprisons me) or they may result from anonymous and impersonal processes and relationships (as when I cannot find a job) (Lukes, 1985, p. 72).

If any given constraint can be classified in terms of each of the three pairs or dichotomies suggested by Lukes, then eight types of constraint are conceivable. (This is so because any conceivable constraint must be internal or external, personal or impersonal, and positive or negative, and there are eight possible combinations – 2x2x2). By abstracting from the positive/negative dimension four basic types of constraint are identified. The rationale for this is that the internal/external and personal/impersonal dimensions can both plausibly be said to refer to the location or source of the constraint whereas the positive/negative dimension describes the way in which it operates. (We will focus on the internal/external and personal/impersonal dimensions in our discussion of mechanisms). This means that each of the four constraint types tabulated below may operate in both a positive and negative form.

Possible constraint types

Personal Internal	Impersonal Internal
Personal External	Impersonal External

Although the three conceptual pairings or dichotomies are introduced by Lukes specifically for the purpose of characterising 'freedom diminishing constraints', it seems plausible to add that the factors impinging on the autonomy of an agent might be similarly characterised. In this case we might refer to 'autonomy diminishing influences'. Such influences would, in some part, determine the purposes of the agent such that these are not self-directed.

Lukes' conceptualisations of autonomy and freedom parallel two possible forms of economic determination. 'Politics' may be explained by 'economics' by showing that the purposes of the state have economic-structural causes and/or by showing that the economic structure imposes limits or constraints on state actions. In other words economic primacy may work by directly explaining the purposes or functions of the state (thereby reducing its autonomy) and/or, whatever its purposes, by restricting the actions it can or must undertake (thereby reducing its freedom). At the same time Lukes' conceptualisation of 'freedom diminishing constraints' seems to map onto conventional conceptual distinctions employed in state theory. The personal-impersonal distinction parallels that between agency and structure and the internal-external distinction closely resembles that between state-centred and society-centred explanations. Lukes' analytical framework can, then, be adapted to elaborate the principal mechanisms of economic determination.

For the state to be shown to be a capitalist state Marxist theory must be able to provide explanations which show that the purposes of the state are in accordance with the maintenance of the economic structure and/or that there are constraints on state action which are sufficiently stringent that the state acts as if such is its purpose. The point is that to show that the state is a capitalist state involves more than showing that the state faces constraints or limits on its actions, that it is not free to pursue its own interests, unless these constraints reduce the feasible set to just those actions which are functional for the capitalist economy. In general Marxist theory requires that the state does do certain things, does perform certain essential functions, and not merely that there are constraints on its actions. For this reason the metaphor which Geras employs (1987, p. 49) to elucidate the concept of relative autonomy seems to provide an analogy for only one, and arguably the least significant, aspect of the question. The man chained to a post is obviously constrained in his actions: the chain determines in a literal sense the space in which he can move, the feasible set of actions open to him. In Lukes' terms the chain involves the constraining of the realisation of the agent's purposes and therefore the diminution of his freedom. However what the chain does not do is determine that he will do certain things. In particular it does not influence what his purposes are and does not, therefore, diminish his autonomy. For this reason the chain metaphor is not adequate to capture the concept of function. For that we need to extend the metaphor. For example we might imagine that while the length of the chain determines the limits to the actor's freedom of movement, at the same time the chain incorporates a wire which is connected to his brain and through which impulses are transmitted which influence his purposes. There we have the two types of explanation working together to provide a fuller account of actions.

It is this second aspect of the question, the ensuring that certain actions are taken, that certain functions are performed, which must be considered crucial. For the state's purpose is to ensure that the requirements of capital are met (Miliband, 1984, p. 94). The task of Marxist theory is to elucidate the mechanism(s) whereby the state's performance of this task is explained.

8
Constraints on the State – Mechanisms of Economic Determination

Introduction

Economic determination may be conceptualised in terms of mechanisms of constraint that limit the potential autonomy of the state. Following Lukes' analysis of freedom and autonomy, four such interrelated mechanisms may be identified by distinguishing internal/external and personal/impersonal constraints. Each of these may be conceived as operating in a positive or negative form. Three of these mechanisms are referred to by Miliband in *The State in Capitalist Society* (1969, p. 79):

- ideological dispositions of governments
- structural constraints imposed upon them by the system
- pressures to which they have been subjected by dominant interests

This analysis suggests two external (or society-centred) mechanisms – structural constraints and pressure exerted by dominant interests – and one internal (or state-centred) mechanism – the ideological dispositions of governments. Miliband also suggests a particular relationship between these mechanisms. Society-centred causal influences are not automatically translated into appropriate state policies but have to be mediated or filtered by the political process and the state system. Thus, in particular, the ideological dispositions of governments make a difference to how they respond to external constraints (making them 'more acceptable') and pressures (making them easier to 'submit to'). It is not clear whether the society-centred causal influences, alone or in combination, would in the end be sufficient to explain state policies, but Miliband argues that specific internal features of the state – the beliefs of office-holders – reinforce these external influences. The passage could be read as an argument that state policies are 'over-determined' by these three causal influences. The mechanisms may also be distinguished in terms of whether they refer to the causal powers of 'structure' (structural constraints) or 'agency' (class, government). And, again, although it is possible that structure or agency alone could be sufficient to explain state policies, this might be conceived in terms of over-determination. There is a fourth mechanism that Miliband does not allude to: the institutional logic or rationality of the state system. This mechanism highlights that governments, whatever their ideological dispositions, operate within a state system with certain structural properties, and that this structural aspect of the state also makes a difference as to how external influences are responded to. Using the distinctions between structure and agency and society- and state-centred explanations, Lukes' four constraints may be presented in a rough schema.

The state-society (internal-external) and structure-agency (impersonal-personal) distinctions are analytical and do not suggest that agents can operate free from structures or that the institutional logic of the state can be entirely independent of the society in which it is located. Rather, in elaborating these four mechanisms it will be important to highlight how they overlap and interconnect.

Mechanisms of Constraint	Agency-oriented	Structure-oriented
State-centred	INTERNAL/ PERSONAL	INTERNAL/ IMPERSONAL
Society-centred	EXTERNAL/ PERSONAL	EXTERNAL/ IMPERSONAL

Mechanism 1 – internal/personal

The idea of an internal/personal mechanism refers to the character of personnel within the state system and, in particular, those who occupy the leading positions within the state. It rests on the claim that the 'people who are professionally concerned with the actual running of the state ...[are]... of crucial importance in the analysis of the relation of the state to society (Miliband, 1969, p. 19). In other words the mechanism relies on the claim that state power is exercised by those people who constitute what Miliband refers to as the 'state elite' (1969, p. 51).[1] However, not only must there be an identifiable elite that exercises state power but, for this to be a mechanism of economic determination, this elite must formulate and implement class-based policies. For example, a 'class conscious political directorate' within the executive and administrative branch of the state (i.e. Cabinet and senior civil service) might be conceived as 'the mechanism by which ... [the longer-term] general interests [of capital as a whole] are mediated and articulated by the state' (Gough, 1979, p. 63).[2]

But, given the institutional separation of the public realm of the state system from the private realm of the capitalist economy, and the associated separation between the state elite and the corporate elite, why should this 'political directorate' be 'class conscious'? Part of the answer is the relationship between state managers and the capitalist class: for example, state managers may have a strong incentive to implement class-based policies because of the threat of sanctions by the capitalist class (investment strike or flight). Ultimately, the indirect power of capital might be conceived in terms of the abstention from, or abdication of, power by the bourgeoisie (Elster, 1985). However these arguments invoke external mechanisms to explain the bias of the state elite.

Part of the answer might be the overlap between the state elite and the corporate elite, that is, the participation of capitalists in the running of the state. However 'colonisation', though important, is limited in extent: only a relatively small proportion of the state elite is made up of capitalists. Especially in conditions of capitalist (liberal) democracy the capacity of the capitalist class to govern directly is clearly limited. If it is not the direct involvement of members of the capitalist class in government and the state that is the most important factor, it is nevertheless a question of

> the social composition of the state elite proper. For businessmen belong, in economic and social terms, to the upper and middle classes – and it is also from these classes that the members of the state elite are predominantly ... drawn (Miliband, 1969, p. 55).

It is, in other words, a question of who the people who are professionally concerned in running the state are in terms of their class origins and what these origins mean for their beliefs and values.

> The assumption which is at work here is that a common social background and origin, education, connections, kinship, and friendship, a similar way of life, result in a cluster of common ideological and political positions and attitudes, common values and perspectives. ... [T]he state elite has tended to share the ideological and political presumptions of the economically dominant class (Miliband, 1977, p. 69).

Expressed most simply, the internal/personal mechanism focuses attention on the social origins and consequent ideological dispositions of the state elite. The task of ensuring that the requirements of the capitalist system are met is performed by the state because people who predominate within the state elite tend to believe in this system because they tend to come from privileged social backgrounds (Domhoff, 1979). This mechanism is, to refer back to Lukes's terminology, personal, internal and positive. Personal, because the mechanism involves the actions of identifiable individuals (agents), interpreted within the framework of a class analysis. Internal, because these individuals occupy leading positions within the institutions of the state. And positive, because these individuals bring to bear definite capacities – beliefs, values, knowledge, powers – in the formulation and implementation of policy. We might also, negatively, consider ways in which policies that are contradictory to the needs of capital are avoided or defeated. This might take the form of 'non-decision making', resistance to such policies or their amendment to lessen or ameliorate the impact on capital.

Notice also that the mechanism connects the state with the economic structure through the emphasis on the class origins of the state elite and connections with the capitalist class proper – it therefore clearly qualifies as a mechanism of economic determination. This also means that this 'internal' mechanism has a crucial 'external' moment: it is the external class origins and social milieu of members of the state elite that largely explain their ideological dispositions. This external connection is needed precisely to explain how a 'separate' state elite could nevertheless come to serve the interests of the dominant class, and thereby to count as a mechanism of economic determination. But the mechanism can be designated 'internal' because it points, in the first instance, to internal factors to explain class-based policies.

Of course the question of the ideological dispositions of state managers is not simply one of people bringing beliefs into the state with them from the outside. For 'appropriate' beliefs and values may be developed and reinforced within the state system through established routines, rules and cultures of state institutions, and processes of recruitment and socialisation into these cultures. In this way ideological dispositions that favour capitalist interests may not require class consciousness as they are rooted in 'common sense' assumptions about what constitute reasonable or sound policies, assumptions that may operate to some extent in an unselfconscious manner. The institutionalised common sense, historically developed, defines reasonableness and soundness in pro-capitalist terms. Such common sense may also be developed and/or sustained to some extent by the very capitalist context in which state managers operate, so that the capitalist system is taken for granted, accepted as given and beyond question. This is what Miliband alludes to when he refers to office-holders not being 'aware that they were helping to run a specific economic system, much in the way that they were not aware of the air they breathed ...' (1969, p. 65). Such unconscious assumptions can, of course, serve both to push 'reasonable' pro-capitalist policies on to the agenda as well as to keep 'beyond the pale' anti-capitalist policies off it. However these ideas point, respectively, towards the 'institutional logic' of the state system and the 'logic of capital' and, therefore, internal and external mechanisms of an impersonal kind.

The ideological dispositions of state managers are important because they do exercise power, but they do not do so in a vacuum and so policy can never be simply a reflection of these dispositions. Other interests are in play in the policy process. To start with, 'political office-holders ... have their own interest in mind when they weigh up policy choices', and there is 'one crucial consideration for people who occupy ministerial office, namely the fact that they very much want to continue doing so' (Miliband, 1984, p. 99). The force of this electoral imperative is reduced by the distinction between government and the wider state system in which it is located and which it formally directs. 'For the other parts of the state, ... which are ... much less vulnerable to popular pressures ... are ... able to act as bulwarks of continuity, stability, 'sound' and 'reasonable' policies' (Miliband, 1984, p. 100) while elected governments come and go. However, it would be putting this argument too strongly to suggest that governments do not formulate policies, and hence electoral considerations do matter. In any case, the idea of interests lodged inside the state extends beyond that of elected office-holders in the poll ratings. More generally, officialdom has a linked interest in securing legitimacy and the governability and stability of society.[3] Pro-capitalist ideological views have to be reconciled with this self-interest. They also have to be reconciled with pressures and demands coming from other social forces and interests, including a plethora of civil society groups but particularly working class 'pressure from below'. These other interests and pressures often conflict with the interests of the capitalist class. For example, in the interests of maintaining political order (and getting re-elected) office-holders may make concessions to working class demands even where these go against capitalist class interests. Therefore the ideological dispositions of the state elite clearly cannot guarantee pro-capitalist policies. But these dispositions will guide the direction of policy and shape the way other pressures are responded to. In other words, capitalist class interests are advantaged, and working class interests disadvantaged, by the ideological dispositions of the state elite. Thus dominant interests may be conceived as a maximand to be pursued by state managers within the constraints of conciliating other demands and maintaining legitimacy/support.

The response to working class demands will depend on the threat posed to capitalist interests. In some cases there may be congruence between the human needs of workers and the needs of capital, allowing a consensus between the major classes on the need for reform. Here 'both of the major classes see these policies as in their interests, but for quite different reasons' (Gough, 1979, p. 66). Pressure from below may be resisted where it poses a threat to capital, though it may be necessary to make concessions to this pressure in some circumstances in order to secure the legitimation of the system. In cases where acceding to demands for reform is seen by the state elite to be necessary or desirable, such reforms will be implemented so as to favour, or not to prejudice, the long-term interests of capital. For example, Saville (1957–8) draws attention to the importance of timing in consideration of the impact of a particular reform: a measure that may be seen as threatening the capitalist system at one moment may be easily accommodated at another. Ginsburg (1979) has argued that reforms, which are in part a response to pressure from below, may be implemented and administered in such a way as, in fact, to meet the needs of capital. In a similar vein Gough (1979) argues that the nature of the state will distort and weaken the ostensible aims of reforms to meet individual needs. For this reason 'the welfare state exhibits positive and negative features within a contradictory unity' (1979, p. 11). It is not that welfare reforms are simply and unambiguously intended to meet the needs of capital, as against individual human need, for they are in part a genuine response to pressure from below. Hence the positive and negative aspects of welfare, the conflict over the organisation and delivery of welfare services, but also, given the ideological dispositions of the state elite, the tendency for the organisation and delivery of services to favour capitalist interests. However the internal-personal mechanism does not, of course, stand alone: it may be 'over-determined' by other mechanisms which we have yet to consider.

Mechanism 2 – internal/impersonal

Marx's argument that the working class cannot simply take control of the existing state apparatus and use it for its own purpose may be taken to indicate that the capitalist bias of the state is not simply a question of the social composition of the state elite. This argument is taken up in Lenin's view that 'the State apparatus in a capitalist society is a distinctly *capitalist* apparatus, organized structurally – in form and content – to serve the capitalist class, and cannot possibly be taken over by the working class to serve its ends' (Carnoy, 1984, p. 59). The key idea here is that it is the very 'form' – or structure – of the state that explains why it serves the capitalist class. This form-determined bias would persist regardless of who is in charge of the state. There are two aspects to this argument. First, there is a general claim that the state, like any other institution or institutional complex, can never be neutral because 'its institutional form does have unequal and asymmetrical effects on the ability of different forces to pursue their interests' (Jessop, 1990, p. 117). All institutions are characterised by particular purposes, rules and practices, which constitute their distinctive 'institutional logic'. This means that institutions are always biased: they advantage certain interests and purposes and, by the same token, disadvantage others. Second, the form-determined bias of specific institutions needs to be characterised and explained. Thus, 'since state forms cannot be neutral, we must explore the structural or strategic selectivity inscribed in specific forms and regimes' (Jessop, 1990, p. 119). If the 'structural selectivity' of the state advantages the interests of the capitalist class this may be defined as an internal/impersonal mechanism of economic determination. Internal, because it is concerned with analysing what goes on inside the 'black box', and impersonal because it is concerned with structural properties rather than the personnel in charge of the state. However, Jessop argues that the idea of structural (or strategic) selectivity means that the state can neither be conceived as neutral nor as a capitalist state, pointing instead to the contingent and relational nature of state power. For Jessop and Lenin, form is important because it always involves 'selectivity' or bias. But for Jessop form 'problematises', whereas for Lenin it more-or-less guarantees, function (i.e. that the state functions in the interests of the capitalist class).

To establish such a mechanism it would be necessary to argue that the state system has its own 'rationality' in virtue of which it systematically tends to favour capitalist interests, regardless of the social composition of the state elite, pressure exerted by the capitalist class, or structural constraints. In other words the claim here would be that form facilitates or promotes function (Poulantzas, 1973; see also Jessop, 1990 pp. 61–72). For this purpose we can conceive the state system, following Jessop, as comprising forms of representation, internal organisation, and intervention. For example it could be argued that the form of representation typical of the modern capitalist state, parliamentary democracy, is functional for capital – a form of class rule. Lenin's claim that this form constitutes 'the best possible political shell' for the capitalist system is an argument of this type, although part of Lenin's argument is that the real business of government takes place away from parliament in the state apparatuses (Lenin, 1917; Hindess, 1980, p. 32) and this invokes the internal personal mechanism of the state elite. Nevertheless, the very form of parliamentary democracy is important in Lenin's argument insofar as this gives the appearance of popular power, thus concealing or mystifying the real mechanisms of power in the state and society (Carnoy, 1984; Wright, 1974–5). Similarly, Miliband emphasises the 'influence of capitalist democracy on labour movements' and claims that democracy 'has played a fundamental role in the containment and defusement of pressure from below', helping to explain why this pressure has been confined within reformist channels. For

> the existence of capitalist democracy has ensured that those who sought to exercise pressure from below did not for the most part feel that they had to look further than the existing constitutional and political system to achieve their purposes ... [T]he predominance of 'reformist' dispositions in the working class ... must surely be attributed to a political system deemed capable of affording remedy and reform (1987, p. 337).

One of the criticisms of Lenin's argument is that he fails to recognise the scope which democracy offers for the effective exercise of pressure from below, an important consideration in Miliband's analysis of the relative autonomy of the state from the capitalist class. However even while recognising this potentiality it is possible to maintain that democracy is beneficial for capital.

As regards the internal organisation of the state, it would be necessary to argue that there is compatibility between the form of state administration and the required functions of the state. This might be understood by conceiving the state system as a structure comprised of roles occupied by office-holders. The roles are positions within the state system defined in terms of specific purposes, powers, practices, and so on. This allows us to conceive state power not so much in terms of decisions by actors who control the power resources institutionalised by the state system, but in terms of the performance of these roles. These roles reveal the formal aspects of state institutions as organisations governed by rules. However institutions are also characterised by informal cultures, values, relationships and practices, and these may be enduring and contribute to shaping institutional 'rationality'. It follows that 'selectivity' will be an effect of these formal and informal aspects, of the balance between them, and their durability. For example, despite the weight normally attached to conventions of neutrality in the higher administrative reaches of liberal-democratic states, 'selectivity' in favour of capitalist interests may be largely explained in terms of informal culture and ideological dispositions, so that neutrality is a mask concealing class interests. Of course, office-holders are not mere personifications or bearers of formal roles or informal beliefs and practices. If this were so the social composition of the state elite would not matter. However, occupation is not the same thing as performance of a role, and not just because of informal influences, and therefore state power reflects the interaction between the composition and associated beliefs of the state elite and the structural properties of the state.[4]

Jessop prefers the idea of 'strategic selectivity' to 'structural selectivity', emphasising that the selectivity of the state is not fixed and not guaranteed to favour capitalist interests. For Jessop 'state power is a mediated effect of the balance of forces among *all* forces in a given situation' (1990, p. 118). Because it is the balance among all forces that matters this rules out state power being merely a reflection of class forces, let alone just the interests of the dominant class. And the possibility of state power reflecting any 'privileged' interests is ruled out by the contingency of the balance among all forces. Thus, although it is a possible outcome that state power is capitalist in the sense that it 'creates, maintains or restores the conditions required for capital accumulation in given circumstances', it could be non-capitalist in the sense of not creating, etc. these conditions (1990, p. 117). What Jessop rejects is 'the search for guarantees that the state apparatus and its functions are necessarily capitalist in all aspects' (1990, p. 118). However, to make his point Jessop aims his critique at an extremely strong version of the capitalist state thesis that possibly nobody believes in. It is not clear that Jessop has very good arguments against a weaker thesis that claims that there is a tendency (not guarantee) that some (not all) aspects of the state apparatus are capitalist in the sense he suggests.

The selectivity of the state has to be understood in relation to the strategies employed by social forces, in two senses. Selectivity is not merely inscribed in the form of the state because which forces are advantaged or disadvantaged depends on the strategies they adopt to gain access and political influence (Jessop, 1990, p. 260). But second, the form of the state is itself the product of past struggles by social forces to transform its structures in order to advantage their own interests – it is 'path-determined'. 'In this sense the current strategic selectivity of the state is in part the emergent effect of the interaction between its past patterns of strategic selectivity and the strategies adopted for its transformation' (Jessop, 1990, p. 261). In other words social forces struggle to use the existing form of the state to their best advantage, and to reorganise or transform the state to their greater advantage. If the balance among these forces, and their relative success in using/transforming the state in their own interests, ebbs and flows, then the selectivity of the state will be indeterminate. It will be necessary to undertake analyses of specific conjunctures in order to capture this selectivity, but it will not be possible to make generalisations from these specific cases precisely because of the ebbing and flowing. This is Jessop's position of contingent necessity. Yet there is no incompatibility between recognising that a multiplicity of social forces contend for political influence and advantage, and the claim that power resources are distributed among these forces asymmetrically. Thus, the balance among all forces may be such as to consistently favour the interests of a dominant interest, that is, the capitalist class. This may be understood as producing a tendency for the 'selectivity' of the state to advantage capitalist interests, a conceptualisation that lies somewhere in between Jessop's open-ended 'contingency' and his straw man 'guarantee'. Further, this does not suggest that this selectivity is an attribute of all aspects of the state. For the functional explanation of the legal and political superstructure only requires those limited aspects of the state that are economically relevant (in the sense supplied by the concept of needs of capital) to be capitalist. Finally, structural selectivity does not have to be conceived in a purely one-sided way. For example, the claim that 'bourgeois democracy' is the 'best political shell' for capitalism does not mean ignoring its two-sided character. In other words, democracy can be harnessed by the working class to press for reforms opposed by the capitalist class. Thus 'democratic forms are both an instrument and a danger for the bourgeoisie' (Carnoy, 1984, p. 51). Selectivity here means that capitalist interests are advantaged and working class interests are disadvantaged, not that the former enjoy 'exclusive political sway'. It can also be added that, for the same reasons, an institution can embody more than one form of selectivity. For example the police force may be institutionally selective in favour of capitalist interests and be, at the same time, institutionally racist. The first form of selectivity contributes to the stabilisation of the economic structure. The second arguably is irrelevant to the needs of capital.

Jessop argues that state power is a reflection of the balance among social forces, and this focuses attention on the strategies employed to use and/or transform the state in pursuit of advantage. However this society-centred emphasis needs to be balanced with recognition of internal, state-centred, processes which tend to embed or institutionalise certain patterns of selectivity through the establishment and reproduction of formal roles and through informal beliefs and practices. This may be reinforced by the tendency of state institutions to become self-referential (Poggi, 1990). This suggests that the state will be somewhat resilient to change, as strategies to transform the state run up against in-built sources of inertia and self-reproduction. Thus, selectivity in favour of capitalist interests can become entrenched and self-sustaining. This is an important internal dimension of selectivity. Nevertheless, there must ultimately be external causes of the state's selectivity and these may be traced, in a Marxist account, to the strategies employed by the dominant class to gain political access and influence, and the adjustment of the state to constraints emanating from the economic structure. Thus, the internal-impersonal mechanism can be located within a theory of economic determination.

Mechanism 3 – external/personal

As noted earlier, the internal mechanisms do not stand alone: in considering how far economic determination extends other mechanisms must be taken in conjunction. Indeed to count as mechanisms of economic determination they must have underlying external economic mechanisms. Miliband says that the ideological dispositions of the state elite have made it easier for them to submit to pressure from above, that is, from the capitalist class.[5] Here we are dealing with an external/personal mechanism: personal because, again, the mechanism involves the actions of identifiable individuals, interpreted within the framework of a class analysis; external, because the capitalist class is separate from and external to the state. Notice also that the class analysis through which this mechanism is explicated clearly connects the state with the economic structure – it therefore clearly qualifies as a mechanism of economic determination.

At one level this mechanism is hard to disentangle from the first, partly because capitalists are directly involved in running the state, albeit constituting a minority only of the state elite as a whole. In addition, members of the state elite, while not being predominantly capitalists, are predominantly drawn from the class to which capitalists belong – what Miliband refers to as the 'upper and middle classes' (1969, p. 55). Elsewhere Miliband further claims that 'in contemporary capitalism, members of the bourgeoisie tend to predominate in the three main sectors of social life- the economic, the political and the cultural/ideological' (1977, pp. 68–9)- and that a 'dominant class' is constituted by virtue of effective control over the three main sources of domination corresponding to these sectors: the means of production; the means of state administration and coercion; and, the means of communication and consent (1987, p. 329). The existence of conflicts within this dominant class is recognised but the dominant class usually remains 'sufficiently cohesive to ensure that their common purposes are effectively defended and advanced' (1987, p. 331). Within this dominant class 'the main sources of power [are identified as] ... corporate power and state power' (1987, p. 329) which are 'institutionally separate, even though the links between the two forms of power are many and intimate' (1987, p. 330). Together big capital (those who control the few hundred largest corporations) and the state elite comprise 'the power elite'. Miliband even conceives the relationship that constitutes this power elite as a 'partnership' (1989, p. 32). These arguments, particularly the locating of corporate and state elites together within a dominant class or power elite, tend to blur the distinction between an internal and external mechanism. However the argument must be that pressure from above would be exerted upon the state whatever the social composition and ideological dispositions of the state elite. The third mechanism here is not predicated upon the first, although it does strengthen it. In Miliband's view the social composition of the state elite does not provide a sufficiently strong mechanism on which to base the economic determination which Marxism asserts and requires. 'In other words, the class bias of the state is not determined, or at least not decisively and conclusively determined, by the social origins of its leading personnel' (1977, p. 71).

This mechanism can obviously be conceived as taking a variety of possible forms. In Lukes' terminology, pressure from above to influence or shape the purposes of governments and office-holders diminishes the autonomy of the state. Resistance to the implementation of policy that prevents the state from realising its aims diminishes the freedom of the state. In either case the mechanism may be positive or negative. Pressure may be exerted, positively, through political parties, campaign contributions, lobbying and public relations efforts, and so on in support of policies which are in the long-term interests of capital and against those which threaten those interests or needs. Negatively, pressure may be brought to bear through resistance to or non-compliance with government policy, withdrawal of co-operation with government, or by the refusal or failure of capitalists to accumulate when public policy is seen as unfavourable.

It can be argued that the external/personal mechanism of pressure from above may operate through the three main forms of power which Miliband identifies: economic, political, and ideological (1987). Politically pressure may be exerted via the forms of representation characteristic of capitalist democracy as a form of state, particularly political parties and campaigns (note again that this external mechanism tends to coalesce with the internal mechanism via links with the state elite). Ideologically pressure may be exerted in virtue of the effective control over the means of communication and consent (the media), either through influence directly over policy-makers or over popular attitudes and beliefs. Economically the capitalist class is able to exert pressure upon the state 'by virtue of its control of the larger part of the country's industrial, commercial, and financial means of activity, and its capacity to make decisions of vital concern not only to the particular firm but to many interests beyond it, up to the whole of society' (1984, p. 95). The decision of most vital concern is of course to renew the circuit of capital and enlarge it via accumulation.

How strong is this mechanism? How far does it take us as a plausible mechanism of economic determination of the state? The claim that the capitalist class constitutes the most powerful 'pressure group' (Miliband, 1984, p. 97) is clearly crucial to this argument. For it entails the rejection of a pluralist understanding of the fragmentation of power and therefore seems to permit the expectation that the capitalist class will normally hold sway.[6] In fact, the mechanism requires that the capitalist class is more than the 'strongest pressure group in the land' if this means that it gets its own way merely more often than other pressure groups, for it arguably must be able to do so routinely, and certainly always in decisive matters touching upon the needs of capital. Related to this, the claim that effective control is exercised over economic, political and ideological sources of power is also crucial for it provides an understanding of the comprehensive means whereby such powerful pressure from above might be exerted. However Miliband acknowledges problems with reliance on this mechanism.

> Capitalist enterprise is undoubtedly the strongest 'pressure group' in capitalist society; and it is indeed able to command the attention of the state. But this is not the same as saying that the state is the 'instrument' of the capitalist class; and the pressure which business is able to apply upon the state is not in itself sufficient to explain the latter's actions and policies (1977, p. 72).

In other words the mechanism is not strong enough to bear the weight of economic determination required by the theory. It is weakened by precisely those considerations which led Miliband to assert the necessity of the relative autonomy of the state from the capitalist class: the disunity of the class and its unwillingness or inability to act strategically. In Miliband's analysis we might say that the two personal mechanisms of economic determination (internal and external) are related in the following way. The relative autonomy of the state from the capitalist class is necessary, in part, because of the inability of the class to govern directly, yet pressure from above is necessary because the social composition of the state elite does not in itself ensure the instrumentality or functionality of the state. The two mechanisms may be said to be mutually reinforcing: any deficiency in the capacity of the class to act as a pressure group is compensated by the ideological dispositions of the state elite, and *vice-versa*. On the other hand the two mechanisms may be said to follow from mutually contradictory premises. The need for the state to be relatively autonomous from the capitalist class follows, in part, from the inability of the class to act as a class and allows the state to act as a capitalist state. On the other hand the need for the capitalist class to act as a pressure group follows, in part, from the possibility that a relatively autonomous state may not act in the long-term interests of capital and presumes that the class does have the ability to act as a class.

Both types of personal mechanism involve a number of implicit assumptions which it is worth making explicit. Briefly, they assume on the part of the individuals involved a high degree of rationality to recognise what the needs of capital are, and both a willingness and capacity to act to meet those needs. If objective interests are to be the basis for the explanation of action there must be a high level of understanding on the part of actors of what these interests are. In short subjective or perceived interests – understandings on the part of actors of what their interests are – must tend systematically to come into line with real – objective – interests. This is, in essence, the idea of 'class-consciousness' upon which the Marxist notion of classes as 'collective actors' ultimately rests. Although there is no automatic correspondence between objective and subjective interests, as agents may misrecognise their true interests, a tendency for such correspondence to emerge is argued on the basis that 'being determines consciousness'. Specifically in relation to the capitalist class and other historical privileged classes, Miliband maintains that 'as a matter of historical fact, privileged classes have always been perfectly class-conscious' (1977, p. 31), at least in the sense of understanding that their true interests 'consist in the maintenance and defence' of the status quo. However the theory clearly requires more than this basic class-consciousness. There must be a capacity to formulate and implement class-based strategies. A particularly important aspect of this problem, given the recognition that there are potential conflicts of interest within the capitalist class and between capital and the state, is the willingness to subordinate sectional interests to the needs of capital as a whole. Either the capitalist class must be able to overcome its internal divisions – an ability over which Miliband casts some doubt – or there must be some agent to act on its behalf. There are two possible candidates to act as agent: the relatively autonomous state (i.e. the state elite) and/or a hegemonic fraction of the dominant class. What is at stake here is not the capacity to identify a set of policies that uniquely express the needs of capital, but to formulate and implement a viable 'accumulation strategy'. Viable accumulation strategies, of which there are always more than one, will tend to advantage certain economic sectors or class fractions at the expense of others while being adequate to secure the necessary conditions for capital accumulation. Assuming rationality and willingness, the personal mechanism of economic determination must assume or claim that the relevant individuals (class, fraction or elite) have the capacity to secure the needs of capital against contradictory interests. What this means, in particular, within the framework of class analysis put forward by Miliband, is that the capitalist class (or its agents) must be successful in the class struggle with the subordinate class. This is fundamentally a question of the power resources controlled by the capitalist class relative to other forces and interests. It is clear that these assumptions are all to some extent problematic, and the external/personal mechanism of pressure from above certainly does not provide a guarantee of state policies adequate to meet the needs of capital. But it may provide a strong tendency. It operates in conjunction with the internal mechanisms, and in the context of the force of structural constraints.

Mechanism 4 – external/impersonal

This mechanism is arguably the most fundamental, underlying the other three. It refers, in Miliband's words, to

> a 'structural' dimension, of an objective and impersonal kind. In essence, the argument is simply that the state is the 'instrument' of the 'ruling class' because, given its insertion in the capitalist mode of production, it cannot be anything else. The question does not, on this view, depend on the personnel of the state, or on the pressure which the capitalist class is able to bring upon it: the nature of the state is here determined by the nature and requirements of the mode of production. There are 'structural constraints' which no government, whatever its complexion, wishes, and promises, can ignore or evade. A capitalist economy has its own 'rationality' to which any government and state must sooner or later submit, and usually sooner (1977, p. 72).

This mechanism is impersonal and external. Impersonal because it involves the rationality of the system as such or, as we have seen Lukes express it (1985, p. 72), 'anonymous and impersonal processes and relationships' rather than 'specified intentional acts by specified

persons'. External because the system, or economic structure, is institutionally separate from the state. Notice that the mechanism establishes
a direct link between the operation of the economic system and the
actions of the state and thus qualifies as a mechanism of economic
determination.

In characterising this mechanism as impersonal it is not meant to
say that acts by persons are not involved, or even that these acts and
these persons cannot be specified. Indeed the system can only work,
and its rationality be expressed, in and through specified acts by
specified persons. Thus the circuit of capital operates through the
relationships and processes of ownership, exchange and production
between capitalists and proletarians. Neither the actors or the acts are
anonymous – their identities are all open to observation. However we
can conceive an 'impersonal' mechanism operating 'anonymously'
in two ways. In the first sense, which seems to be what Lukes has in
mind in his example of 'when I cannot find a job' (1985, p. 72), my
purpose being prevented from being realised is an unintended aggregate outcome or effect of the interaction of a large number of decisions
by independent actors. The mechanism is anonymous and impersonal
because my plight is not the intended outcome of a specified act and
responsibility for it cannot be attributed to specified persons. However
Miliband, and Marxism generally, invokes a second and stronger sense
of an external/impersonal mechanism. It is impersonal and anonymous in the same sense that structural constraints are effects of the
system, not attributable as intended effects of specified acts. The crucial
difference lies in the claim that the system has its own rationality.
This rationality is seen as being quite apart from, and indeed logically
prior to, the purposes and actions of individual agents. In this
view, expressed in Marx's characterisation of capitalists as 'capital personified', agents act in a particular way because of the positions or roles
they occupy in the economic structure – 'being determines consciousness'. Structural constraints emerge as necessary effects of structures of
a particular type.

It should be clear that this mechanism is not predicated on the
others we have discussed – the structure will impose constraints upon
the state regardless of who is in the leading positions within the state,
its institutional logic, or what pressure is exerted from above. Indeed
Miliband suggests that these constraints are themselves sufficient
to guarantee that the state is a capitalist state – in virtue of the constraints, which cannot be evaded, it 'cannot be anything else'. In
this view the state appears to have no room for manoeuvre – its own

purposes are as nothing in face of the structural constraints. If the constraints really were that stringent we would have here all the explanation – all the economic determination – of the state that the theory needs. But arguing along these lines leads into what Miliband, in his response to Poulantzas, refers to as the '"hyperstructuralist" trap', which he is careful to avoid.[7] In Miliband's more modest but somewhat non-committal view, 'There are "structural constraints" – but how constraining they are is a difficult question' (1977, p. 73). Indeed this is the central question, and in order to answer it we need to know rather more about what these constraints consist of and how they constrain: the 'explanation is relatively empty if the nature of these "structural constraints" cannot be specified' (Gough, 1979, p. 43).

There seem to be two main understandings of the notion of structural constraint. In the passage from Miliband quoted above the understanding we are given is in terms of 'the nature and requirements of the mode of production'. At another point we have seen that reference is made to the 'imperative requirements of capital'. Thus, the notion of structural constraints may be understood as a form of expression for the needs of capital. In that case the point about the impersonal mechanism is that it suggests that these needs impinge directly on the state as well as being articulated through the personal mechanisms we have discussed. They impinge directly in virtue of the dependence of the state on revenue generated in and extracted from the capitalist sector. The second understanding is expressed in the idea of there being limits to state action or reform. It is this understanding which figures in Miliband's elaboration of the notion of structural constraint when he says that

> the strength of the 'structural' explanation is that it helps us to understand why governments act as they do – for instance why governments pledged to far-reaching reforms .... have more often than not failed to carry out more than at best a very small part of their reforming programme (1977, p. 73).

The first understanding purports to explain why governments *do* certain things – responding to imperative needs of capital – while the second purports to explain why they do *not* do other things – failing to implement reforms in the face of structurally determined constraints which impose limits on what they can do. In other words structural constraints determine what the state must do as well as what it cannot do. The two understandings are not mutually exclusive and are, in fact, closely related. This can be seen through consideration of the idea of the crisis of the welfare state. The long postwar boom created the conditions for the growth of social expenditure. On the one hand rapid accumulation allowed state revenues to increase and created the space in which reforming governments (or governments willing to sustain programmes of reform in response to popular pressure) could commit resources to an expanding welfare state. At the same time it can be argued that these welfare policies were a response to the needs of capital, particularly for the reproduction of labour power. The end of the long boom and the onset of crisis created conditions of crisis of the welfare state. As accumulation faltered governments faced a growing fiscal crisis from around the early 1970s – a tendency for expenditures to outrun revenues – and found that the space for reform was eroded. Hence cuts and retrenchment within the welfare state. These conditions also created a crisis of social democracy as an ideology and programme principally associated with the welfare state. At the same time cuts in social expenditure can be seen as part of a strategy to restore conditions of accumulation – hence as a response to the needs of capital. Hence the crisis of the welfare state can be interpreted both as effect of the economic crisis (and so illustrative of the limits to state action understanding of structural constraints) and as response to economic crisis to restore profitability (illustrative of the requirements of capital understanding) (see Gamble, 1988; Mishra, 1984; Taylor-Gooby, 1985).

Expressed in Lukes' terms structural constraints can be understood as both positive – the requirements of capital are experienced as imperatives – and negative – limits to state action result from a deteriorating revenue base. The requirements of capital impose certain purposes on the state and thus impinge on its autonomy, while the structural limits to state action may be said to diminish its freedom. Both forms of the external/impersonal mechanism work through the nature of the structural relationship between the state and capital. The state is both excluded from the circuit of capital and the process of capital accumulation in virtue of the institutional separation of the state and economy and, at the same time, dependent on capital for its own revenues (Offe, 1984, p. 120). Exclusion from the circuit of capital means that the state cannot organise production for its own ends. Its consequent dependence on private capital accumulation to generate revenues for the state means both that it has to implement policies that are conducive to accumulation, and that there are fiscal limits to its freedom of action according to the volume of revenue that can be withdrawn from the circuit. Governments must both secure the needs of capital and confine their programmes within limits consistent with the pace of accumulation for fear, as Elster puts it, of 'killing the goose that lays the golden eggs'. The basic claim that is being made here is that all governments, whatever the detail of their own purposes and commitments, have a self-interest in securing the needs of capital since the health of the economy determines their own freedom of manoeuvre and capacity to realise their own objectives, whatever they are (Offe, 1984, p. 120; Held, 1989, p. 71).

As to the question of how constraining these constraints are, part of the answer is obviously that they loosen and tighten with the rhythm of boom and slump of the economic cycle. Within that cyclical pattern Miliband, we have seen, argues that structural constraints never determine absolutely and decisively what governments do – there is always some room for manoeuvre, or 'relative autonomy'. Nevertheless if the concept of the needs of capital is a plausible one, if there really are objective conditions which must be met if capitalism is to continue as a system, then these constraints must be seen as binding. The strong understanding of the concept of need as a condition of existence of the system can only permit limited flexibility or discretion on the part of the state.[8] Whatever else the state does within the fiscal limits imposed by the accumulation process, these conditions must be secured.

As with the other mechanisms discussed this one does not stand alone – all four may be said to be mutually reinforcing. Although the impersonal mechanism is not predicated on the personal ones and seems to be independent of them it is worth considering the relationship between them. Taking the internal/personal mechanism first, we have come across the idea that the purposes of office-holders may be shaped by the context in which they formulate and implement policy. The economic structure may exercise a 'dull compulsion' over office-holders insofar as they take this context as given and become habituated to operating according to its requirements and within its limits. In this way the rationality of the capitalist economy may not in fact be experienced as something to which governments must sooner or later 'submit', as imposing artificial constraints, but more as a natural order. In a similar way structural properties of the state – its internal rules and practices – may adjust to these external constraints, perhaps through a trial-and-error search for the best institutional fit.

The relationship to the external/personal mechanism, the exercise of economic power by capitalists to exert pressure from above, seems more problematic. We appear to have here two contradictory understandings of the operation of the capitalist economy. One emphasises the capacity of capitalists as agents to take decisions concerning the circuit of capital and accumulation so as to bring pressure to bear on the state (e.g. through investment strikes or capital flight). The other emphasises that the system has its own rationality. In one the functioning of the system is the outcome of the actions of capitalists; in the other the actions of capitalists are the outcome of the functioning of the system. At root we are dealing here with the structure-agency dilemma. The two mechanisms can be reconciled by arguing that capitalists, and other economic agents, are not merely 'bearers' of objective economic relations. In other words it is necessary to argue that the actions of capitalists are very strongly determined by the positions (roles) they occupy in the capitalist system of production (sufficiently so that the system can be said to exhibit its own rationality), but to allow space for agency so that capitalists do exercise choice and discretion (sufficiently so that economic power can constitute a form of pressure from above). However, in exercising pressure on the state capitalists carry over into the political sphere interests that are shaped or determined by the roles in the economic structure that constitute their being.

Summary

We have now completed our discussion of conceivable 'mechanisms' of economic determination which purport to show how the state (insofar as it is part of the superstructure) is functionally explained by the nature of the economic structure. The four mechanisms we have discussed, classified using Lukes' conceptual framework for understanding freedom and autonomy, are tabulated below.

Mechanisms of Economic Determination	PERSONAL	IMPERSONAL
INTERNAL	Ideological Dispositions of State Elite	Rationality of State System
EXTERNAL	Pressure From Above	Structural Constraints

These mechanisms can be related to our analysis of the nature of the economic structure. It was argued that the concepts of 'class interests' and 'needs of capital', derived from an analysis of the nature of the economic structure, provide starting points or foundations for a Marxist theory of the state. The relation between these two concepts is that 'needs of capital' constitute a subset of dominant class interests. Both are structural concepts since needs are defined in terms of the rationality of the system and interests are objectively defined by the nature of the relations of production which comprise the economic structure. This chapter has shown that the structural (impersonal) explanation of the state invokes a mechanism wherein 'structural constraints' impinge directly on the state, whereas class struggle (personal) explanation invokes a mechanism wherein the needs of capital are mediated by some form of class agency. In both cases the foundation concepts are structural and thus we would maintain that structural (functional) explanation is primary.

9
Globalisation, History and the State

Introduction – The challenge of globalisation

What connection is there between globalisation and the central concerns of this book? It is certainly true that the globalisation debate looms large in much recent state theory, and it is certainly of prime interest to Marxists. On these accounts it seems to merit some consideration here. The central 'problem' analysed in state theory is the disjuncture between the stretching of social interaction that is the hallmark of globalisation and the territorial confinement of the nation-state. Or, between political power and other forms of social power. Thus far we have not considered the nation-state explicitly and the argument has largely been conducted in abstraction from the spatial dimension. This is because our focus has been on the state in the theory of history, as an aspect of the superstructure, and we have followed Cohen's highly abstract exposition of the theory. In considering the nature and implications of globalisation we can integrate a spatial dimension into the theory of history. This is particularly appropriate for an analysis of the capitalist state, given the close connection between capitalism and globalisation.

The concept of globalisation (if not the word itself) is central to Marx's characterisation of capitalism as an economic system. Indeed, 'Marx has some claim to the status of the first major theorist of globalisation' (Bromley, 1999, p. 280). However, even if Marx's analysis of capitalist globalisation is accepted as broadly valid, this does not mean there is consistency with other areas of Marxist theory. In particular it is worth enquiring whether there is a proper connection between the analysis of economic globalisation and the theory of history and the theory of the state.

If globalisation is seen as essentially an economic process, connected to the nature of the relations of production, this raises questions about the functional relationships between the forces and relations of production, and between the base and superstructure (i.e. stage 1 and stage 2 of the theory of history). The question here is: is there a plausible account of economic globalisation that is consistent with the central claims of the theory of history and, more specifically, the theory of the state? Or, does globalisation undermine these areas of Marxist theory?

What is globalisation?

'Globalization, simply put, denotes the expanding scale, growing magnitude, speeding up and deepening impact of transcontinental flows and patterns of social interaction' (Held and McGrew, 2002, p. 1).[1] Scale refers to the spatial or geographic reach of social interaction. Thus the term 'refers to a shift or transformation in the scale of human organization that links distant communities and expands the reach of power relations across the world's regions and continents' (ibid.). Similarly Bromley defines globalisation in 'general and abstract terms ... [as] ... the disembedding of social interaction from particular local contexts and its generalised extension across space' (1999, p. 281).[2] In other words, globalisation involves the 'stretching' of social relations in space.[3] We can say that expanding scale or reach is the essence of globalisation, being contrasted with more limited scales such as, notably, the national. In this sense the notion of 'the global' is largely synonymous with 'beyond the national'. For example, the idea of an emerging global economy may be contrasted with a previous era of national economies. Thus the process of globalisation can be defined in terms of 'the expansion and intensification of economic, political, social and cultural relations across borders' (Sorensen, 2004, p. 23), meaning across *national* borders. Much of the debate about globalisation and its implications concerns precisely this disjuncture: between social interaction that reaches across the world's regions and continents, and a world that is divided up into territorial nation-states with borders. The challenge this poses is one of regulation and control, where the reach of economic and other relations and interactions is increasingly moving beyond that of the territorially bounded nation-state as the still predominant form of political power.

Although globalisation involves the stretching of social relations across borders beyond the national scale, Jessop says it denotes 'multiscalar' processes – 'it emerges from actions on many scales' (2002, p. 113). In fact, neither 'national' nor 'global' can really be said to refer to a specific or determinate spatial scale of social interaction. For example, the concept of a national economy encompasses economic interactions on many scales at the sub-national level. What makes for a 'national economy' is that the national level constitutes the limit or horizon for many, or most, interactions. Of course, the idea of a closed national economy is a fiction, and economic interactions across borders are certainly not novel. But globalisation also, as Jessop points out, involves actions on many scales, not all of which are truly global (whatever that means). So we might conceive of economic interaction as tendentially global in the sense, again, that a global reach is the limit or horizon of action (Jessop, 2002, p. 116). In this view globalisation is not a condition but a process of increasing globality. For example: 'While globalization obviously develops unevenly in both space and time, it can be said to increase insofar as the covariation of relevant activities is spatially more extensive and/or occurs more rapidly' (Jessop. 2002, p. 114).

'Speeding up' (in the definition from Held and McGrew given above) is important in part because transnational or transcontinental interaction becomes more feasible, and so can grow in volume or magnitude, as it becomes faster (and, we should also add, cheaper).[4] For example, transatlantic travel and trade was possible in the sixteenth century but was restricted by the length, cost and hazardous nature of the sea passage. Hence globalisation is made possible by technological revolutions in the fields of transport and communications making for increased speed and/or lower cost. 'Growing magnitude' is part of the definition insofar as globalisation denotes that transcontinental flows are not merely marginal within the overall pattern of social interaction but assume a growing weight and intensity. Thus they have a 'deepening impact'.

There are, of course, many forms of social interaction, meaning that globalisation, on this definition, is multi-faceted. It involves, 'in the broadest sense, … economic, political, social and cultural relations' (Sorensen, 2004, p. 23; Gill, 2003; King & Kendall, 2004). Thus globalisation does not denote a single process but a set of processes that may interact in complex ways. Similarly, Jessop sees globalisation as multi-causal – 'it results from the complex, contingent interaction of many different causal processes' (2002, p. 114). This is what Sorensen refers to as a broad concept of globalisation 'involving all aspects of social reality', contrasted with a narrow concept which sees it as 'a primarily economic process' (2004, p. 25). Marxism's commitment to economic determination means that it focuses on economic globalisation. But this is not a narrow concept in the sense that it focuses on the economic dimension to the exclusion of the 'broader sociological process' (Sorensen, 2004, p. 25). Rather, globalisation is a primarily economic process in the sense, and to the extent, that it drives forward and shapes other types of social interaction across borders. For example, cultural interactions and influences are largely carried by international trade in cultural goods and services and the activities of multinational corporations (MNCs) in the culture industries. The transformation of states will also, in this view, largely be explained as an effect of, or response to, economic globalisation. This does not preclude the many ways in which states may be seen as 'authors' of economic globalisation, but it does not see globalisation as 'both a cause and a consequence' (Sorensen, 2004, p. 23) insofar as this entails an interactionist view of the relation between the economic and political dimensions. Rather, it assigns causal primacy to the economy and emphasises the inherent developmental tendencies of the capitalist economy, driven forward by profit-oriented firms in a competitive environment.

This intrinsic connection between economic globalisation and the nature of a capitalist economy is identified by Marx and Engels in *The Communist Manifesto* (Renton, 2001). The transition from feudalism to capitalism (the manufacturing system) is attributed to 'the growing wants of the new markets' (Marx & Engels, 1976, p. 485) opened up by European expansion, and the subsequent establishment of Modern Industry goes hand-in-hand with that of 'the world market' (and the conquering by the bourgeoisie of 'exclusive political sway') (p. 486). Economic globalisation is seen as an expression of the inherent dynamism of capitalism. Just as 'the bourgeoisie cannot exist without constantly revolutionising the instruments of production' (p. 487), at the same time:

> The need of a constantly expanding market for its products chases the bourgeoisie over the whole surface of the globe. ... The bourgeoisie has through its exploitation of the world market given a cosmopolitan character to production and consumption in every country. ... In place of the old local and national seclusion and self-sufficiency, we have intercourse in every direction, universal interdependence of nations. ... [The bourgeoisie] creates a world after its own image (pp. 487–8).

The Communist Manifesto characterises capitalism as a tendentially global system in the sense that the global level constitutes the limit or horizon of action of profit-oriented capitalist firms. It follows that economic globalisation is nothing new. However the analysis errs both in overstating the extent to which economic globalisation had already progressed in the mid-nineteenth century, and in characterising it too one-sidedly as an ineluctable process. In overstating the level of globalisation the *Communist Manifesto* can be seen as looking forward, so that 'the world transformed by capitalism ... is recognisably the world in which we live 150 years later' (Hobsbawm, 1998, p. 31). Thus globalisation can be seen as novel in the sense of new *forms* and/or an unprecedented *level* of globalisation in recent decades.[5] Yet the image of the bourgeoisie being chased over the whole world needs to be tempered by recognition of inhibiting factors, some of which are intrinsic to the nature of a capitalist economy. In other words, there are advantages and disadvantages to foreign trade and investment. For example, though the search for constantly expanding (or 'newly emerging') markets chases the bourgeoisie over the whole surface of the globe, on the other hand international trade is still dominated by those areas of the surface where markets are well developed, that is the advanced capitalist economies. At the same time the globalising tendency of capitalism requires favourable external conditions for its realisation and can be checked by unfavourable conditions or external shocks.

Thus a globalising tendency inherent in capitalist relations of production may be consistent with some of the claims of the 'sceptics': that the level of economic interdependence between countries today is similar to that of the so-called *'belle epoque'*, and that the world today is characterised by regionalisation or triadisation. For the globe can constitute the horizon of action while economic interaction is still dominated, in practice, by the regional level. And the underlying globalising tendency can be held in check by unfavourable conditions, such as the two world wars and great depression that followed the 'belle époque' in the period 1914–45. In contrast the postwar decades provided favourable economic and political circumstances.

Summarising, globalisation can be seen as a primarily economic process. Although this process is multi-scalar it can be understood in a limited way as the stretching of economic interaction beyond the nation-state, that is across national borders. This approach cuts short the debate as to whether a truly global economy has yet emerged (or will do so).[6] Economic globalisation is a tendential process linked to the basic character of capitalist relations of production and the accumulation process – profit-oriented capitals operating in a competitive environment. In other words 'capitalism, as a social order, has a pathological expansionist logic' (Held & McGrew, 2002, p. 4). In this sense economic globalisation is nothing new, but there may be novel aspects in terms of its specific forms and/or overall level. From a Marxist perspective, based on economic determination, the key question is to what extent economic globalisation shapes other dimensions of social interaction, especially the state and political power.

Globalisation and the theory of history

The theory of history concerns the relationship between the productive forces, the set of production relations that a society has, and the character of its legal and political superstructure. The theory comprises two stages of functional explanation:

Stage 1 – the stage of development of the forces of production functionally explains the nature of the relations of production

Stage 2 – the nature of the relations of production functionally explains the character of the legal and political superstructure

Relations of production are selected because, and persist so long as, they are forms of development of the productive forces. In turn, laws and other phenomena that make up the superstructure are selected, and persist so long as, they are functionally effective in stabilising the economic structure. In this theory history is fundamentally a story of productive progress. It is so because of some aspects of human nature. Humans are rational and intelligent and will take advantage of opportunities for productive progress (improved labour productivity) to reduce scarcity. These opportunities are choices of appropriate production relations that, given the stage of development of the productive forces, will drive productive improvement. And related choices of appropriate laws that will stabilise these relations and so secure the desired productivity gains.

What are the implications of globalisation for the theory of history? In order to see these it is useful to pose the question in a more general way. The more general question is: how is a spatial dimension incorporated in the theory of history? Space is included by Cohen in the set of productive forces, although his arguments for this designation are questionable. Of course it is true that everything that happens,

happens in space, and so space 'is certainly indispensable to putting in hand any productive process' (Cohen, 1978, p. 51). This means that ownership or, more strictly, effective control of space is necessary for any productive process. For this reason it may be accepted that 'Ownership of space certainly confers a position in the economic structure'. Of course, that position can be as subordinate producer (e.g. serf) or member of the dominant class, according to the overall pattern of ownership of labour power and means of production. As Cohen shows, a proletarian can, in principle, own space or land which is used for production, but remain a proletarian because this space, and other means of production, can only be used as a means of livelihood by contracting with a capitalist (1978, pp. 70–3). Conversely it is not necessary for a capitalist to own land, and neither are landowners necessarily capitalists. Capitalists may rent land from private landlords or from the state. Finally, it is not effective control of just any space that is necessary for production, but only space that is productively useful. Ownership of space that is not productively useful clearly does not confer a position in the economic structure.[7]

However although space is clearly productively useful (indispensable) it is not clear that it is used in production in the relevant sense. Obviously space is used in the sense that it is occupied by the direct producers, the instruments of production they work with and the raw materials they work on. But space is not used in the same way that instruments and materials are used. Specifically, space does not have 'productive power, the power to make or be made into products', which is characteristic of productive forces (Cohen, 1978, p. 37). Space is simply where productive power is exercised but does not partake of that exercise.[8]

Cohen says that 'something like a development of space does occur' and cites 'the conquest of new spaces' and 'improved use of existing spaces' (1978, pp. 51–2). It is certainly true that both of these processes contribute to expansion of the ability to produce by having more space to use for production and by getting more production out of each portion of space. Insofar as space is a finite resource and using any portion of it cannot leave 'as much and as good' left for others, using space more efficiently contributes to expansion of ability to produce (i.e. development of the productive forces) in the same way as using other scarce resources more efficiently.[9] But although it is customary to speak of developing new sites (conquest) it is arguable that the space itself is not developed, only that development takes place within it.[10]

If space is not included in the set of productive forces because it lacks productive power, then its ownership cannot confer a position in the economic structure, because 'Persons and productive forces are the terms of production relations' (Cohen, 1978, p. 34). Yet it is clearly the case that ownership of space may be a source of economic power because of its indispensability to production. Cohen's presentation seems to go wrong in seeing relations of economic power as being based only in effective control over things that possess productive power. Whereas in fact economic power is based on control of any resources which are necessary for production, and that evidently includes space.

Although it is useful to distinguish analytically between space and its contents so that space is conceived as contentless, this is not conventional usage. Space customarily refers to a portion of the surface of Earth (which is customarily thought to include the earth below and the airspace above the surface, etc.). In this usage a portion of space is described by its location and by its material properties or contents, such as the character of the soil or rock. Larger spaces (countries, regions, continents) may be characterised also in terms of their climatic conditions. This notion of space is tantamount to geography and plays a fundamental role in the theory of history. For history is the result of a struggle with nature, with the physical environment in which humans find themselves. History – which is fundamentally the growth of human productive power – happens because 'man's environment is – generally hostile to him' (Cohen, 1978, p. 23). In other words humans occupy a generally hostile space. Space is a requisite of all human activity, but it is also the contents of the specific spaces that humans occupy with which they have to struggle, which they strive to transform, and from which they secure their material needs and 'produce their life' (Marx, quoted in Cohen, 1978, p. 23). Of course, while being generally hostile, the particular and varied spaces occupied by humans will be more or less so, that is more or less productively useful. Different spaces are, for example, more or less rich sources of energy and raw materials. This variability of environmental conditions will go some way to explain why productive development occurs earlier or faster in some areas than in others (Diamond, 1998; Carling & Nolan, 2000).

In sum, space plays two related roles in the theory of history. In the first it is defined inclusive of its contents, and in the second in abstraction from its contents, as pure space. In the first meaning space denotes geography or nature, the struggle against which is the basis of history as productive development. In this sense space is the original source of raw materials which are productive forces, used (worked on) by producing agents to make products (Cohen, 1978, p. 32). Second, abstract or pure space is a requisite of production and its ownership, or effective control, confers economic power (though it is questionable whether space is a productive force and so whether it is a term of production relations).

However the spatial dimension needs to be incorporated in the theory of history in a more thorough-going way. The concept of space as productively useful and, consequently, a source of economic power does not tell us anything about the spatial scale or level of social interaction. This is a missing dimension of Cohen's presentation of the theory of history.[11] The spatial scale of social interaction has complex effects on social integration and system integration.[12] For example:

- Spatial proximity or distance may influence opportunities for communication, feelings of community and shared identity, and the possibilities of collective action (social integration)
- The spatial reach of different institutional orders (e.g. the market and the state) may enable or hinder their integration (system integration)

Questions about the implications for social and system integration are prominent in the globalisation debate, seen, for example, in discussions of an emerging global civil society, the influence of international non-governmental organisations in global governance, and the disjuncture between national politics and global economics.

Cohen's concept of the economic structure incorporates space only insofar as ownership of space confers a position in that structure, but it does not analyse the distinctive spatial dynamic of capitalist production relations. This means that the implications of this spatial dynamic for the development (and ultimate fettering) of the productive forces are not considered. Similarly there is no analysis of the spatial dimension of the legal and political superstructure. Consequently, the spatial dimension of system integration between base and superstructure is not analysed. Cohen's conception of economic structure cannot analyse its spatial dynamic because, in this conception, it does not have one. For '[t]he economic structure is not a way of producing, but a framework of power in which producing occurs' (Cohen, 1978, p. 79). Yet it is precisely as a 'way of producing' that capitalism displays a distinctive spatial dynamic. And it is as a way of producing that capitalism must be stabilised as it is through the process of production that the productive forces are developed. Such is the role of laws and other superstructural phenomena. According to the theory of history, laws are developed that match basic powers and so legitimate and stabilise them. But there is a spatial as well as a functional aspect to this matching. Put simply, laws that secure private property must be implemented in all the locations or areas (spaces) in which capitalists exercise effective power over persons and productive forces.

Capitalism's spatial dynamic consists in it being a tendentially global system, meaning that the global level constitutes the limit or horizon of action of profit-oriented capitalist firms. Capitalism and globalisation go hand-in-hand. Just as competition and the profit motive drive the constant revolutionising of the instruments of production, so they drive the continual search for new markets and for favourable locations for production. The bourgeoisie 'must nestle everywhere, settle everywhere, establish connections everywhere' (Marx & Engels, 1976, p. 487). In the *Communist Manifesto* this tendency is clearly depicted as part and parcel of capitalism's progressive historical role: expanding markets foster industrial development and economic growth, and international competition compels all nations to emulate capitalist development (Marx & Engels, 1976, p. 488). Thus capitalist relations of production tend to spread throughout the world, displacing existing economic systems through the coercive force of competition, and so generalising productive development to all nations.[13] In theory of history terms, globalisation is part of capitalist progress, carrying forward the historical struggle with nature. Capitalist globalisation thus brings forward the day when the struggle with nature will be at an end.

The theory of history stipulates that this will be when capitalism is fully developed and has exhausted its potential for productive development (i.e. when capitalist production relations have become fetters on the productive forces), and when the new higher production relations have matured within the existing society (Cohen, 2000, p. 389). Interpreting this second condition, Cohen suggests that 'whatever else is required for such relations to have matured within capitalism, there surely must exist ... a large proletariat within the capitalist society in question' (2000, p. 390).[14] These conditions are supposed to coincide: both are necessary, neither alone sufficient.[15] Marx and Engels use these indicators in the description offered in the *Communist Manifesto* of the rise of capitalism from the ruins of feudalism, and the 'similar movement ... going on before our own eyes' (1976, p. 489) towards the demise of capitalism in a socialist revolution. Thus the productive forces have become 'too powerful' for capitalist relations of production 'by which they are fettered' (p. 490). At the same time capitalist development engenders the development of the proletariat as a growing class, to become a movement of 'the immense majority' (p. 495). Thus the two conditions coincide: capitalist relations become exhausted and new production relations mature.

Marx's theory of history and characterisation of capitalism can be set out in abstract terms leaving out the spatial dimension (as in Cohen's presentation of the theory of history). The purpose of the theory is to show that the underlying reason for the rise and fall of economic structures is a trans-historical tendency for the productive forces to develop, rooted in facts about the nature of humans (intelligence, rationality) and the historical situation (scarcity) they face. The reason *why* history occurs can be explained without reference to the particular spatial level at which economic structures and their societies are organised, and it might be possible to defend such an abstract theory by reference to the broad record of history. Yet for the theory to have explanatory and/or descriptive purchase on historical events the two stipulated conditions for one social formation to perish and be replaced by a higher form need to be capable of being applied empirically. However this will be difficult because the definitions of the conditions are rough. Neither makes any reference to the spatial scale at which they are supposed to apply. Yet if we wish to elucidate *how* history happens by showing plausible mechanisms for the rise and fall of economic structures their spatial organisation needs to be taken into account. For conditions and mechanisms that are found at one spatial level (e.g. national) might not be found at another (e.g. global).

Cohen has applied the two historical materialist conditions to the collapse of the Soviet Union, seen as a test of the theory (2000, pp. 389–95). In this discussion Cohen considers the issue of spatial scale, suggesting two possible construals of historical materialism. The two conditions can be asserted 'of each society taken singly' or 'of world-scale or at least multi-national social systems'. On the first construal the 1917 revolution and its aftermath does not, according to Cohen, contradict the theory. This is because the revolution did not inaugurate a truly socialist society, and capitalism merely receded (rather than perished) only to be restored in the collapse of the Soviet Union.

Cohen introduces the 'global' construal of the theory in considering Marx's advice that a revolution could succeed in Russia if it became 'the signal for a proletarian revolution in the West' (quoted by Cohen, 2000, p. 393). Marx's reasoning seems to be that a successful socialist revolution could not take place in Russia alone because one or both of the conditions stipulated by the theory of history were not met. It is an argument about economic backwardness – in Russia the productive forces were not sufficiently developed to enable higher production relations to be installed successfully as forms of productive development, and/or the new relations had not matured as gauged by the development of the proletariat. Marx seems to believe that a series of revolutions within multi-national social systems (i.e. within the advanced West) could compensate for this economic backwardness. Socialist production relations could be successfully installed in backward Russia assisted by friendly socialist countries in the West or as part of a new pan-European socialist economic area. In Cohens' view this advice goes against historical materialism because only one of the two conditions was satisfied at the time. Although 'the proletariat was sufficiently developed across Europe as a whole' there was 'as history shows ... enormous scope for further [productive] development under capitalism in Europe' (Cohen, 2000, p. 394).

Here 'global' seems to mean taking a number of societies together and conceiving simultaneous and complementary revolutions in each of these societies. In fact this is really a multi-national conception which it is misleading to counterpose to the national or single-society construal of historical materialism.

It is instructive to compare this analysis to the *Communist Manifesto*. Here Marx and Engels depict the development of the class struggle at a primarily national scale culminating in 'one national struggle between classes' (1976, p. 493).[16] In this view the proletariat must conduct the struggle against capitalism within the historically developed framework of national economies and nation-states. It is first of all at the national level that the proletariat of each country must 'settle matters with its own bourgeoisie' (p. 495) and 'acquire political supremacy' (pp. 502–3). At the same time, it is emphasised that it is 'in form' though not 'in substance', and only 'at first', a national struggle (p. 495). In substance the struggle is really about 'the common interests of the entire proletariat, independently of all nationality' (p. 497). Indeed, 'United action, of the leading civilized countries at least, is one of the first conditions for the emancipation of the proletariat' (p. 503).

The *Communist Manifesto* is thus consistent with a 'multi-national' construal of historical materialism like that which Cohen sketches in relation to Marx's advice on the prospects for a successful revolution in Russia. Although there is some ambiguity, the emphasis seems to be on the two conditions maturing (or not) within each society or nation-state and the development of national struggles. The major difference is that the *Communist Manifesto* envisages revolution in the leading capitalist economies only, whereas the Russian case allows the possibility that a successful revolution can occur in a backward country so long as it is part of united action with economies where capitalism is fully developed. In the first case the conditions must be present in each country separately, and united action may be necessary primarily for political or military reasons rather than economic ones. In the second case the conditions must be present within the countries taken as a whole, and united action is needed for the backward country for economic reasons (as well as political-military ones).

Cohen says that Marx's advice to the Russian socialists was contradicted by his own theory of history because we can now see what enormous scope there was for productive development in Europe under capitalist auspices. Of course the error is not inconsistency between the theory and the politics, but bad judgement about capitalism's potential. The same mistaken belief that capitalist relations of production were becoming fetters upon the productive forces is also the basis of the mistaken revolutionary optimism of the *Communist Manifesto*. However this points up a real difficulty with the historical materialist condition that capitalism will only perish when its productive potential is exhausted: how would we recognise the onset of exhaustion? It is not clear that it is possible to foresee the potential of capitalist globalisation for further productive development (as opposed to viewing it in hindsight).

A more fundamental challenge to the theory comes in the claim that the contemporary limits to capitalism are not at all revealed in its incapacity to develop the forces of production but, on the contrary, its tendency to continue productive development beyond the point where it becomes counterproductive in some sense. The most prominent form of this claim links capitalist globalisation to deepening ecological crisis. In this view environmental limits to productive development along capitalist lines are reached before economic limits in the form of fettering by the relations of production. If true, this would mean that one of the conditions for the transition to higher relations of production – that there is no more room for productive development under capitalism – is unattainable (Wetherly, 1999).[17]

Even if we set aside this challenge to the theory of history, capitalist globalisation presents a challenge to the 'multi-national' conception of revolution. The problem with the *Communist Manifesto* is that, despite the emphasis given to the creation of the world market, it essentially describes a world of nation-states and national economies. It is a world in which *exchange* is increasingly moving beyond the confines of national borders creating interdependence of nations, but in which *production* remains national in character. It is a world, therefore, in which each country has its own bourgeoisie 'in a constant battle ... with the bourgeoisie of foreign countries' (Marx & Engels, 1976, p. 493). It is also therefore a world in which the overthrow of capitalism can be conceived, at first, on a national basis. However globalisation in its contemporary forms undermines this analysis insofar as it undermines the concept of national capitalist classes with which the working classes of each country can first of all settle accounts. Related to this, it undermines the conception of a national economy in which a higher set of production relations can be successfully installed. Where the *Communist Manifesto* appears to advocate united action of the leading capitalist countries on essentially political-military grounds, it is arguably now necessary for economic reasons – not because of backwardness but because advancement has created unprecedented interdependence. That the struggle for political supremacy should focus on the nation-state reflects the fact that it was, and indeed remains, the primary locus of political power. But the *Communist Manifesto* reflects an age in which the nation-state was ascendant, whereas our age is, allegedly, one of 'crisis' for the nation-state (see Wallace, 1994; Strange, 1996; Van Creveld, 1999).

The precise implications of globalisation for the nation-state are contested. It is clear, however, that the nation-state no longer presides over a national economy as it once did and, in consequence, individual nation-states are less able to regulate and control economic life. An important aspect of this has been the rise of multi-national corporations and the tendency for *production* to become increasingly global in character. The extent to which these companies have become truly global or still rely on the advantages derived from national bases is disputed, but it is clear that there has been a shift in the balance of power between capital and the state, and of course the labour movement, in favour of the former (Goldblatt et al., 1997, p. 74). The implications for socialism are serious insofar as it is the nation-state that has, in line with the *Communist Manifesto*, constituted the predominant framework within which inroads against capital have been devised or attempted. The *Communist Manifesto* envisages an emergent international movement to overthrow capitalism in the form of a number of essentially national economies, whereas the modern world has witnessed essentially national-based socialist movements in the context of an emergent global capitalism.

Globalisation and the state

Within Marxist theory and politics, and socialist thought more generally, the state is considered from two aspects:

- As a set of institutions whose function is to stabilise and maintain capitalist relations of production
- As a vehicle for reform and/or socialist revolution

This dual perspective tends to produce an ambivalent view of the state – as in some ways good, and in some ways bad – or to see the state as an inherently contradictory phenomenon. It is contradictory because, for example, it is subject to contradictory influences and pressures – from the capitalist class to consolidate capitalism and from the working class to reform it. According to the theory of history, state institutions (insofar as they are superstructural) are functionally explained by the nature of the economic structure. This leaves less room for a contradictory conception of the state, for the theory emphasises the functional correspondence (or 'system integration') of base and superstructure. In this view a state exists because and so long as the needs of development of the productive forces dictate forms of production relations in which the direct producers are subordinate, and the form of state changes in compliance with changes in the economic structure. But the essential function of the state to stabilise production relations does not rule out the possibility of reform. The state is, as we have seen, relatively autonomous and there is scope for reform consistent with securing the needs of capital. Further, a more revolutionary possibility is that state actions go against the needs of existing production relations so that new production relations (favoured by the productive forces) can be established (Cohen, 1978, pp. 225–30).

As has been noted, Cohen's (1978) presentation of the theory of history does not analyse the distinctive spatial dynamic of capitalist production relations, or the spatial dimension of the legal and political superstructure. Yet there is clearly a spatial as well as a functional aspect to the matching of, say, superstructural rights with basic powers. Indeed, a functional match obviously depends on a spatial match (it is no good having appropriate laws to stabilise capitalism operating at a different spatial location and/or scale). A disjuncture between the territorial basis of the nation-state and the stretching of economic interactions across national borders is precisely the challenge apparently posed by capitalist globalisation.

However we should note that much of the discussion of this 'challenge' takes the perspective of the state, so to speak. In other words, claims to the effect that the sovereignty of nation-states is being eroded by globalisation are primarily concerned with the capacity of the state to manage the economy and sustain welfare expenditures. However the theory of history is not immediately concerned with the *reformist* capacity of the state, and so is not embarrassed by these claims. The claim that the superstructure is functionally explained by the nature of the base is only threatened where reform that is functionally required is not enacted or is enacted for reasons unconnected to the base, or where reform that is dysfunctional for the economic structure is enacted. Thus, if state sovereignty is eroded as a consequence of globalisation, the historical materialist question is whether this undermines the *functional* capacity or adequacy of the nation-state form for capitalist production relations. This is a much more specific question than whether states have lost (or gained) power in some general sense.

Roughly considered, this question concerns two types of state: existing capitalist states which have been used to presiding over a national capitalist economy and which now face the spatial expansion of capitalist relations of production outward beyond/across national borders; and, non-capitalist states used to presiding over non-capitalist economic structures and which now face the spatial expansion of capitalist relations of production inward within their national borders. The first case apparently concerns the *moving away* of capitalist relations of production and the challenge of an *erosion* of the capacities of capitalist states. The second case apparently concerns the *moving in* of capitalist relations of production and the challenge of the need to *install* a capitalist state. In the first case capitalist relations of production are typically dominant, while in the second they typically co-exist with non-capitalist production relations (which they may or may not tend to displace). In both cases, however, there is the same disjuncture between a territorially-bound nation-state and tendentially global capitalist relations of production.

If globalisation induces the retreat of the nation-state (erosion of sovereignty, weakening of functional capacity, etc.) this would present a challenge to the theory of history if the claim that 'bases need superstructures' equates to 'capitalist relations of production need a nation-state'. However this equation does not hold, at least as a general statement. The theory stipulates only that capitalism requires a super-structure (comprised of non-economic phenomena that function to stabilise the production relations), and there are good reasons to suppose that there is some overlap (but not equivalence) between 'superstructure' and 'state' (e.g. in the area of law, such as in the requirement for rights to stabilise basic powers). Thus the theory explains the *functions* of the state, but it needs to explain the *form* of the state only insofar as there must be compatibility between the state's form and functions. The theory cannot tolerate incompatibility for in that case the performance of functions required for the stability of the economic structure would be inhibited or blocked, which would in turn inhibit productive development. Thus the theory predicts that if the form of state is not compatible with the performance of func-tions required by the economic structure it will be transformed, and such transformation will be explained by the needs of the economy.[18] For example, the consolidation of nation-states might be explained by the needs of capitalism at an early stage of development, such as for a unified legal framework and integrated market. On the other hand, it could, consistent with the theory of history, just so happen that capi-talism developed in a world comprised, for independent reasons, of nation-states and that these turned out to provide compatible frame-works of political power. In either case it might be argued that nation-states proved to be functionally effective frameworks of political power for capitalist development until recent times. More specifically, the claim might be that the tendential process of economic globalisation that is bound up with the nature of capitalist production relations has progressed to a 'tipping point' at which it has begun to undermine the nation-state form.

The theory of history predicts that the nation-state will be trans-formed only *if* it is incompatible with the functional requirements of globalising capitalism, *and* if globalisation is necessary for productive development. If globalisation is not necessary for productive develop-ment there is no reason, on historical materialist grounds, to expect superstructural adaptation. There may, of course, be good reasons to expect the state to carry out an 'international function' (Miliband, 1977, p. 90). In this area the rhetoric of advancement of the national interest may be cover for the advancement of capitalist interests, for example in helping to secure the opening up of overseas markets or locations for investment. However if these capitalist interests are essentially 'benefits' then they are not strictly relevant to the theory of history because that theory concerns functional requirements or 'needs' of capital. Capitalists might desire, and organise politically to secure, access to overseas markets in the service of improved profitability, but this does not show that such forms of globalisation are essential to the reproduction of capitalist production relations. However two considerations suggest that globalisation is necessary. In the first place globalisation is, as we have seen, intrinsically linked to the nature of a capitalist economy – it is the manifestation of capitalism's 'pathological expansionist logic'. This suggests that it is not possible to decouple capitalism and globalisation or, at least, that the globalising tendency of capitalism – its global horizon of action – is very difficult to constrain.[19] Thus there is a powerful tendency for states to adapt to this logic. Further, globalisation may be seen as carrying forward capitalism's progressive historical role of developing the productive forces. This is true insofar as globalisation involves the spread of productivity-enhancing capitalist production relations throughout the globe (and displacement of less productive economic systems), and tends to enhance the overall productivity of the capitalist economy at a global level as an effect of firms seeking out locational advantages and more efficient firms driving out less efficient ones in global competition.[20]

The coupling of capitalism and economic globalisation – capitalist globalisation – means that superstructural phenomena must be adapted to the tendential spatial extension of the production relations. Globalisation can be seen as a 'way of producing' involving the spatial extension or stretching of the circuit of capital. Since it is only as a way of producing – through the activity of production rather than through mere ownership – that the relations of production constitute forms of development of the productive forces, it follows that the role of the superstructure in the theory of history must be to stabilise the circuit of capital.[21]

The functional adequacy of the nation-state concerns its capacity to secure the external conditions of accumulation (needs of capital). If functional adequacy is weakened this is because globalisation affects the needs of capital with the effect that it becomes harder for nation-states to secure them. This is not because a global capitalist economy has a different set of needs to a national capitalist economy. The abstract conceptualisation of needs set out earlier, such as 'bourgeois legal order and money', applies at any spatial scale. It is precisely the spatial dimension of these needs that globalisation alters. There are two aspects to this. The first is that these conditions or needs must be secured in new locations (i.e. new national territories) as the bourgeoisie obeys the imperative to 'nestle everywhere, settle everywhere'. The sensitivity of multi-national corporations to 'political stability' in deciding locations for investment may largely turn on whether bourgeois legal order is established and compliance secured. The second aspect, associated with the first, is that the circuit through which capital is expanded and accumulated is increasingly a circuit that extends across national borders, connecting national territories. This means that the need for bourgeois legal order and money must be secured *inter*nationally, not just within the territory of each nation-state. And this is what individual nation-states, just because of their territoriality, cannot secure. Securing these needs requires new forms of intergovernmental cooperation and/or new international agencies and regulatory frameworks – such as those governing currency exchange, trade and property rights.

However this does not entail the end of the nation-state, just as globalisation does not mean the end of national economies. If globalisation is conceived in terms of the 'horizon of action' of capitalist firms and as an intrinsic tendency of capitalism as a 'way of producing', it is consistent with the 'sceptical' claims that economic activity is still primarily organised on a national basis and that 'the fate of firms ... [including MNCs] ... is still primarily determined by local and national competitive advantages' (Held & McGrew, 2002, p. 42). Expressed in the language of the needs of capital, the point is that some of these – such as regulation of the capital-labour relation and provision of general material conditions – are still secured primarily at a national level.

Insofar as globalisation does require new forms of intergovernmental cooperation to secure needs of capital, this is sometimes expressed in terms of the erosion of sovereignty and retreat of the nation-state. There are some things that states cannot do by themselves but only in concert with other states. Nation-states can secure conditions for market exchange within their territories but self-evidently cannot secure the conditions for the operation of the international trading system. Further, as the weight or intensity of international trade increases so the intergovernmental level of political action increases in importance relative to the national.

The globalisation/anti-globalisation debate tends to rehearse the debate between society-centred and state-centred views of the state. The sceptics tend to adopt a state-centred approach, emphasising the dependence of capital on national conditions governed by states and the consequent bargaining power of states. States do not all respond in the same way to pressures or constraints coming from globalisation and, further, international economic governance is dominated by the most powerful states. States are, in other words, seen as architects or authors of globalisation. In contrast, globalists tend to adopt a society-centred approach, emphasising the pressure on states to adapt to global competitive conditions. In consequence states have reduced autonomy and bargaining power, and there is a tendency towards convergence in economic and social policy. Rather than states being seen as architects of globalisation, 'global corporate capital ... exercises decisive influence over the organization, location and distribution of economic power and resources in the contemporary global economy' (Held & McGrew, 2002, pp. 53–4). States are, in other words, forced to retreat in the face of globalisation.[22]

This dichotomy obviously simplifies the debate, concealing more of a spectrum of views. The argument of this book has been that a society-centred account of the state, such as contained in the theory of history with its commitment to economic primacy, should be developed in non-reductionist form. This means that society-centred causal mechanisms constrain but do not obliterate the autonomous capacity of the state. This is captured by the idea of relative autonomy. Both the globalist and sceptical interpretations of globalisation err in asserting the (now-past or still-continuing) primacy of states, exemplified in the idea of the state presiding over a national economy. For globalists this primacy has been eroded by economic globalisation, whereas for sceptics the myth of globalisation conceals its continuation. In contrast to both of these approaches there never was, according to the theory of history, a 'golden age' of nation-states, for they were always capitalist states. The sceptics are right that capital depends on the state to secure conditions of accumulation (needs of capital) but wrong to infer from this that states exercise power over capital. For the fact that bases need superstructures does not entail the primacy of the state in relation to the economy. The historical materialist claim that the nature of the economic structure (or base) *functionally* explains the character of the legal and political superstructure shows how the truth that capital depends on the state is compatible with *economic* primacy. The state stabilises the economy (secures needs of capital) because the economy requires that it does so.

The globalist approach is mistaken insofar as it emphasises economic constraints on the state as a novel condition connected to globalisation, as opposed to a chronic condition linked to the dominance of a capitalist economy. The theory of history also involves a reframing of the debate, in contrast to claims that globalisation has forced the retreat of the state. For, according to the theory, the state does not retreat in the face of globalisation but continues to perform its functional role of securing the needs of capital. In this view, the form of state will be transformed in compliance with the needs of a globalising capitalism, where necessary acting in concert with other states. Thus certain new forms of global governance may be functionally explained as, in Jessop's phrase, constituting a new spatio-temporal fix for capitalist production relations 'as a means of stabilising accumulation' (Jessop, 2002, p. 113). However, as a non-reductionist claim, this approach must allow for the relative autonomy of the state. Thus the causal mechanisms that sustain the functional explanation need to be powerful enough to constrain or block the autonomy of the state where this would threaten the base-superstructure connection set out in the theory of history. For example the state might be conceived as having an interest in sustaining its sovereignty or independence, and the essentially anarchic international society of states may be conceived, as in a realist view, as tending to a struggle for power among rival state interests rather than new forms of co-operation mandated by the needs of capital.

The question for the theory of history then is how does globalisation affect the causal mechanisms that serve to sustain the functional explanation of the legal and political superstructure by the economic base? Or, how far do the causal mechanisms rely upon the existence of a national economy? Although the theory of history, as set out by Cohen, abstracts from the spatial dimension, the theory of the capitalist state often depends implicitly on a (national) capitalist class able to convert economic power into political power and a developed capitalist economy upon which the state depends for revenue. The problem is that globalisation apparently creates a disjuncture between the spatial reach of economic power and political power, and therefore makes the translation of the former into the latter more problematic.

These issues require more considered treatment than can be offered here.[23] On the one hand globalisation seems to undermine the conditions for the existence of a cohesive national capitalist class whose interests are bound up with the success of the national economy. This suggests that the class struggle mechanism will tend to weaken. Crucially, the incentive to organise to influence or control 'your own' state becomes weaker as de-nationalised firms can shop around, pursuing global strategies and locating investment where conditions are most favourable. This also suggests a growing division between a fraction of capital with a global horizon of action and a national fraction. On the other hand, globalisation may foster the emergence of a transnational capitalist class able to influence and control nation-states and international agencies.[24] The general point is that globalisation introduces a further element of complexity into an instrumental account of the state. For in place of a rough congruence between a national capitalist class and a nation-state there are national and global fractions of the capitalist class and national and supranational levels of governance.

However the spatial mobility of multi- or transnational companies – their opportunities to 'shop around' – tends to increase the structural power of capital in relation to nation-states. States depend on capital accumulation to generate tax revenues, and this fiscal dependence is the source of the structural power of capital. This dependence is based on the logic of capital or the market and the structural coupling of the state and the capitalist economy. Policies to secure the needs of capital are implemented because they serve indirectly state interests, regardless of the effectiveness of the political organisation of the capitalist class. Capitalist globalisation does not create this dependence but it does heighten it. This is because states have more room for manoeuvre – more autonomy – within a national economic framework since capitalist firms do not have an exit option. In the context of globalisation firms do have an exit option and this will tend to raise the 'business confidence' threshold. This is exemplified in notions of tax competition and the 'race to the bottom' that highlight the increased pressure on states to reduce welfare and other spending commitments that do not support capital accumulation and to focus more on those that do. The claim here, as Held and McGrew put it, is that '... governments are increasingly unable to maintain existing levels of social protection or welfare state programmes without undermining the competitive position of domestic business and deterring much-needed foreign investment' (2002, p. 55). Of course this does not mean that states respond to globalisation in precisely the same way – states still retain variable degrees of autonomy and face policy choices. But it does suggest a movement in the direction of greater sensitivity to the needs of capital. It is less clear how inter-governmental organisations (IGOs) are constrained by the enhanced structural power of capital, since they do not face the same direct revenue dependence and, further, do not face the same legitimacy constraints as states. However this does not make such organisations autonomous with respect to the needs of capital. For they may be conceived as instruments of capitalist states, sharing a pro-capitalist ideology, and subject to pressure and influence from the transnational capitalist class.

Finally, the enhanced structural power of capital in relation to the state that is a consequence of globalisation may exacerbate the dilemma faced by states in trying to balance or reconcile accumulation and legitimation. The structural dependence of the state on capital accumulation derives form the connection between legitimacy or popular support and the ability of the state to manage a 'healthy economy' and, through tax revenues generated by economic growth, to sustain welfare programmes to meet human needs. This has always involved a balancing act because the needs of capital and human needs often pull in different directions (Gough, 2000). For example, although economic growth creates space for reform, measures to promote profitability and growth may require attacks on the 'social wage' or workers' rights. Insofar as globalisation does induce a 'race to the bottom' to sustain competitiveness and attract inward investment states face a heightened accumulation-legitimation dilemma. Indeed the anti-globalisation movement and the decline of trust in government are based in part on the perception that governments are increasingly servants of big business and do not represent the interests of the people (Hertz, 2001).

Notes

Prelims

1. The first stage is the functional connection between the forces of production and the relations of production that comprise the economic structure.

Chapter 1

1. In this book references to the original work are given for the first (1978) edition. References to the second (2000) edition are given only for the added Introduction and ChXV 'Marxism After the Collapse of the Soviet Union'. Other chapters added to the 2000 edition are referred to from the book *History, Labour and Freedom* (1988).
2. The relationship between structure and agency is discussed in chapter 4. See Roemer (ed.) (1986), Mayer (1994) for discussions of analytical Marxism.
3. This is, for example, a criticism of Althusser's (1969) concept of 'ideological state apparatuses'.
4. Conversely, the superstructure, which includes parts of the state, is explained functionally as comprising all those non-economic phenomena whose effect is to stabilise the economic structure. The question is to what extent these are phenomena of the state, i.e. specific state institutions and/or policies.
5. Of course it does not, and cannot, do this completely. But it asserts or claims a monopoly of physical force and seeks to allow the use of physical force by private agents in civil society only within limits prescribed by state authority (i.e. typically in law).
6. It should be noted that Weber does not provide a simple narrow concept of the state in which the naked use of coercion is all. Rather he points to coercion clothed in legitimacy, and also emphasises that coercion is not the normal, everyday, means of the state.
7. Economic power operates in all societies, but it is only in class societies that economic power is embodied in production relations giving rise to a conflict of interests between a dominant class and a class of subordinate producers. Marxism, as a politics of emancipation, is chiefly concerned with socialism, but the theory of history is chiefly concerned with the sequence of class societies through which humankind progresses towards it.
8. Wright (1993) distinguishes three 'nodes' of Marxism, adding 'Marxism as class emancipation' to the 'class analysis' and 'theory of history' nodes. The class analysis node constitutes 'independent-variable Marxism' in which 'Marxists can study virtually anything' (p. 18). That is not to say that 'virtually anything' can be explained, for it will be the case that 'class is not very important for certain problems' (p. 18). However its explanatory ambit will be much wider than 'dependent-variable Marxism' constituted by the theory of history. Here the specific focus is 'the inherent

tendencies of historical change to follow a particular trajectory with a specific kind of directionality' (p. 18). See also Wright, Levine and Sober, 1992, pp. 179–191.

9. For important early statements of a state-centred view see Skocpol (1979 and 1985). On the 'organisational realist approach' see Barrow (1993), and on statism and new institutionalism see Cammack (1990).

10. In this approach the potential autonomy of the state is real. The theory has to show how, despite this, state actions are functionally explained by the needs of capital. In other words the theory demonstrates how the real (potential) autonomy of the state is constrained. This is in contrast to the argument that the state must have a degree of autonomy in order to serve capitalist interests – this being, in effect, a kind of pseudo-autonomy.

11. For such surveys see Jessop (1984), Clarke (1991), Barrow (1993). For a more wide ranging discussion of state theory see Smith (2000), Knuttila and Kubik (2000), Jessop (2001a).

12. This is, in other words, a general claim about the relationship between the nature of the economic structure and certain non-economic phenomena (including important aspects of the state) in capitalist society.

Chapter 2

1. Marx, K. and Engels, F. (1976) Collected Works, vol. 6, pp. 477–519.
2. Marx, K. and Engels, F. (1979) Collected Works, vol. 11, pp. 99–197.
3. Miliband's 'primary' and 'secondary' may be plausible as interpretation of what Marx said (and many other commentators make the same contrast), but the distinction is still unsound.
4. See Skocpol (1985).
5. Callinicos (1991) also characterises historical materialism as a general theory.
6. The parentheses are important here, indicating that, because of the distinction between base and superstructure, the claim is not that Marx provides a single theory or explanation of the state as such. Aspects of the state that are non-superstructural are beyond the reach of the theory of history. Following a distinction that Cohen, following Wright, makes between the theory of history and Marxist sociology, this does not mean that they are beyond the reach of Marxism, though some may be.
7. Marxist sociology involves economic determination but it might not make use of functional explanation. For example, the argument that the car industry is able to use its economic power to secure favourable political decisions is a form of economic determination but need not be a functional explanation. The favourable decisions might not contribute to securing the functional requirements of the economic structure.
8. That is, again, of the superstructural attributes or elements of the state. This might be referred to as a 'structural-functional' explanation.
9. It is worth noting that an instrumental view is compatible with differing, and non-Marxist, answers to the questions who controls the state?, and in whose interests? The state could be conceived as an instrument (in a liberal view) of society as a whole and the common good or (in a feminist view) men. Note also that Marx's 'instrumentalism' is not as simple as it may

appear. The formula 'the common affairs of the whole bourgeoisie' implies that there are particular interests of fractions of the class. This then suggests a conception of the capitalist class as potentially fractured rather than monolithic. Elsewhere Marx makes the idea of class fractions central to his analysis (1979, pp. 99–197). The concept of common affairs is compatible with that of 'needs of capital' or functional requirements. Although the reference to the exclusive political sway of the bourgeoisie seems to allow no possibility of other classes or social forces influencing the state, it should also be noted that some effect of 'pressure from below' is compatible with the state successfully managing the bourgeoisie's common affairs. An example of this is Marx's analysis of the Factory Acts in volume 1 of *Capital*.

10. Though note that in later writing, Marx takes the view that the working class cannot simply lay hold of the existing state apparatus and use it for their own purpose (Marx, 1986). This idea is taken up in Lenin's argument, in *The State and Revolution*, that it is necessary to smash rather than capture the state (1917, in Collected Works, vol. 25).

11. That is, a more expansive understanding of what is required for the 'stabilisation' of the economic structure.

12. Marx, K. and Engels, F. (1986) Collected Works, vol. 22, pp. 307–59.

13. The term is mainly associated with Poulantzas' state theory (1973).

14. As already noted, two distinctions are conflated in this primary-secondary contrast. Specifically, instrumentalism is conflated with a reductionist view of the state. But instrumentalist theory can be non-reductionist. And reductionist theory can be non-instrumentalist.

15. There is some inconsistency in Elster's discussion of autonomy. First, the absence of class interest explanation is conflated with the more precise absence of explanation by the interest of the *dominant* class. Second, this sense of autonomy, in either case, is different from the sense associated with the analysis of Bonapartism since in the latter, but not the former, autonomy means specifically the ability of the state to assert itself.

16. The forces of production constitute the third component of the model but do not comprise a structure in the sense that is being used here. Rather the productive forces are embraced by relations of production that constitute the economic structure.

17. That is, those aspects of the state that are included in the superstructure.

Chapter 3

1. See McGrew (1992) for a discussion of society- and state-centred approaches. On the Marxist-pluralist dialogue see McLennan (1989).

2. This formulation is derived from Norman Geras. In response to Laclau and Mouffe's (1985) rejection of relative autonomy Geras argues that 'between explaining everything and determining nothing, there are real determinants able merely to account for a great deal' (1987, p. 50; also Laclau and Mouffe 1987, Geras 1988). See also Wetherly (2001, 2002).

3. Though this does not imply that Miliband's analysis is reducible to the instrumentalist approach.

4. Although there has been a 'vast inflation' of the state's activity in advanced capitalist societies as Miliband notes, the modern state has

always been a powerful instrument in virtue of its claimed monopoly of coercion.

5. Though there may be limits to the ends or purposes that may be pursued by a particular form of state. In other words the state may be, to use Jessop's term, 'strategically selective'.

6. However, Miliband also characterises the relationship between corporate power and state power as a 'partnership' (1989, p. 32).

7. Whether power is 'decisive' can only really be reckoned in relation to particular interests or purposes, e.g. the interests of the capitalist class or 'needs of capital'.

8. Poggi doesn't distinguish very clearly between *groups* who deploy power resources and *forms* of power. Groups seem to be identified with specific forms of power that they have 'built up'. Barrow, in contrast, focuses more sharply on rivalry between groups rather than forms of power. And while groups are defined in terms of particular power resources, groups may also control a portfolio of power resources. 'Relative amounts of power are indicated by the degree to which those who control a particular resource (e.g., wealth) are able to monopolise (1) the control of that key resource which defines them as a social group, and (2) the control of other key resources that potentially supply other groups with competing sources of power' (1993, p. 14). Poggi emphasises the *relational* aspect of power while Barrow seems to conceive it more in terms of a *quantum*. A combination of these approaches is needed. Power should be conceived in relational terms between groups, each of which controls a quantum of power resources which may comprise a portfolio of different forms of power.

9. An instrumental theory of the state is thus, more specifically, an instrumental theory of power with a particular focus on the state as one among other institutional 'power containers'.

10. This means that the 'instrumentalist' conception of power has a 'structural' dimension.

11. The added clause is in italic (Barrow, 1993, p. 14).

12. A number of familiar, though contentious, examples may be given. First, individual police officers internalising the racist 'canteen culture' of the police force: what may be referred to as institutional racism. Second, women entering male-dominated professions or occupations and internalising or exhibiting masculine behavioural norms to get by or get on: institutional sexism. Third, the conservative outlook or bias of top civil servants: 'the knowledge which civil servants have of what is expected, indeed required, in ideological and political terms is likely to be more than sufficient to ensure that those of them who might be tempted to stray from the narrow path they are expected to tread will subdue and suppress the temptation' (Miliband, 1969, p. 124). This might be called institutional conservatism. In all these cases individuals or agents conform to what is expected or required of them within particular institutional roles.

13. The connection with voluntarism is that instrumentalism relies on 'conscious historical agency to explain state policies' (Barrow, 1993, p. 45). At the extreme 'theories of agency view individual action in terms of unconstrained choice. Individuals have the ability to act, or not to act, as they wish, dependent largely on their own volition' (Luger, 2000, p. 26). In this

form they may be 'closely associated with the notions of indeterminacy, contingency, voluntarism, and, above all, methodological individualism' (Hay, 1995, p. 195).

14. In terms of Cohen's interpretation of Marx we have: a) occupants of economic roles are divided into 'classes bearing antagonistic interests', b) the 'ideas [of persons] are more or less determined by their economic roles' and c) their 'actions are inspired by their ideas' (1988, p. 46). This is a rough definition of the Marxist concept of class consciousness.

15. This is not to deny an element of choice. To the extent that there is recruitment into the capitalist class individuals may choose, or not, to (try to) join it. And individuals who are members of the capitalist class can conceivably choose to leave it, and to forsake the lure of the profit motive. It might then be argued that the reproduction of the capitalist system is to be explained, in voluntarist fashion, by the fact that a sufficient number of individuals do choose to become and remain capitalists. And, from this, that the system would grind to a halt if an insufficient number made this choice. Yet the longevity of capitalism suggests that its reproduction cannot be explained as the contingent result of individual choices. If these choices could have been different why haven't they been? That longevity lends weight to the claim that those choices reflect interests and purposes that are systemic.

16. More accurately, the superstructure comprises non-economic phenomena (Cohen, 1988).

17. Carling argues that 'one should not expect capitalism *as a consequence of its basic principles of operation* to uphold or to favour moral principles *of any kind,* beyond those strictly required for the maintenance of private property relationships' (1999, p. 223).

18. Thus Block suggests that divisions within the business community 'impede the process of developing common interests and common programs' (1987, p. 9).

19. 'Class interests' and 'needs of capital' are analysed in chapter 6.

20. Though note that the whole explanatory burden does not fall on the instrumental account insofar as it is combined with a structural view.

21. The concept of accumulation strategy is employed extensively in Bob Jessop's work on state theory (Jessop, 1990; 2002).

22. This formulation is repeated at p. 160 but the important qualification registered by the word 'wholly' is omitted: 'Interests are not pre-given but must be defined within the context of specific accumulation strategies'.

23. Also the 'interconnected elements of the value-form define the parameters in which accumulation can occur ... [but] ... the value-form itself does not fully determine the course of capital accumulation' (Jessop, 1990, p. 197). Thus accumulation occurs within the parameters of the circuit of capital and this in turn depends on certain external conditions. But the constraint imposed on accumulation by the value-form and the needs of capital is a minor theme in Jessop whose major theme is the contingency of competition between alternative possible accumulation strategies.

24. 'Despite all ... [the] vagaries [of the course of accumulation] ... capital continues to circulate. It seems as if, whatever happens to particular capitals, capital in general somehow or other survives' (Jessop, 1990, p. 152). The

survival of capital in general may be attributed largely to the functional relationship between the needs of capital and accumulation strategies.

25. The point that there are fundamental class interests in terms of the needs of capital and that these constitute parameters within which specific interpretations of class interests in terms of rival accumulation strategies operate can be made in a more general way. Thus Miliband notes that 'there are of course innumerable differences and disputes over specific items of policy and strategy which arise between members of dominant classes. But however sharp these may be, they do not seriously impair an underlying consensus about the essential goodness and viability of the system itself' (1989, p. 34).

26. On this see Cohen's discussion of 'Restricted and Inclusive Historical Materialism' (1988) and the corresponding distinction between the theory of history and Marxist sociology in the same article.

27. It is clear that the micro- and macro- levels of analysis are closely interconnected. Thus although Luger's analysis of the power of the automobile industry is ostensibly conducted at the micro level insofar as it is not overtly concerned with the interests of capital in general, such an analysis could be located within the wider framework of Fordism as an accumulation strategy (Luger, 2000).

28. Some of the categories cut across the state-civil society (or public-private) distinction e.g. engineers, sociologists.

29. This is the idea of a principal-agent relationship rejected by Miliband, or the idea of the process of representation of interests as an automatic transmission belt rejected by Jessop.

30. In effect Jessop thus ignores the effect of the institutional separation of state and civil society.

31. On pluralism see Smith (1995).

32. Cohen, 1978, p. 69.

33. This does not mean that the middle class is closed off to recruitment from below. But the limits of this upward mobility should be emphasised together with the processes of selection and socialisation (e.g. see Miliband, 1969, pp. 64–5).

34. In this work, separated from *The State in Capitalist Society* by a period of twenty years, Miliband makes no explicit reference to colonization.

35. '... a dominant class may be so designated by virtue of the effectiveness and cohesion it possesses in the control of the three main sources of domination: ... the main means of economic activity ...; ... the means of state administration and coercion; and ... the means of communication and persuasion. The dominant class of advanced capitalist societies, and notably their power elites, do have the requisite effectiveness and cohesion' (Miliband, 1989, p. 27).

36. Though the exercise of hegemony may normally require material concessions.

37. The special interest process is obviously closely related to the policy planning process. And the mechanisms of collective representation cited here could be incorporated within the concept of a corporate policy-planning network. However it useful to retain the distinction between the insider status of capital in the policy planning process and the additional capacity to exert pressure and influence outside of this process.

38. The investment strike also features in structural explanations of the political power of capital. e.g. see Jessop, 1990, p. 146.
39. On the other hand they must not be so independent that they become detached. Of course there may be many in these categories who are detached from, or even hostile to, capitalist interests. But, again, the theory requires only a sufficient degree of attachment.
40. If Jessop is correct this 'making itself heard' could not amount to putting forward a viable accumulation strategy. It could take the primordial form of a claim of importance and demand for recognition as in 'a strong economy requires a healthy manufacturing sector'. Or it could take the pre-strategic form of the assertion of particular interests and demand for particular policies, e.g. a demand for exchange rate devaluation or protectionist measures to aid manufactured exports. An obvious problem here might be the possibility of the organic intellectuals being captured by a specific fraction and articulating its particularistic interests.

Chapter 4

1. There is, says Barrow, 'reliance on conscious historical agency to explain state policies' in the power structure methodology (1993, p. 45).
2. E.g. Hay (2002) identifies 'intentionalist' and 'structuralist' approaches.
3. Though Marsh suggests that 'there is a tendency throughout the social sciences for authors to favour structural or agency explanations' (Marsh, 1999, p. 14). Against such 'simplistic' approaches Marsh argues that 'the relationship between structure and agency is dialectical' (p. 14). See also, in the same volume, Kerr's and Marsh's argument for a 'multidimensional approach' to explaining Thatcherism incorporating 'an appreciation of the importance of both ... structural and intentional factors' (Kerr & Marsh, 1999, p. 175); and the similar approach in Marsh 1995.
4. Social structure is merely a term for aggregate social phenomena. Where social structures appear to exert causal powers, e.g. in constraining feasible actions, in fact the constraint is always reducible to 'other individuals' (King, 1999, p. 217). 'In principle' means that we may speak of social structure having a causal effect only in a holding operation when individualist explanations have not yet been supplied. Thus although King rejects the concept of structure in principle in favour of 'the reduction of society to individuals', it is not always going to be possible to reduce society in this way because of practical constraints on the research process and so 'practically, a heuristic concept of structure can be usefully maintained' (1999, pp. 222–3).
5. Methodological collectivism, in Elster's definition, 'assumes that there are supra-individual entities that are prior to individuals in the explanatory order. Explanation proceeds from the laws either of self regulation or of development of these larger entities, while individual actions are derived from the aggregate pattern' (1985, p. 125).
6. Thus rejecting methodological individualism (MI) does not entail embracing methodological collectivism (MC) in Elster's senses of these terms. As Callinicos argues, 'all those who deny MI are not ipso facto methodological collectivists. All that the opponent of MI has to say is that social structures

have explanatory autonomy ... [i.e.] ... that they cannot be eliminated from the explanation of social events' (1989, p. 83). In fact Elster's MI approach allows for the causal efficacy of social structure. Specifically, 'rational-choice explanation ... must be supplemented by an account of how preferences and beliefs emerge from within the social structure' (Elster, 1985, p. 28). Yet this concession appears inconsistent with the MI claim that individuals are prior to social structure in the explanatory order (Wetherly, 1992a, pp. 121–31).

7. For example, Archer's 'morphogenetic sequence' is based on an ontological distinction or separation between structure and agency (Archer, 1995; for discussion see McAnulla, 2002 & Hay, 2002).

8. The three approaches can be seen as advancing different ontological claims. In the first approach reality consists only of structures or only of agents. In the second both structures and agents are real. In the third 'neither agents nor structures are real, since neither has an existence in isolation from the other' (Hay, 2002, p. 127). The second view is based on an ontological, and the third a merely analytical, distinction between structure and agency.

9. This definition is contrasted with an alternative view according to which 'institution' is synonymous with 'organisation'.

10. Thus, in distinction from Jessop, structure does not include practices. In other words, Cohen distinguishes between the 'occupation' and 'performance' of a role.

11. The material or physical environment obviously influences behaviour, not least through its implications for the feasible set of possible actions.

12. The point here is that determinism is not synonymous with structuralism. Even if determinism is defensible this indicates that structuralism isn't since some non-structural elements of the social are likely to exert causal effects.

13. The idea that some elements of social life fall outside of 'structures' can also be seen in slightly different form in Jessop's distinction between a 'self-organizing ecology of instituted systems' (such as the economic and political systems) and 'a rich and complex lifeworld ... which is irreducible to such systems and their logics' (2002, p. 8). Similarly, Scott makes a distinction between 'structures of domination [that] rest upon the organised positions or locations that people occupy in institutional and relational structures, [and] patterns of interpersonal power [that] derive from the personal characteristics and attributes that people have' (2001, p. 135).

14. The theory of history seems to rely on an objective idea of scarcity whose historical purchase continues right up to (and perhaps through) the threshold of massive surplus achievable within socialism. Against this claim it might be argued that scarcity, at least for much of this historical span, reflects a cultural norm more than an objective situation.

15. It should be added that social theory is also concerned with the effects or outcomes of action or conduct, involving the interaction between individuals. Elster refers to this as 'causal explanation of aggregate phenomena' (1985, p. 4). In Archer's morphogenetic sequence this is the final stage (which is also the first phase of a new cycle) of 'structural elaboration' (Archer, 1995). The circuit of capital can also be analysed in terms of the effect of the 'interaction' between capitalists and workers in reproducing or modifying the economic structure.

16. Archer (1995) argues, along these lines, for an ontological distinction between structure and agency.
17. Numbering has been added.
18. Or that it really involves a more structuralist starting point.
19. Jessop also defines the strategic-relational approach in terms of its 'radical "methodological relationalism", that is, its insistence on treating social phenomena in terms of social relations' (2001, p. 1223).
20. Though this statement may be qualified by the recognition that some behaviour occurs outside of, and/or is not oriented to, any structural context.
21. The notion of 'strategy' is, in effect, the mutual element in the 'mutual constitution' of agency and structure.
22. Jessop suggests that 'structured coherence' may arise from 'a structurally inscribed strategic selectivity that rewards actions that are compatible with the recursive reproduction of the structure(s) in question' (2001, p. 1225). But such reward will depend largely on position within the structure, e.g. for exploiters rather than the exploited.
23. Indeed, 'the strategic-relational approach ... argues that subjects have no free will' (Jessop, 1990, p. 266).
24. This is distinguished from Hay's definition of structuralism as 'explanation ... exclusively in terms of structural or contextual factors' (2002, p. 102). Thus a structuralist explanation need not involve the claim that explanation can be given *exclusively* in terms of structural constraint.
25. This does not mean that the structuralist explanation makes no reference to the conduct of politicians, officials and other members of the state elite, or the ways they respond to structural constraints, just that the existence of the constraints is independent of the particular individuals who comprise the state elite.
26. Lindblom and Woodhouse (1993) argue from a non-Marxist standpoint that business occupies a 'privileged position'.
27. These other purposes may even be motivated by hostility towards capitalist interests. Thus Meynaud, quoted by Miliband, claims that 'the concept of the "bias of the system" makes it ... possible to understand that ... measures taken to remedy the derelictions, shortcomings and abuses of capitalism result ultimately ... in the consolidation of the regime. It matters little in this respect that these measures should have been undertaken by men sympathetic or hostile to capitalist interests ...' (1969, p. 79).
28. The other two answers, or mechanisms, being the character of the state's leading personnel and the pressures exercised by the capitalist class (1977, p. 73).
29. According to Miliband 'whatever the state does ... has to run the gauntlet of the economic imperatives dictated by the requirements of the system' (1977, p. 97). However he does not explain the nature of these requirements.
30. In other words, a structuralist explanation does not entail a concept of functional requirement.
31. '[T]here is no single best solution to to the regularization of capital accumulation' (Jessop, 2002, p. 22).
32. Where 'a is a function of b' means something like 'the occurrence of b causes, contributes to or is favourable for the occurrence of a'. So, the

prosperity of capitalist enterprise is favourable for the strategic capacity of the state (1), and state actions contribute to the prosperity of capitalist enterprise (2).

33. In other words 'the more ... etc.' the stronger is the structural thesis, whereas 'the less ... etc.' the weaker is the structural thesis. 1) and 2) both must be true to some degree for the structuralist thesis to have any strength. A further dimension of the constraint involves the inducement for policy-makers to avoid policies that may be damaging to accumulation, and here we need to take account of how resilient the accumulation process is to such potentially harmful policies. Thus, the more dependent is accumulation on positive state actions and the less resilient to negative actions, the stronger the constraint faced by the state.

34. We can make sense of this in terms of the distinction between holding (structure) and exercising (agency) power. 'An agent who has this capacity to affect others [holds power] may, however, be able to achieve this without actually having to do anything at all [exercising power]. This occurs when others anticipate their intentions and their likely actions and act in relation to these' (Scott, 2001, p. 4).

35. Anybody can threaten an investment strike but to be plausible such a threat must be backed up by control over investment. And although such a threat involves a choice, such a choice is always related to the interests generated by the role of control of investment.

36. 'Structural power' may be defined as 'unconscious power'. Gough and Farnsworth quote this characterisation from Strange (1996). But some of their own formulations tend to blur the structure-agency distinction, for example the claim that 'capital disposes of structural power' (p. 81) seems to equate capital with an actor and the operation of structural power with a decision.

37. In each case mobility is relative to the scale of analysis.

38. The structural power of capital over labour is seen in the limits to trade unionism. E.g. see Coates (1975, 1980).

39. See also Goldblatt et al. (1997).

40. These two cases are interrelated insofar as the second explains the existence of private property rights that reinforce the power of capital over labour described in the first, i.e. bases need superstructures.

41. The subordination of the worker to the capitalist occurs because 'he can ensure his survival only by contracting with a capitalist whose bargaining position enables him to impose terms which effect the worker's subordination' (Cohen, 1978, p. 70).

42. The performance of labour can be secured through forms of repression and coercion, but this is not the normal case. A range of worker rights and benefits have been more or less institutionalised within welfare states, and in part this reflects the 'structural power' of labour.

43. Of course, it would pose a challenge to the structural argument if state managers have an interest in cutting budgets and rolling back the state.

44. The agency-structure distinction is misleading when it is seen as synonymous with the instrumental-structural distinction. The problem with that usage is not the distinction between agency and structure but the equation or conflation of each term with a specific type of explanation. For instru-

mentalism, as a species of structural explanation, is not synonymous with agency. Both instrumentalism and structuralism emphasise causal influences that operate at the level of social structure. A better approach is to see structure and agency as chronically implicated in the explanation of behaviour, so that explanation always involves some combination of these influences (and others besides, such as non-structural social influences, or human nature). Thus pressure is not simply a phenomenon of agency but also involves a critical structural dimension. Likewise, constraint is not simply a phenomenon of structure but also involves a dimension of agency.

45. For example property rights are functionally explained by their making legitimate, and so stabilising, basic powers. But this functional explanation does not stipulate every detail of property rights. These details can and do vary, and this variation may be due to a range of causal influences.

46. This follows Cohen's important discussion of 'Restricted and Inclusive Historical Materialism' (1988).

47. Scott characterises pressure as a form of 'counteraction' undertaken by those who are 'members of the political system, but not of the state itself' (2001, p. 26). Pressure is classed as counteraction because it is a 'demand to be heard' from those who are subject to the power of command exercised by members of the state. Yet pressure does not always come from groups who in other respects are subordinate or weak in society. It can be a mechanism for powerful groups to defend and reinforce their privilege.

48. Thus 'the [economic] structure may be seen not only as a set of relations but also as a set of roles' (Cohen, 1978, p. 36) and the occupants of roles may be said to bear interests (Cohen, 1988, p. 46). Cohen adds that 'for Marx, a person's social being is the economic role he occupies' (1988, p. 45), and thus the phrase 'economic role' may be substituted for 'social being' in the claim that 'social being determines consciousness'. This claim means that the beliefs people have about society are 'more or less determined by their economic roles' (Cohen, 1988, p. 46).

49. Agency is not the only other factor here. The economic structure should be seen in the context of other causal influences.

50. Similarly, Cohen suggests that actions are 'inspired by' ideas that are 'more or less determined' by roles. This allows that the strong connection between roles-ideas-actions is not such that ideas and actions are merely reducible to roles. Similarly 'production relations do not mechanically determine class consciousness'. However this is consistent with production relations strongly determining consciousness.

51. This merges two of Jessop's five dimensions that contribute to the 'ecological dominance' of capitalism.

Chapter 5

1. This explanation presupposes a distinction between base and superstructure. Cohen distinguishes between base and superstructure on the basis of a distinction between powers and rights, such that 'to have a right over some productive force is to stand in a superstructural relation of law, to have a power over some productive force is to stand in a basic relation of production'

(1988, p. 34). And Cohen shows, against criticism from Lukes (1983), that this distinction is compatible with recognition that, in general, rights are indispensable to powers.

2. Or, more generally, non-economic phenomena. For 'when we think about the superstructure, our fundamental concept should be of a superstructural fact or phenomenon, rather than a superstructural institution, the latter idea being insufficiently general and insufficiently abstract' (Cohen, 1988, p. 178).

3. Although it is not clear whether the accumulation of confirming instances can establish the truth of the general claim, or how many confirming instances are needed. Capitalism might be a confirming instance, but without evidence from other types of society it could, for all we know, be historically peculiar in displaying this relationship between base and superstructure. To the extent that the record of history is consistent with the truth of the development thesis then it can be argued that economic structures must have been transformed to suit the developing forces and, by extension, that superstructures must have changed to stabilise the changing structures.

4. In other words it is the *performance* and not just the *occupancy* of the roles that must be stabilised.

5. However labour power is better conceptualised as a 'fictitious commodity'. This means that it 'has the form of a commodity (in other words, that can be bought and sold) but is not itself created in a profit-oriented labour process' (Jessop, 2002, p. 13). In other words labour power is not (re)produced within the circuit of capital, and this fact has important implications for the 'stabilisation' of the circuit. Jessop identifies three other categories of fictitious commodity: land (or nature), money and knowledge (ibid.).

6. Conceivably this exchange could take the form of proletarians hiring means of production from capitalists or capitalists hiring labour power from proletarians, but of these the latter is clearly the historically dominant or 'normal' form and the one with which we will be concerned.

7. Thus, 'the formal subordination of "commodified" labour-power to capital through the emergence of the market for wage-labour was reinforced historically when the exercise of labour-power in production was brought directly under capitalist control through machine-pacing in the factory system' (Jessop, 2002, p. 15).

8. They might, on this argument, be Marxist sociological explanations.

9. Though, of course, this does not mean all aspects of the economy.

10. Assuming commodities sell at their full values.

11. Though the extraction of surplus labour is not a sufficient condition for the achievement of a satisfactory rate of profit, which also depends on realisation conditions.

12. For example, see Marx's analysis of 'The Working Day' in vol. 1 of *Capital* (1976). For discussion see Wetherly, 1992.

13. The circuit can be analysed from the perspective of any of the three forms of capital, but for our purpose it is convenient to analyse it in terms of the circuit of money capital, that is, beginning and ending with money.

14. As opposed to being caused by exogenous 'shocks'.

15. The circuit also expands spatially – see the discussion of globalisation in chapter 9.
16. In other words, 'Individual persons, whether capitalists or workers, are pressed by the "dull compulsion of economic forces" to undertake actions which result in the [dynamic] tendencies [of the system]' (Gough, 1979, p. 29). Better to say 'compulsion of economic *relations*'.
17. And largely outside the ambit of the theory of history.

Chapter 6

1. Or, we might say, its disposition to be stabilised by superstructural phenomena of that type.
2. Another term that could be used here is 'system needs'. The needs of capital are system needs of a capitalist economy.
3. Doyal and Gough's (1991) theory of human need not only provides a catalogue of basic and intermediate needs but also specifies a standard of need satisfaction – a concept of 'optimum' levels of health and autonomy. However this aspect of the theory is problematic (Wetherly, 1996). The theory of the needs of capital will focus on the qualitative dimension.
4. See Elster (1980, 1982, 1986), Cohen (1980, 1982).
5. In functional explanations it seems that system needs will usually figure as first- or second-order goals, i.e. as ends in themselves or means to ends. It is difficult to see how functional explanations can work through the unintended and/or unrecognised consequences of actions, since the satisfaction of needs would then be fortuitous. For example, a person could consume food for pleasure without intending or recognising the contribution its nutritional value makes to the satisfaction of her basic need for physical health. But in that case the need plays no role in explaining the behaviour that leads to its satisfaction, which is purely fortuitous.
6. For discussion of models of capitalism see Coates (2000).
7. The need to regulate competition is an example of the potential conflict between the interests of capital in general and particular capitals.
8. The rationale for this move is that from the standpoint of capital the wage is a reproduction cost.
9. The same point applies to other fictitious commodities that enter into the circuit of capital: land, money and knowledge (Jessop, 2002).
10. Although housewives may sometimes be treated as part of the reserve, the distinction between potential and reserve segments mirrors the conventional distinction between economically inactive and economically active.

Chapter 7

1. See 'Restricted and Inclusive Historical Materialism' in Cohen, 1988.
2. Though 'stabilisation' may cover a range of specific functional requirements.
3. In other words it is the *non-self-stabilising* nature of the economic structure that functionally explains the character of the superstructure – it is the

structure's need for stabilisation, and its disposition to be stabilised, by certain non-economic phenomena that explains their occurrence.

4. A wider conception is 'the absence of explanation by the nature of the economic structure' or, more simply, 'the absence of economic explanation'.

5. Since 'the state' is too vague as an object of explanation we should refer to specific aspects of the form and functions of the state.

6. Or, at least, that the relative unity of the state system is achievable.

7. Cohen does not accept (though does not reject) the determinist label. In a footnote (1978, p. 147, n1) he says 'Technological determinism is, presumably, two things: it is technological, and it is determinist. ... Our version of historical materialism may be called technological, but the issue of determinism will not be discussed in this book'.

8. In effect Jessop rejects the idea of a 'superstructure' since no *general* statements that certain non-economic phenomena are explained by the nature of the economic structure are admissible.

9. For further discussion see Wetherly 2001 and 2002.

10. Freedom arguably presupposes autonomy: freedom to determine the means to ends that are not truly my own may be felt to be so restricted as not to count as true freedom.

Chapter 8

1. Which does not mean, of course, that state power is simply reducible to the decisions and actions of this elite.

2. It is claimed that 'the long-established, career-oriented British Civil Service, together with a powerful Treasury, provides a relatively centralised instrument for formulating and implementing longer-term class-based policies' (Gough, 1979, pp. 63–4).

3. Of course, governability is much more than merely a question of the current poll ratings and electoral prospects of existing Ministers.

4. State power must also reflect, to some degree, the scope for agency and choice, not reducible to either social origin or position within the state.

5. And similarly pressure from above may reinforce the state's in-built structural selectivity.

6. The then conventional pluralist theory was Miliband's target, but the theory also provides an alternative to Jessop's pluralistic style of argument.

7. See Poulantzas (1969), Miliband (1970, 1973).

8. This flexibility extends, for example, to selecting from a range of potentially viable accumulation strategies. These rival strategies are functional alternatives.

Chapter 9

1. A review of the ever-growing globalisation debate is beyond the scope of this discussion. See Held et al. (1999), Hirst and Thompson (1996), Held and McGrew (2002).

2. There is some degree of consensus on the general idea of globalisation. Bromley suggests that the definition given here 'is more or less common

ground'. Held et al. refer to 'a general acknowledgement of a real or perceived intensification of global interconnectedness' (1999, p. 2).

3. Goldblatt et al. define globalisation in terms of 'growing global interconnectedness; a stretching of social relations across space ... such that day to day activities in one part of the globe are increasingly enmeshed with events happening on the other side' (1997, p. 62).

4. Although Jessop sees globalisation as multi-temporal (2002, p. 113), this is compatible with speeding up on average.

5. In this vein Bromley refers to 'the particular intensity of modern globalisation compared with the more general interaction across space that has characterised much of world history' (1999, p. 280).

6. Sklair (2002) distinguishes between 'the inter-national, the transnational, and the global ... The global signifies an already achieved state of globalization but ... this is still fairly uncommon' (p. 35).

7. Similarly, ownership of obsolete instruments of production would not confer a position in the economic structure (though whether instruments of production that are obsolete still count as instruments of production is questionable).

8. Against this, Cohen claims that 'a portion of space may be more or less productively useful' and that this is 'more pertinent' (1978, p. 51). One cause of variation in productive usefulness is location, and Cohen gives the example of a space adjoining a source of energy. But it would be, say, the coal that has productive power and not the space that adjoins it, any more than the space that contains it has productive power itself. Similarly, some times (of the day, of the year) are more productively useful than others, but this does not show that the temporal location of production has productive power. Any productive process takes place in time and space, and we may say that time and space are used in production. Further, some times and some spaces are certainly more productively useful than others. But time and space do not, on that account, constitute productive forces.

9. The criterion that 'there is enough, and as good left in common for others' comes from John Locke's defence of property in whatever is removed from nature and has labour mixed with it (reproduced in Rosen and Wolff, 1999, p. 191).

10. The content of the space, e.g. the soil it contains, may be developed, but , as Cohen himself asserts, space is to be defined 'in abstraction from whatever it contains' (1978, p. 50).

11. There is, for example, no mention of globalisation or other concepts of spatial scale in the first (1978) edition of *Karl Marx's Theory of History*. The second (2000) edition does include an additional chapter on 'Marxism After the Collapse of the Soviet Union' that considers a 'global construal of historical materialism' (p. 393), discussed in more detail below.

12. This distinction is taken from Lockwood (1964).

13. In the displacing of pre-capitalist economic systems 'the concentrated force of the state [also] played a central role' (Bromley, 1999, p. 288).

14. Cohen recognises that the existence of a large proletariat only goes part way to answering what is required to demonstrate that higher production relations have matured, and that 'a complete answer to that question might be difficult to supply' (1978, p. 390). This is, of course, a serious omission

for a theory that purports to supply persuasive reasons why capitalism will be replaced by socialism.

15. Though this does not mean that the two conditions appear simultaneously. For example, the proletariat could be sufficiently developed before capitalism is fully developed.

16. Or, similarly, 'the national struggles of the proletarians of the different countries' (p. 497).

17. There are, of course, other rival conceptions of contemporary capitalism's distinctive limits or contradictions. Prominent among these are: that capitalist globalisation inhibits rather than promotes productive development in poor countries and regions, tending to increase global inequality, and that capitalism's output expansion bias is at the expense of a possible and desirable reduction of toil (Cohen, 1978, ch. XI). Both of these contradictions may bite before capitalism has exhausted its productive potential.

18. In other words, the theory of history deals not only with transformations of 'the entire immense superstructure' due to changes of the 'economic foundation' (e.g. from a feudal state to a capitalist state) but with transformations within, say, the capitalist type of state in compliance with the changing requirements of a developing capitalist economy.

19. This does not mean that globalisation moves ineluctably along a single path. On the contrary, there is more than one possible path of globalisation, and the forms, extent and speed of globalisation processes are contested. The point is that globalisation is a very strong tendency of capitalist production relations.

20. These are obviously very large and contentious claims, and they deserve greater scrutiny than they are given here.

21. This is different to Cohen's approach. In his view 'the economic structure is not a way of producing, but a framework of power in which producing occurs' (1978, p. 79). Since the superstructure is restricted to those non-economic phenomena that are functionally explained by the nature of the economic structure, that is the need of the structure to be stabilised, this deprives the superstructure of any role in securing the conditions necessary for producing to occur. Yet it is only through ensuring that producing occurs that the productive forces are developed. Ensuring the stability of the framework of power is necessary but does not seem to be sufficient.

22. This summary draws on Held and McGrew, especially chapter 4 'A Global Economy?' (2002, pp. 38–57).

23. See Panitch (1994) for a more extensive analysis.

24. See Sklair (2001) for a discussion of the concept of a transnational capitalist class.

Works Cited

Althusser, L. (1969) *For Marx*, London: Allen Lane.

Altvater, E. (1978) 'Some Problems of State Interventionism', in Holloway, J. and Picciotto, S. (eds) *State and Capital: a Marxist Debate*, London: Edward Arnold.

Archer, M.S. (1995) *Realist Social Theory: The Morphogenetic Approach*, Cambridge: Cambridge University Press.

Barrow, C. (1993) *Critical Theories of the State. Marxist, Neo-Marxist, Post-Marxist*, Wisconsin: University of Wisconsin Press.

Berki, R.N. (1989) 'Vocabularies of the State', in Lassman, P. (ed.) *Politics and Social Theory*, London: Routledge.

Bhaskar, R. (1991) 'Determinism', in Bottomore, T. et al. (eds) *A Dictionary of Marxist Thought*, Oxford: Blackwell.

Block, F. (1987) *Revising State Theory*, Philadelphia: Temple University Press.

Bobbio, N. (1983) 'Politica', in Bobbio, N. et al. (eds) *Dizionario di Politica*, Turin: UTET.

Bottomore, T. (1971) *Sociology. A Guide to Problems and Literature*, London: George Allen and Unwin, (2nd ed.).

Brewer, A. (1984) *A Guide to Marx's Capital*, Cambridge: Cambridge University Press.

Bridges, A.B. (1973) 'Nicos Poulantzas and the Marxist Theory of the State', *Politics and Society* 2.

Bromley, S. (1999) 'Marxism and Globalisation', in Gamble, A. et al. (eds) *Marxism and Social Science*, Basingstoke: Macmillan.

Burden, T. and Campbell, M. (1985) *Capitalism and Public Policy in the UK*, London: Croom Helm.

Burnham, P. (1994) 'The Organisational View of the State', *Politics* 14(1).

Callinicos, A. (1989) *Making History. Agency, Structure and Change in Social Theory*, Cambridge: Polity Press.

Callinicos, A. (1991) *The Revenge of History: Marxism and the East European Revolutions*, Cambridge: Polity Press.

Cammack, P. (1990) 'Statism, New Institutionalism, and Marxism', *The Socialist Register*, London: Merlin Press.

Campbell, M. (1981) *Capitalism in the UK*, London: Croom Helm.

Carling, A. (1997) 'Analytical and Essential Marxism', *Political Studies*, vol. 45, no. 4.

Carling, A. (1999) 'New Labour's Polity: Tony Giddens and the "Third Way"', *Imprints*, vol. 3, no. 3.

Carling, A. and Nolan, P. (2000) 'Historical materialism, natural selection and world history', *Historical Materialism*, no. 6.

Carnoy, M. (1984) *The State and Political Theory*, Princeton: Princeton University Press.

Catephores, G. (1989) *An Introduction to Marxist Economics*, London: Macmillan.

Clarke, S. (ed.) (1991) *The State Debate*, Basingstoke: Macmillan.

Coates, D. (1975) *The Labour Party and the Struggle for Socialism*, Cambridge: Cambridge University Press.

Coates, D. (1980) *Labour in Power? A Study of the Labour Government 1974–1979*, London: Longman.

Coates, D. (2000) *Models of Capitalism: Growth and Stagnation in the Modern Era*, Cambridge: Polity Press.

Cohen, G.A. (1978) *Karl Marx'sTheory of History: A Defence*, Oxford: Clarendon Press.

Cohen, G.A. (1980) 'Functional Explanation: Reply to Elster', *Political Studies*, vol. 28, no. 1.

Cohen, G.A. (1982) 'Reply to Elster on "Marxism, Functionalism and Game Theory"', *Theory and Society*, vol. 11, no. 4.

Cohen, G.A. (1988) *History, Labour and Freedom*, Oxford: Clarendon Press.

Cohen, G.A. (2000) *Karl Marx's Theory of History: A Defence*, 2nd edition, Oxford: Clarendon Press.

Diamond, J. (1998) *Guns, Germs and Steel. A Short History of Everybody for the Last 13,000 Years*, London: Vintage Book.

Domhoff, G.W. (1979) *The Powers That Be: Processes of Ruling Class Domination in America*, New York: Vintage Books.

Doyal, L. and Gough, I. (1991) *A Theory of Human Need*, Basingstoke: Palgrave.

Dunleavy, P. and O'Leary, B. (1987) *Theories of the State. The Politics of Liberal Democracy*, London: Macmillan.

Elster, J. (1980) 'Cohen on Marx's Theory of History', *Political Studies*, vol. 28, no. 1.

Elster, J. (1982) 'Marxism, Functionalism and Game Theory', *Theory and Society*, vol. 11, no. 4.

Elster, J. (1985) *Making Sense of Marx*, Cambridge: Cambridge University Press.

Elster, J. (1986) 'Further Thoughts on Marxism, Functionalism and Game Theory', in Roemer, J. (ed.) *Analytical Marxism*, Cambridge: Cambridge University Press.

Evans, M. (1975) *Karl Marx*, London: George Allen and Unwin.

Fine, B. (1975) *Marx's Capital*, London and Basingstoke: Macmillan.

Fine, B. and Harris, L. (1976) 'State Expenditure in Advanced Capitalism: A Critique', *New Left Review*, 98.

Fine, B. and Harris, L. (1979) *Reading Capital*, London: Macmillan.

Foley, D. (1991) 'Labour power', in Bottomore, T. et al. (eds) *A Dictionary of Marxist Thought*, Oxford: Blackwell.

Gamble, A. (1988) *The Free Economy and the Strong State*, Basingstoke: Macmillan.

Geras, N. (1987) 'Post-Marxism?', *New Left Review*, 163.

Geras, N. (1988) 'Ex-Marxism Without Substance: Being A Real Reply to Laclau and Mouffe', *New Left Review*, 169.

Giddens, A. (1976) 'Functionalism: Apres la Lutte', *Social Research*, vol. 43.

Giddens, A. (1984) *The Constitution of Society. Outline of the Theory of Structuration*, Cambridge: Polity Press.

Gill, G. (2003) *The Nature and Development of the Modern State*, Basingstoke: Palgrave.

Ginsburg, N. (1979) *Class, Capital and Social Policy*, Basingstoke: Macmillan.

Goldblatt, D. et al. (1997) 'Economic Globalization and the Nation State: The Transformation of Political Power?', *Soundings*, Issue 7.

Gough, I. (1979) *The Political Economy of the Welfare State*, London: Macmillan.

Gough, I. (1992) 'What Are Human Needs?', in Percy-Smith, J. and Sanderson, I. *Understanding Local Needs*, London: IPPR.

Gough, I. (2000) *Global Capital, Human Needs and Social Policies*, Basingstoke: Palgrave.

Gough, I. and Farnsworth, K. (2000) 'The Enhanced Structural Power of Capital: A Review and Assessment', in Gough, I. *Global Capital, Human Needs and Social Policies*, Basingstoke: Palgrave.

Gramsci, A. (1971) *Selections From Prison Notebooks*, London: Lawrence and Wishart.

Hall, J.A. and Ikenberry, G.J. (1989) *The State*, Milton Keynes: Open University Press.

Hall, S. (1977) 'The "Political" and the "Economic" in Marx's Theory of Classes', in Hunt, A. (ed.) *Class and Class Structure*, London: Lawrence and Wishart.

Hall, S. (1984) 'The State in Question', in McLennan, G. et al. (eds) *The Idea of the Modern State*, Milton Keynes: Open University Press.

Hay, C. (1995) 'Structure and Agency', in Marsh, D. and Stoker, G. (eds) *Theory and Methods in Political Science*, Basingstoke: Macmillan.

Hay, C. (1996) 'Marxist Theories of the State: Horses for Courses?', Muirhead Working Paper, University of Birmingham.

Hay, C. (1996a) *Restating Social and Political Change*, Milton Keynes: Open University Press.

Hay, C. (1999) 'Marxism and the State', in Gamble, A. et al. (eds) *Marxism and Social Science*, Basingstoke: Macmillan.

Hay, C. (2002) *Political Analysis. A Critical Introduction*, Basingstoke: Palgrave.

Held, D. (1984) 'Central Perspectives on the Modern State', in McLennan, G. et al. (eds) *The Idea of the Modern State*, Milton Keynes: Open University Press.

Held, D. (1984a) 'Power and legitimacy in contemporary Britain', in McLennan, G. et al. (eds) *State and Society in Contemporary Britain*, Cambridge: Polity Press.

Held, D. (1989) *Political Theory and the Modern State*, Cambridge: Polity Press.

Held, D. et al. (1999) *Global Transformations*, Cambridge: Polity Press.

Held, D. and McGrew, A. (2002) *Globalization/Anti-Globalization*, Cambridge: Polity Press.

Hertz, N. (2001) *The Silent Takeover: Global Capitalism and the Death of Democracy*, London: Heinemann.

Hindess, B. (1980) 'Marxism and Parliamentary Democracy', in Hunt, A. (ed.) *Marxism and Democracy*, London: Lawrence and Wishart.

Hirst, P. and Thompson, G. (1996) *Globalization in Question*, Cambridge: Polity Press.

Hobsbawm, E.J. (1998) 'Introduction', in Marx, K. and Engels, F., *The Communist Manifesto. A Modern Edition*, London: Verso.

Hoffman, J. (1995) *Beyond the State*, Cambridge: Polity Press.

Holloway, J. and Picciotto, S. (1977) 'Capital, Crisis and the State', *Capital and Class*, no.2.

Holloway, J. and Picciotto, S. (1978) *State and Capital: a Marxist Debate*, London: Edward Arnold.

Howard, M.C. and King, J.E. (1975) *The Political Economy of Marx*, Harlow: Longman.

Jessop, B. (1977) 'Recent Theories of the Capitalist State', *Cambridge Journal of Economics* 1.

Jessop, B. (1984) *The Capitalist State*, Oxford: Blackwell.

Jessop, B. (1990) *State Theory. Putting Capitalist States in their Place*, Cambridge: Polity Press.

Jessop, B. (1996) 'Interpretive Sociology and the Dialectic of Structure and Agency', *Theory, Culture and Society*, vol. 13(1).

Jessop, B. (2001) 'Institutional re(turns) and the strategic-relational approach', *Environment and Planning*, vol. 33 (7).

Jessop, B. (2001a) 'Bringing the State Back In (Yet Again): Reviews, Revisions, Rejections, and Redirections', *International Review of Sociology*, vol. 11, no. 2.

Jessop, B. (2002) *The Future of the Capitalist State*, Cambridge: Polity Press.

Kerr, P. and Marsh, D. (1999) 'Explaining Thatcherism: Towards a Multidimensional Approach', in Marsh, D. et al. (eds) *Postwar British Politics in Perspective*, Cambridge: Polity Press.

King, A. (1999) 'Against structure: a critique of morphogenetic social theory', *The Sociological Review*, vol. 47, no. 2.

King, R. and Kendall, G. (2004) *The State, Democracy and Globalization*, Basingstoke: Palgrave.

Knuttila, M. and Kubik, W. (2000) *State Theories. Classical, Global and Feminist Perspectives*, London: Zed Books.

Laclau, E. and Mouffe, C. (1985) *Hegemony and Socialist Strategy*, London: Verso.

Laclau, E. and Mouffe, C. (1987) 'Post-Marxism without Apologies', *New Left Review*, 166.

Lenin, V.I. (1917) *The State and Revolution*, in *Collected Works*, vol. 25, London: Lawrence and Wishart.

Lindblom, C. and Woodhouse, E.J. (1993) *The Policy-Making Process*, Englewood Cliffs: Prentice Hall.

Lockwood, D. (1964) 'Social Integration and System Integration', in Zollschan, G.K. and Hirsch, W. (eds) *Explorations in Social Change*, London: Routledge and Kegan Paul.

Luger, S. (2000) *Corporate Power, American Democracy, and the Automobile Industry*, Cambridge: Cambridge University Press.

Lukes, S. (1983) 'Can the Base be Distinguished from the Superstructure?', in Miller, D. and Siedentop, L. (eds) *The Nature of Political Theory*, Oxford: Clarendon Press.

Lukes, S. (1985) *Marxism and Morality*, Oxford: Oxford University Press.

Mandel, E. (1978) *Late Capitalism*, London: Verso.

Mann, M. (1986) *The Sources of Social Power: Volume 1. A History of Power From the Beginning to AD1760*, Cambridge: Cambridge University Press.

Mann, M. (1986a) 'The Autonomous Power of the State: Its Origins, Mechanisms and Results', in Hall, J.A. (ed.) *States in History*, Oxford: Blackwell.

Mann, M. (1988) *States, War and Capitalism*, Oxford: Blackwell.

Marsh, D. (1995) 'Explaining Thatcherite Policies: Beyond Uni-dimensional Explanation', *Political Studies*, vol. 43, no. 4.

Marsh, D. (1999) 'Explaining Change in the Postwar Period', in Marsh, D. et al. (eds) *Postwar British Politics in Perspective*, Cambridge: Polity Press.

Marsh, D. (1999a) 'Resurrecting Marxism', in Gamble, A. et al (eds) *Marxism and Social Science*, Basingstoke: Macmillan.

Marsh, D. and Stoker, G. (eds) (1995) *Theory and Methods in Political Science*, Basingstoke: Macmillan.

Marx, K. (1976) *Capital*, vol. 1, Harmondsworth: Penguin.

Marx, K. (1985) 'Inaugural Address of the Working Men's International Association', in Marx, K. and Engels, F. Collected Works, vol. 20, London: Lawrence and Wishart.

Marx, K. (1986) *The Civil War in France*, in Marx, K. and Engels, F. Collected Works, vol. 22, pp. 307–59, London: Lawrence and Wishart.

Marx, K. (1987) *A Contribution to the Critique of Political Economy*, in Marx, K. and Engels, F. Collected Works, vol. 29, pp. 257–65, London: Lawrence and Wishart

Marx, K. (1979) *The Eighteenth Brumaire of Louis Bonaparte*, in Marx, K. and Engels, F. Collected Works, vol. 11, pp. 99–197, London: Lawrence and Wishart.

Marx, K. and Engels, F. (1976) *The Manifesto of the Communist Party*, in Marx, K. and Engels, F. Collected Works, vol. 6, pp. 477–519, London: Lawrence and Wishart.

Mayer, T. (1994) *Analytical Marxism*, London: Sage.

McAnulla, S. (2002) 'Structure and Agency', in Marsh, D. and Stoker, G. (eds) *Theory and Methods in Political Science*, Basingstoke: Palgrave.

McGrew, A. (1992) 'The State in Advanced Capitalist Societies', in Allen, J. et al. *Political and Economic Forms of Modernity*, Cambridge: Polity Press.

McLellan, D. (1980) *The Thought of Karl Marx*, 2nd edition, London and Basingstoke: Macmillan.

McLennan, G. (1989) *Marxism, Pluralism and Beyond*, Cambridge: Polity Press.

McLennan, G. (1996) 'Post-Marxism and the "Four Sins" of Modernist Theorizing', *New Left Review*, 218.

Miliband, R. (1965) 'Marx and the State', in Miliband, R. and Savill, J. (eds) *The Socialist Register*, London: Merlin Press.

Miliband, R. (1969) *The State in Capitalist Society*, London: Weidenfeld and Nicolson.

Miliband, R. (1970) 'The Capitalist State: Reply to Nicos Poulantzas', *New Left Review*, 59.

Miliband, R. (1973) 'Poulantzas and the Capitalist State', *New Left Review*, 82.

Miliband, R. (1977) *Marxism and Politics*, Oxford: Oxford University Press.

Miliband, R. (1984) *Capitalist Democracy in Britain*, Oxford: Oxford University Press.

Miliband, R. (1987) 'Class Analysis', in Giddens, A. and Turner, J. (eds) *Social Theory Today*, Cambridge: Polity Press.

Miliband, R. (1989) *Divided Societies. Class Struggle in Contemporary Capitalism*, Oxford: Oxford University Press.

Mills, C.W. (1959) *The Power Elite*, Oxford: Oxford University Press.

Mills, C.W. (1962) *The Marxists*, Harmondsworth: Penguin.

Mintz, B. (1989) 'United States of America', in Bottomore, T. and Brym, R.J. (eds) *The Capitalist Class: An International Study*, New York: New York University Press.

Mishra, R. (1984) *The Welfare State in Crisis. Social Thought and Social Change*, Brighton: Wheatsheaf.

O'Connor, J. (1973) *The Fiscal Crisis of the State*, New York: St Martin's Press.

Offe, C. and Ronge, V. (1982) 'Theses on the Theory of the State', in Giddens, A. and Held, D. (eds) *Classes, Power and Conflict*, Basingstoke: Macmillan.

Offe, C. (1984) *Contradictions of the Welfare State*, London: Hutchinson.

Panitch, L. (1994) 'Globalisation and the State',*The Socialist Register*, London: Merlin Press.

Pierson, C. (1996) *The Modern State*, London: Routledge.

Plant, R. et al. (1980) *Political Philosophy and Social Welfare. Essays on the Normative Basis of Welfare Provision*, London: Routledge and Kegan Paul.

Poggi, G. (1990) *The State. Its Nature, Development and Prospects*, Cambridge: Polity Press.

Poulantzas, N. (1969) 'The Problem of the Capitalist State', *New Left Review*, 58.

Poulantzas, N. (1973) *Political Power and Social Classes*, London: New Left Books.

Przeworski, A. and Wallerstein, M. (1988) 'Structural dependence of the state on capital', *American Political Science Review*, 82(1).

Renton, D. (2001) *Marx on Globalisation*, London: Lawrence and Wishart.

Roemer, J. (ed.) (1986) *Analytical Marxism*, Cambridge: Cambridge University Press.

Rosen, M. and Wolff, J. (1999) *Political Thought*, Oxford: Oxford University Press.

Runciman, W.G. (1989) *A Treatise on Social Theory: Volume II. Substantive Social Theory*, Cambridge: Cambridge University Press.

Sassoon, A.S. (1980) *Gramsci's Politics*, London: Croom Helm.

Saville, J. (1957–8) 'The Welfare State: An Historical Approach', *New Reasoner*, 3.

Schwartz, M. (ed.) (1987) *The Structure of Power in America*, New York and London: Holmes and Meier.

Scott, J. (2001) *Power*, Cambridge: Polity Press.

Shaikh, A. (1991) 'Economic Crises', in Bottomore, T. et al. (eds) *A Dictionary of Marxist Thought*, Oxford: Blackwell.

Sklair, L. (2001) *The Transnational Capitalist Class*, Oxford: Blackwell.

Sklair, L. (2002) *Globalization. Capitalism and its Alternatives*, Oxford: Oxord University Press.

Skocpol, T. (1979) *States and Social Revolution*, Cambridge: Cambridge University Press.

Skocpol, T. (1985) 'Bringing the State Back In: Strategies of Analysis in Current Research', in Evans. P. et al. (eds) *Bringing the State Back In*, Cambridge: Cambridge University Press.

Smith, M. (1995) 'Pluralism', in Marsh, D. and Stoker, G. (eds) *Theory and Methods in Political Science*, Basingstoke: Macmillan.

Smith, M.J. (2000) *Rethinking State Theory*, London: Routledge.

Sorensen, G. (2004) *The Transformation of the State*, Basingstoke: Palgrave.

Stokman, F., Ziegler, R. and Scott, J. (eds) (1984) *Networks of Corporate Power*, Cambridge: Polity Press.

Strange, S. (1996) *The Retreat of the State: The Diffusion of Power in the World Economy*, Cambridge: Cambridge University Press.

Sweezy, P. (1942) *The Theory of Capitalist Development*, New York: Monthly Review Press.

Taylor-Gooby, P. (1985) *Public Opinion, Ideology and State Welfare*, Routledge and Kegan Paul.

Van Creveld, M. (1999) *The Rise and Decline of the State*, Cambridge: Cambridge University Press.

Wallace, W. (1994) 'Rescue or Retreat? The Nation State in Western Europe', *Political Studies*, vol. 42 (Special Issue).

Weber, M. (1991) *From Max Weber: Essays in Sociology*, edited by Gerth, H.H. and Mills, C.W., London: Routledge.

Wetherly, P. (1988) 'Class struggle and the Welfare state: some theoretical problems considered', *Critical Social Policy*, Vol. 22.

Wetherly, P. (1992) 'The Factory Acts: Class Struggle and Functional Requirement in the Explanation of Legislative Intervention', in Wetherly, P. (ed.) *Marx's Theory of History: The Contemporary Debate*, Aldershot: Avebury.

Wetherly, P. (1992a) 'Mechanisms, Methodological Individualism and Marxism: A Response to Elster', in Wetherly, P. (ed.) *Marx's Theory of History: The Contemporary Debate*, Aldershot: Avebury.

Wetherly, P. (1996) 'Basic Needs and Social Policies', *Critical Social Policy*, vol.16(1).

Wetherly, P. (1998) 'A Capitalist State. Marx's Ambiguous Legacy', in Cowling, M. (ed.) *The Communist Manifesto. New Interpretations*, Edinburgh: Edinburgh University Press.

Wetherly, P. (1999) 'Marxism, "manufactured uncertainty" and the ecological crisis', *Contemporary Politics*, vol. 5, no. 3.

Wetherly, P. (2001) 'Marxism and economic determination: clarification and defence of an "old-fashioned" principle', *Review of Radical Political Economics* 33.

Wetherly, P. (2002) 'Making Sense of the "Relative Autonomy" of the State', in Cowling, M. and Martin, J. (eds) *Marx's 'Eighteenth Brumaire'. (Post)modern Interpretations*, London: Pluto.

Wetherly, P. and Carling, C. (1992) 'An Analytical Outline of Historical Materialism', in Wetherly, P. (ed.) *Marx's Theory of History: The Contemporary Debate*, Aldershot: Avebury.

Wright, E.O. (1974–5) 'To Control or to Smash Bureaucracy: Weber and Lenin on Politics, the State, and Bureaucracy', *Berkeley Journal of Sociology* 19.

Wright, E.O. (1993) 'Class Analysis, History and Emancipation', *New Left Review*, 202.

Wright, E.O., Levine, A. and Sober, E. (1992) *Reconstructing Marxism*, London: Verso.

Index